MAN-CHILD

MAN-CHILD

A Study of the Infantilization of Man

David Jonas and Doris Klein

JONATHAN CAPE
THIRTY BEDFORD SQUARE LONDON

FIRST PUBLISHED IN GREAT BRITAIN 1971
© 1970 BY McGRAW-HILL, INC.

JONATHAN CAPE LTD, 30 BEDFORD SQUARE, LONDON WC1

ISBN 0 224 00566 9

The passages on pp. 27-9 are freely adapted from *Ring of Bright Water* by Gavin Maxwell, © 1960 by Gavin Maxwell; the passage on pp. 29-30 is freely adapted from *The Rocks Remain* by Gavin Maxwell, © 1963 by Gavin Maxwell; both books published by Longmans, Green & Co. Ltd. The authors gratefully acknowledge the permission of Peter Janson Smith Ltd. to adapt these passages.

The authors gratefully acknowledge permission to quote from the following works:
    The Mind of the Dolphin by Dr John Cunningham Lilly. © 1967 by Dr John Cunningham Lilly. Reprinted by permission of Doubleday & Company, Inc.
    'The Rigors of Play' by Mihaly Csikszentmihalyi. © 1969 by The Nation Associates, Inc., New York, N.Y. 10014. Reprinted by permission of *The Nation*.

PRINTED IN GREAT BRITAIN BY
LOWE AND BRYDONE (PRINTERS) LTD LONDON
ON PAPER MADE BY JOHN DICKINSON AND CO. LTD.
BOUND BY G. AND J. KITCAT LTD LONDON

To Our Children

Anne and Pamela
Francis and Jill
we dedicate this book, our latest child,
and hope they will enjoy
having it in the family

Acknowledgments

In the preparation of this book, the works of many writers and the reports of many scientists have been read, and some of their thoughts and ideas have been incorporated into our text.

For the most part we have included their names and the titles of their works in the text, but in some cases, where we have felt that it would interrupt the flow of the reader's attention, we have not done so. We have listed every book we have read, referred to, or quoted, in the bibliography, and we ask their writers, or other owners, to accept our grateful acknowledgments here.

A special word of thanks is due to Jill Klein, who read our copy and who informed us in no uncertain terms when she thought we had used a technical term or concept that might not be intelligible to the general reader without further explanation.

Contents

FOREWORD: AN APOLOGY TO SPECIALISTS   xiii

§PART I

CHAPTER ONE: INTRODUCTION   3

CHAPTER TWO: INTELLIGENCE AS A REGRESSIVE FACTOR   10
    EVOLUTION OF INTELLIGENCE   10
    INTELLIGENCE IN OTHER SPECIES   22
    THE MODULATING EFFECT OF INTELLIGENCE ON EMOTIONAL DEVELOPMENT   36

CHAPTER THREE: GENIUS   45

CHAPTER FOUR: IDEALS, MORALS, AND ESTHETIC APPRECIATION   51

CHAPTER FIVE: ART AS AN INDICATOR   61

CHAPTER SIX: THE EXPANDING NURSERY   77
    HOME   77
    COOKERY   81

Contents

SHELTER	83
CLOTHING	88
A THOUGHT ON WOMAN	95

CHAPTER SEVEN: PLAY — 97
DEVELOPING PATTERNS	97
PLEASURE	101
HOBBIES	103
PURITANISM	105
TOYS	106
EQUIPMENT AS TOYS	109

CHAPTER EIGHT: SEX — 119

CHAPTER NINE: THE MATTER OF COURAGE — 142

CHAPTER TEN: THE ELEMENT OF PLEASURE IN BEING DESTRUCTIVE — 147

CHAPTER ELEVEN: VIOLENCE — 150
CIVIL STRIFE AND WARFARE	150
CHANGING SOCIETY	160

CHAPTER TWELVE: POLITICAL LIFE — 166
GOVERNMENT	166
POLITICS	173
THE LIBERAL APPROACH	176
POLITICIANS AND LEADERS	179

CHAPTER THIRTEEN: PSYCHOLOGICAL FACTORS — 189
INTRODUCTION	189
THE INDIVIDUAL VIS-À-VIS SOCIETY	191
PSYCHOSOMATIC MECHANISMS AND COPING MECHANISMS	204
FAMILY THERAPY	212

PARENT-CHILD RELATIONS	216
A PORTRAIT OF THE MAN-CHILD	218
TESTS	223
CONCLUSIONS	224

CHAPTER FOURTEEN: AN ASPECT OF CROWDING 228

CHAPTER FIFTEEN: CULTURAL TRENDS: THE "NORMAL" AND THE "DEVIANT" 238

§PART II

CHAPTER SIXTEEN: REGRESSIVE EVOLUTION 255

INTRODUCTION	255
THE FACT: ANATOMIC CONFIRMATION	257
THE MECHANISM: HORMONES	270
THE CAUSE: THE VIRUS: DEUS EX MACHINA	285
THE RESULT: NEW SPECIES	310
THE HISTORY	325

CHAPTER SEVENTEEN: THE FUTURE 328

CHAPTER EIGHTEEN: A SUMMING UP 338

FOREWORD

An Apology to Specialists

Inductive natural science always starts without preconceptions from the observation of individual cases and proceeds from this toward the abstract law which they all obey.
—*Konrad Lorenz*

It may with some justification be asked by what right a psychiatrist and a writer presume to offer explanations in a field which spreads over into several highly specialized disciplines. We feel that some explanation—even an apology—for our presumption is due.

Carl Rogers, the noted psychologist, asked: "How does it happen that the deeper we go into ourselves as particular and unique, seeking for our own individual identity, the more we find the whole human species?"

This question expresses a concept which is of the essence. The history of the universe is compressed into every single atom. Had we the necessary tools we could infer all known phenomena from what we observe in this small unit of the cosmos. In the same way we could infer from what we observe, either in a single generation or in the sum of generations that constitutes the whole of man's history, a trend that may offer clues to all that went into molding his present form. Even more specifically, the observation of the nature of emotional dysfunctions in modern man provides the first clue toward an hypothesis of human evolution. The discrepancy between man's technological advances, the growing social disintegration, and the progressive prolongation of youthful behavior in mankind begged for a search as to whether there is not a physiological and anatomical counterpart. As we searched for such elements, the confirmatory evidence became overwhelming. It was almost too good to be true. We looked for flaws, but whenever one appeared and we checked into it, we found that it was only information that had been missing. As our knowledge was filled in, the picture fell more and more into shape.

A psychiatrist sees manifestations of human behavior not readily apparent to others. All human beings maintain in the presence of others a façade which their society or culture demands. But no matter to what extent an individual is successful, a pillar of his society, or respected by the world, in the intimacy of his home or in a psychiatrist's office he presents a totally different picture. This becomes particularly apparent in the course of family therapy. As no man is a prophet in his own country or a hero to his valet, so the immediate family of any individual knows the façade for what it is and with uncanny accuracy punctures it. Almost invariably, behind the façade—no matter how intelligent, dignified, or learned the person—one finds childlike behavior. This contradiction became the guiding beacon.

For a writer the route is different. A writer, too, must be an observer of human behavior and an analyst of its motivations, but the field of observation is more in the social and cultural areas. A writer spends a lifetime in generalized reading and research, and acquires some knowledge of many diverse fields. This writer was particularly impressed not only with the increasing youthfulness of the aspect and behavior of adults today, but also with the way these youthful attitudes had permeated every field of artistic, cultural, and social activity, and she undertook research to see whether an explanation could be found on an evolutionary basis.

Much has been said and written in recent times along the lines of the definition of the specialist as one who knows "more and more about less and less until in the end he knows everything about nothing" and of the need for interdisciplinary studies, with which we most wholeheartedly agree. On the principle of "the onlooker seeing most of the game" we think that sometimes an over-all view from the outside may very well throw light on a subject that is obscured at closer range—like the forest by the trees.

Without wishing to add to our presumption by putting ourselves into the same company, we should nevertheless like to point out that Darwin himself was only twenty-two years old, fresh out of Cambridge (where he had been preparing for a career in the church), and rather unsure about what he wished to do with his life when he boarded the *Beagle* as a naturalist in 1831 as a result of a chance friendship with the Rev. Professor J. S. Wenslow of Cambridge, a botanist, who recommended him. The *Beagle*'s captain, Captain Fitzroy, was a traditionalist with a Fundamentalist belief in the book of Genesis, who conducted daily Bible readings throughout the voyage, forcing comparisons between conventional belief and the observations Darwin so industriously made, until he reached the stage when he wrote: "At last gleams of light have come, and I am almost convinced (quite contrary to the opinion I started with) that species are not . . . immutable."

To use another of the clichés of folk wisdom, we hope that we shall not be condemned as the opposites of the specialists—as generalists who know less and less about more and more until in the end they know nothing about everything—but that we shall, by stepping back and taking a wider view, perhaps have contributed a little to the understanding of our very complex species.

David Jonas
Doris Klein

New York, 1970

PART I

CHAPTER ONE

Introduction

Often, in the springtime, when looking with delight on the sprouting foliage, considering the lilies of field, I have asked myself whether there is no power, being, or thing, in the universe, whose knowledge of that of which I am so ignorant is greater than mine. I have said to myself, can man's knowledge be the greatest knowledge—and man's life the highest life?
 —*John Tyndall in* Crystals and Molecular Force

When those of us who are now in our middle years first learned geometry at school, we were taught some comfortingly positive definitions. A straight line was the shortest distance between two points on the same plane, for example; parallel lines never met. It was only later that we were faced with the fact that there is no such thing as a straight line, and that even if there were, two of them, no matter how parallel they might seem, must eventually meet.

Not only in geometry have our old certainties evaporated,

but so have they in almost all the areas of knowledge. Solid matter has dissolved into molecules, atoms, electrons, and protons until matter itself, under ever closer scrutiny, disappears from view in a swirl of electric charges. Space and time have ceased to be trustworthy mile after mile or minute after minute, adding up to the days and years of our lives and civilizations, but have become relative concepts depending upon the point or scale of our observation.

One of the most widely accepted tenets of the days of our youth was man's emergence as the culmination and crown of a long process of evolution beginning with the most elementary forms of life and, through processes of adaptation, mutation, selection, and heredity lasting for more than two billion years, and by way of aquatic, amphibian, airborne, and terrestrial stages, finally achieving the apes and their most complex and glorious descendant, Man. It was an axiom that evolution would continue through him, and that the development and enlargement of his phenomenal brain would separate him further and further from his animal origins until his remote descendants achieve godlike powers and wisdom. No longer, however, do scientists believe that "man descends from the ape." We are told that man probably emerged, along with the apes, from a common ancestor, and that adaptability and the heredity of acquired characteristics do not necessarily constitute a means of evolution, but only one of transformation, and may end in blind alleys, monsters, and regression.

We have pondered on these thoughts. There is no doubt that adaptation can lead to temporary advantage, but if a creature is well adapted to its environment and circumstances, is it not apt to stagnate? When the adaptation is excessive, does it not lead the species to extinction? Is it not within the realm of possibility that human intelligence, a supreme adaptation, may be recessive in this way?

Introduction

Nature's favorite form seems to be that of the circle. In the same way that a straight line is an optical illusion and becomes a segment or arc of a circle in the context of space; that matter, seen closely, resolves into orbiting electrical charges; that space and time are governed by the spherical properties of the universe; that the galaxies rotate in stately waltzes in a universe which itself, no doubt, spins as it expands; so man's life and social forms follow circular principles. The cycles of birth and death; of disintegration into the earth and the arising of new life from the earth; the rise and fall of dynasties, of nations, of civilizations, of species all tend to support this view. Why should the development of man alone in the universe follow a straight path from slightly differentiated living matter to miraculously complex intelligent forms and proceed forever in a linear manner to further and further progress? Is it not more probable that his destiny, like that of everything else, is to follow a circular course, and that as he approaches an apogee, the forces of life will spin him back to his beginnings?

Dr. John Mulholland has noted that man's intellectual progress is marked by a reaction or resistance to fundamentally new knowledge or thoughts. This reaction at times has been unreasoned and panicky, sometimes so strong as to include hostility toward the innovator. Bitter antagonisms were aroused by such iconoclastic thinkers as Galileo, Mendel, and Darwin. Outbursts of this kind, as a response to discovery, are not unlike an animal's response to danger. When threatened, its survival mechanism is brought into play. There is an immediate coordinated provision for preservation of life and species, in which no activity related to reason is evident. Perhaps this is what Albert Szent-Györgyi meant when he said "The human brain is not an organ of thinking but an organ of survival, like claws and fangs. It is made in such a way as to make us accept as truth that which is only advantage."

The advantages of closing one's mind to a fundamentally new truth include release from the burden not only of learning something new but also of unlearning something secure and comforting. This is why young minds, uncluttered with experience, can tolerate change while old minds cling to what has served them well. Change is threatening. And, since our emotions also influence our thought processes, we largely think what it suits us to think and believe what it pleases us to believe.

It appears to man that an intelligent principle has been guiding the process of evolution. From where we stand as men, all the pathways of the development of living matter seem to lead to the place we are occupying. We seem, to ourselves, to be the culmination of a long process that had us as its aim.

The suggestion that it is possible that the species Man is perhaps not in the main line of evolutionary development evokes an immediate reaction of total disbelief. The authors themselves strongly resisted the idea at first, but the accumulating evidence so impressed them that they decided at least to collect it and put it into some order. In the process of doing so they have felt that some tendencies are sufficiently strongly pointed up to bear presentation to the general public.

It is true that the prevailing opinion of evolutionary biologists is that Man is at the culmination of about two to three billion years of life on earth, and that from and through his development the most progressive of the life forms of the future will come into being. Perhaps it is not surprising that this should be the case, for the evolutionary biologists are, after all, of the species Man. No doubt if a poll of prevailing opinion had been taken at any time during the one hundred and forty million years of the Triassic, Jurassic, and Cretaceous periods, it would have been considered that evolution was likely to proceed through the development of the dinosaurs. There are many features of Man's development, adaptation, and modification that would make it seem to an impartial observer that the current prevailing opinion may also be mistaken. On the contrary, it would appear that, if anything, Man may be a product of regressive rather than progressive evolution.

Evolution is an abstract concept of the methods of nature by and through which all matter and life has come to take on its present forms. Ever since Man began to develop theories on the subject of his origin and to record them, he has assumed that he himself is at the peak of its ladder.

One of the earliest of his theories was that of special creation, as expounded in the book of Genesis, in which—even if only six days were required to produce the universe—the undertaking nonetheless proceeded in order from inorganic to organic development and ended with Man. Each subsequent theory, down to Darwin's of natural selection, modified this early one, but all left intact the final assumption.

Yet how do we know what the processes of nature are? How do we know that there is a method, or even any aim? Do we not make these inferences because our rational minds need a sense of order in the world around us? Do we not interpret *a posteriori* a sequence of events as evolution leading to us because we are what we are and we stand where we stand, in much the same way as a passenger on the deck of a moving ocean liner at night sees the path of moonlight on the water leading directly from the moon to him, no matter how fast or in which direction the liner is carrying him, by reason of principles of optics relating to his power of vision?

Our brain, a product of this process we call evolution and

formed by it, tries to understand the force which brought it into being. And yet any concept it forms is determined by its own structure and nature, and by the nature of the stimuli it is capable of registering. To some extent we are aware that "there are more things in heaven and earth... than are dreamt of in [our] philosophy." We know that there are colors in the spectrum we cannot see; that even though man's eyes can only relay messages of red, orange, yellow, green, blue, indigo, and violet to his brain, there is a color before red and another after violet, and other eyes, more delicate than ours, perceive infrared and know the color of ultraviolet. Perhaps they have detected the existence of still other hues.

We also know that sound waves exist that we cannot hear. Yet some other animals hear them. The cetaceans not only hear sounds on wave lengths of a frequency too high for our receptors to record but also use them for communication through the dense medium of their watery environment. Then there are, among others, short waves, and X-rays, of which we have only recently in our history as a species obtained inklings through our developing technology. Bats and dolphins, among many other species, obtained information by echolocation long before we discovered the possibilities of radar or sonar.

The knowledge we have, the ideas of reality we form, and the conclusions we draw from them are all collated, governed, limited, by the nature of our structure, by the form we have taken, by the degree of sensitivity of our receptive apparatus, by the physical functioning of our brains. It is as though a fluid were poured into a bottle. It takes the shape of the bottle, but only for so long as the bottle contains it. The shape of the bottle is not its reality. So it is with all reality: that part of it we perceive takes shape in the vessel of our consciousness, unmodified by any awareness of the part we do not perceive.

We have no means of knowing whether the ideas we have

formulated about evolution (or any other matter) even approximate the actual processes of nature. Some few of us believe that nature is a mechanistic reaction between blind chemical forces inevitably following the laws of their properties. George Gaylord Simpson wrote in his *The Meaning of Evolution:* "Man is the result of a purposeless materialistic process that did not have him in mind. He was not planned. He is a state of matter, a form of life, a sort of animal, a species of the order Primates, akin nearly or remotely to all of life and indeed to all that is material."

Why should plants and animals struggle? What is it that repels some animals from some environments and impels them to seek another? Is the instinct for self-preservation the only reason for an animal to fight and adapt for survival? Why should there have been an evolution at all? There was no need for primitive life to develop any further. Its very existence is an indication of its ability to live in compatibility with its environment. Is it not possible that mutant, sick, or regressive forms were those that were spurred to new adaptations?

Let us speculate.

CHAPTER TWO

Intelligence as a Regressive Factor

EVOLUTION OF INTELLIGENCE
It would appear that through the principle of natural selection a species would tend to assume more and more efficient forms, refine its adaptability to its environment, and continue to improve its evolutionary progress indefinitely. Ever since the time of Darwin it has been generally assumed that this was the way of nature. Accumulating studies of the race histories of species, however, tend to show that we must modify our thoughts on such conclusions. There comes a point in the development of any species when it is perfectly adapted to its environment, and no further development is necessary. Thus the societies of ants, for example, achieved their optimum adaptation some fifty million years ago, and they have remained more or less unchanged ever since.

On the other hand, if within the species—either through

disease or mutation—a variant appears on the scene, it will not possess the adaptability of its healthy progenitors and its fellow creatures. It will then either perish or be forced to find a new adaptive mechanism geared to its special condition to make it possible for it to maintain its existence. If this particular animal should then not only manage to survive but also to find a mate, it will transmit its own defective genes to its offspring and thus put them, too, at a disadvantage vis-à-vis the rest of the species.

For these offspring the danger of succumbing before reaching maturity will be an ever-present threat. However, some chance discovery may provide a new adaptive mechanism which then, in time, may become a characteristic of a new species.

One could imagine, for example, a herd of goats grazing in a lush valley. Through mutation or sickness a small number of these animals have developed a weakening abnormality which sets them apart from the others. Their weakness has lessened their fighting spirit, and in any case they are outnumbered, so they are easily pushed from their habitual feeding grounds by the stronger members of their group. Little by little, having been pushed to the edges of the herd in the valley, they have no choice but to graze on the higher ground. The grass may be sparser there, but there is less competition for it. As time goes on, a variety of offspring will descend from these aberrant animals. Many of them will be unable to cope with the difficulties of their condition and environment and will perish. Some may just manage to maintain themselves in an uneasy *status quo*. But there will be a few, with stronger muscles, perhaps, who will be able to avail themselves of the more extensive, even if less rich, grazing land of the higher region. After many generations, during which the inevitable natural selection will have had time to preserve those favorable adaptations that will have arisen from time to time within the group, a new subspecies will be seen bounding among the inhospitable boulders of the upland and nourishing itself on whatever vegetation is to be found there. By the time this stage is reached, it would be difficult for any onlooker to identify these animals as the distant offspring of weak and sickly progenitors as he observes their powerfully built bodies, magnificently adapted to climbing and leaping over the rocks with great agility, and which have come to be known as mountain goats.

It is quite possible that in some such way as this some maladapted mutants or sickly individuals of the primate family may have had to relinquish their tree habitat, no longer having the necessary endowments for arboreal life. An infection by any one of the many viruses which affect the nervous system may have been a cause. As a delayed consequence of this type of infection animals (and human beings, too) may eventually lose their coordinated muscular skills. Such a handicap would make it difficult if not impossible to swing from branch to branch, and therefore these marked primates would have had to accommodate themselves to a new type of life on the ground—and, what is more, with a brain functioning inadequately because of the disease process.

A vivid example of the ravages that may be inflicted on a population, animal or human, by a virus disease, is given by Peter Farb in his book on Indian cultures in North America. In regretting that only meager information about the primeval cultures of two groups of Canadian subarctic populations exists, he notes that, along with the fur trade, the whites also brought diseases which wrought a devastation difficult to imagine today:

Lacking any immunity to smallpox, the entire Indian population of Canada was very nearly eradicated by a single epidemic occurring about 1780. A Hudson's Bay Company explorer reported that this epidemic alone wiped out nine tenths of the population of Chipewyan Indians, and this was only one of many epidemics. The Ojibway, originally one of the largest Indian groups north of Mexico, met with such a succession of disasters that as early as 1670 their numbers had dwindled to about one hundred and fifty.

The results of such epidemics could not have been very different for our earliest ancestors. For the few surviving individuals there would have been no alternative but to find a way to compensate for their deficiencies, and, as is often the case when any creature with a defect compensates by the development of superior ability in another field, it is not unusual for the goal to be overshot. The result is overcompensation.

The brain of all mammals is composed of several parts. Basically man's brain is the same in its general construction as all others, and differs from them only in the greater complexity of some of the parts. This is especially true of the neocortex, the latest-developed part of man's brain (as the name implies) and in effect the part which distinguishes him as a species. The neocortical structure is present in other primates, but only in a rudimentary form; whereas in man the surface is increased by multitudinous convolutions, it appears in the lower mammals as a few lobes. The most important part of the brain of lower mammals is the paleocortex. The paleocortex still persists in the brain of man and has important functions, but it is slowly being superseded by the neocortex.

Any disease process affecting a complex organ is likely to damage the most highly functioning part of it. In early primates the paleocortex would have been the most highly functioning part, and therefore it would have been the first victim when a disease disturbed normal brain functions. When, by some freakish chance, an early primate survived such a brain disease, the neocortex would have been the only available organ capable of carrying on the higher functions of the brain. (In certain virulent diseases, where the total brain is affected, the less differentiated parts have a greater chance than the more specialized of recuperation in the recovery period.)

All these factors would have tended to spark the neocortex into action in such a rare circumstance as an animal's survival of a brain-damaging disease, and would have been an important stimulus to its growth and development.

Not being able to reach the tree fruits that until then had been the main staple of their diet (although they were able to digest and did sometimes eat some animal components such as birds, birds' eggs, lizards, spiders, insects, and frogs), our hypothetical primates, involuntarily grounded, would then have had to become carnivorous at least in part to supplement their diet. When necessary they would gradually have extended this to small and then to larger mammals as their digestive system accommodated itself slowly to the more frequent utilization of animal proteins. They must also have begun to eat grasses at this time.

Like their arboreal ancestors, they too had to organize into groups for better protection, especially since their physical endowments were definitely inferior to those of the many predatory animals now surrounding them. But the earliest neocortical growth, although still primitive, would have given them a sufficient edge over stronger adversaries by leading them to realize the possibilities of the use of stones, rocks, or branches as weapons. Moreover, mutations or virus infections obviously are not isolated occurrences. They recur at intervals in animal populations just as epidemics do in ours. A similar sequence of events probably took place again and again. Each time a number would have perished and among the few survivors there would have been some who found ways to overcompensate for physical defects by the extension of their primitive intelligence to the point where it led them to realize the possibilities of the use of sticks and stones as tools. We can imagine a sickly forerunner of man, half-paralyzed, physically incapacitated, playing around with stones and discovering the cutting property of the sharp edges of some of them. As he used his hands to make use of those sharp stones, the effect was a new round of stimulation on that lately developing part of his brain.

At this point it should be repeated that there is actually no new structure to be found in the brain of man that is not found in other mammalian species. The differences between the brains of the highest and lowest primates lie in progressive elaboration and differentiation. Different parts of the brain did not expand equally. The areas which are largest are the ones of greatest functional importance. For example, the area which governs the hand increased vastly more than that for the foot, a fact that supports the idea that the increase in the size of the brain occurred after the use of tools and that selection for more skillful tool-using reinforced the changes in the proportions of the hand and the parts of the brain controlling the hand. That is to say, our brains are not just enlarged, but the increase in size is directly related to tool use, speech, and increased memory and planning. In its basic pattern it is similar to the brain of other primates. The uniqueness of the human brain lies not only in its larger size, but also in the particular areas which are enlarged. From the immediate point of view, this human brain makes culture possible. But from the long-term, evolutionary point of view, it is culture which creates the human brain. The part of the brain which controls the eyes, too, almost as much as that for the hands, stimulates its complexity.

To come back to our sickly forerunner discovering the cutting potential of sharp stones, it could very well have been in this fashion that in succeeding generations the weaker members of those prehistoric groups must have come to depend more and more on their ingenuity, establishing a never-ending cycle of the brain affecting the action and the action stimulating the brain. This became the ascending factor in the evolution of man. On the descending side we see many anatomical, physiological, and psychological features becoming regressive as a result of the changed genes transmitted by generations of sickly and mutant ancestors. This pattern of parallel development—intelligence increasing in the same degree as bodily and social abilities decrease—has become the outstanding characteristic of human evolution. And since we have not yet done so, we might mention here that intelligence has been defined as problem-solving, recognition of patterns, storage of information, combination of information, programming and processing information, learning ability, and exploratory behavior. Superior brainpower has allowed man, as it did his forerunners, to cope with the dangers of a threatening environment despite defective physical attributes, which would otherwise have led to the extinction of the species.

In this way there must have developed an ever-growing pool of physically inadequate individuals who were forced to overcompensate in the area of intelligence in order to be useful to the total group. Since they could not be hunters, it is very likely that it was from among them that the first toolmakers came, and, later on, the craftsmen, artists, and shamans.

A fact that would tend to confirm this speculation is the high esteem that brain-injured epileptics have enjoyed in primitive tribes of man. Almost every messianic movement around the world came into being as a result of the hallucinatory visions of their founders.

Peter Farb's work lends support to this theory. Describing the Eskimo, he wrote:

> An Eskimo shaman ... dresses no differently from anyone else, and he lives like the rest of the community. He hunts, or he joins a whaling crew; he may be married and have children. He has no special privileges or insignia. ... There are, however, ways to recognize him. Search out the least skilled hunter in the group, one who is also physically or mentally handicapped and who makes nervous movements with his hands or feet. You have probably located your man. The shaman actually is different from everybody else. ... He is meditative and introverted; he may have fits or fainting spells; he is disturbed by dreams and suffers from hallucinations and hysteria. The shaman is a psychological type known as the neurotic borderline schizoid—which is perfectly all right with the Eskimo, since he believes the shaman needs extraordinary abilities in his traffic with the supernatural.

And even in less primitive societies from the earliest until modern times, subtle or more pronounced damage to the brain has allowed some individuals to rise to great heights of leadership, especially in the religious and political arenas, through visions or the intensity of their paranoid delusions. Here we see the roots of the paradox in which a man endowed with superior ability to manipulate others and to make far-reaching decisions is nevertheless emotionally immature, possibly due to a combination of genetic and environmental factors. We shall go into this more fully in later chapters.

To sum up this projection, a circular feedback has been operating in man from the very beginning of his emergence as a separate species: sickness leading to mutations and intelligence have promoted the obsolescence of many physical features; the condition of inadequate physical function has demanded an ever-growing intelligence to compensate, and even to overcompensate, for the functional losses. This process appears inexorable, and it will no doubt continue into the far future.

As we have just stated, since the earliest ancestor of man began to use his mind rather than his muscles, it was inevitable that in each succeeding generation the deviant or psychologically unstable individual would have had to have improved on this particular ability to ensure survival for himself. To squeeze the last drop of advantage out of this potential, it was necessary for the neocortex to remain uncommitted for a long time. This is to say that only a very small portion of its potential is utilized in the earliest years of life. Its full potential is only brought into play by learning and experience, little by little, throughout the course of life.

Only by this means could the young learn the many complex skills and symbols which cannot be transmitted by heredity. *Without recourse to any other possible direction, inevitably childhood had to be prolonged.* This, and this only, allowed for the acquisition by man of a progressively increasing storehouse of knowledge.

What we call evolution is the outcome of nature's failures overcompensating for shortcomings resulting from illness, deprivation, or mutation. A normally developed organism, suitably adapted to its environment, would remain stable indefinitely in all the generations of its descendants. Thus we see two distinct trends—one for an organism to find an optimum relationship with its environment, leading to stable forms; the other, the nonstable creatures which survive only through a series of overcompensations. It is the latter which gradually brings about the changeovers to new species. One could venture to say that it is not the survival of the fittest animal that is responsible for evolution, but rather that it is the occasional unstable creature which achieves new forms through a series of overcompensations in himself and his descendants, while the fit achieve slow modification in making themselves even fitter to remain what they already are.

In nature the sick animal has little chance to survive; only rarely can such an animal find new ways not only to stay alive but then to be able to transmit such ways to its offspring. In man today we find almost the reverse to be the case. Improved methods of healing keep the sick from dying, and in this way a disproportionately large number of faulty genes are transmitted to the next generation. For this reason man shows more rapidly occurring evolutionary changes than any other animal. Included in this accelerated evolution are also man's domestic animals and his pets, since veterinary medicine keeps otherwise unstable forms alive.

Sometimes the casual remarks of a man of vision bring into sharp focus an idea that otherwise would escape general attention. In the course of a Congressional hearing in February 1970, Nobel Prize-winner Dr. Glenn Seaborg said:

I believe that one of the characteristics of the human race—possibly the one that is primarily responsible for its course of evolution—is that it has grown by creatively responding to failure.

Dr. Seaborg was speaking in another context, but he certainly stated the case we have been making very concisely with these words.

The method of overcompensation is an observable phenomenon in man on many levels. All of us know of such examples as a one-legged man who develops superior skills in some sport; a puny or short youngster who builds himself up to the figure of a Hercules through weight-lifting or other exercises; someone with a speech impediment who practices until he is able to make a career as an actor or politician; or, on the other hand, a physically handicapped person who becomes intensely involved in intellectual pursuits and excels in this way. The reverse is also true. When individuals are endowed with what is esteemed in their particular group, they often fail to develop other faculties. We do not expect a woman who is beautiful to be intelligent, nor do we expect a brilliant mind from a physically well-endowed man. We are surprised if a pretty blonde is not "dumb," and taken aback if an athlete or, say, a tenor, makes intelligent conversation. These people are well adapted to their group through their good looks or physique, and they have no need to develop intelligence to gain the esteem of their peers.

Here we must note an ever-widening circle in which the growth of the neocortex depended upon elaborate protection of the sick, deviant, or unstable members of the human group. By mating among themselves they produced genetically inferior specimens who, to a large extent, became extinct. However, the few who managed to continue their lines had to overcompensate in the only area that promised a better place in their society: intelligence. Since this group harbored many defective genes, a large variety of chronic diseases of both the body and the mind appeared on a scale never seen anywhere else in nature. When, through such circumstances as geographic isolation or social separateness imposed by religious or political doctrines, inbreeding becomes a factor, this development is accelerated. A good example of this situation is the Jewish ethnic group, which harbors a comparatively large reservoir of hereditary diseases (some of which, like Burger's disease, are seen only in Jews) on the one hand, and a percentage of outstanding scholars and intellectuals in many fields out of all proportion to its numbers on the other.

When the gene pool of inbred groups becomes too small (there appears to be an optimum number below which no overcompensation can be effective), eventual extinction is inevitable. C. D. Darlington, in his book *The Evolution of Man and Society,* traces the fall of past dynasties and kingdoms.

Intelligence as a Regressive Factor

They all vanished, he states, for fundamentally the same reason: once a ruling class fixed itself in power, it sought to conserve that power by inbreeding—by denying the infusion of new genetic patterns that might have refreshed the stock. It was this practice, says Darlington, that expedited the decline of the Pharaohs, the Ptolemies, and the Caesars. It might also have contributed to the disappearance of the Mayans.

To return to the Jews, it may be of interest to note that in our generation, as a result of the lowering of religious and social barriers, widespread intermarriage has occurred between the Jewish people of the Western world and members of the dominant groups among whom they live, thus diluting their gene pool. The effect of this may well be that the spectacular achievements of the Jews in intellectual and creative fields may have seen its peak and that in the future their contributions in these areas will be less phenomenal. The only part of the world today where exclusive inbreeding among a comparatively small Jewish group exists is in Israel, and there, too, has been seen remarkable accomplishment. At the moment the Israeli population, which until recently consisted almost exclusively of European Jewish groups, is in the process of absorbing a population of immigrants from North African and Oriental communities, which may have the effect of reducing nature's recourse to excessive intellectuality for some time. However, unless the gene pool remains sufficiently large once the present immigration has been absorbed, there is a possibility that a new dependence on the intellect for survival may produce another great flowering there.

The accumulation of defective genes creates a potential for disturbed behavior which can be triggered by environmental influences—parental, educational, and socio-economic pressures may add further dimensions. For example, whereas an acute distress in a genetically sound person may provoke only a transient attack of anxiety, in one genetically handicapped it may initiate an anxiety neurosis. The emergence of disturbed behavior then feeds on itself as offspring learn neurotic patterns from their parents, creating an ever larger group of individuals responding to situations of everyday life in a neurotic way. (This subject is amplified in a later chapter.) Just as steady noises cease to be noticed, so have we, historic man, accepted as inevitable the many aberrations and irrational aspects of our species—wars, violence, murder, cruelty, thievery, deceit, disloyalty to the group, and so on—none of which are seen elsewhere in the animal kingdom, except to a relatively minute degree in isolated and exceptional cases.

Parallel in its intensity has been the growth of the only overcompensatory mechanism available to man, his intelligence, by means of the continuous development of the neocortex. This suggests progress, but only in terms of intellectual achievement. Whether it constitutes true progress for the species is open to interpretation. In terms of harmonious group living, as seen in animal societies, we are certainly on a downtrend, with no end in sight. Attempts through the ages to foster better group living, such as have been made by the establishment of religions; philosophies; laws; political solutions of the type of the League of Nations, United Nations, the International Court; socio-economic arrangements like democracy, socialism, communism, dictatorship, theocracy, or monarchy have all, until now, failed. Dissension in its various forms is part of all our lives.

INTELLIGENCE IN OTHER SPECIES

What constitutes the difference between genetically carried instinctive patterns and intelligent behavior in animals is difficult to define. Actually, as Darwin pointed out in his *Descent of Man*, there is no fundamental difference between man and the higher mammals in their mental faculties, and there is the same variability between individuals of the same species as there is, say, between a Fuegan primitive and a Newton. Man has the same senses as other animals and many of the same instincts, though man has somewhat fewer instincts. According to Herbert Spencer the first dawnings of intelligence developed through the multiplication and coordination of reflex actions operating on the brain, but Darwin wrote that though many simpler instincts graduate into reflex actions, more complex instincts originate independently of the mind. On the other hand he noted that instinctive actions may lose their fixed character in some instances, and some "intelligent" actions may become converted into instincts in time. A. R. Wallace argued that much of the intelligent work done by man is due to imitation (i.e., learning) and not to the exercise of reason. But Darwin considered that there is a great difference between man's actions and those of most other animals in that a man cannot make a stone hatchet or canoe at first trial, by imitation. He has to practice. But a bird can make a nest or a spider its wonderful web quite as well the first time it tries as when it is old and experienced.

Nowadays we generally define intelligence as the ability to solve problems, and we see it exercised by many species, not merely by mammals. The authors have, for example, placed pieces of plant stems or small twigs in positions blocking the entrances to anthills and watched in fascination as individual ants, discovering them, summoned help and devised means to remove them. Bees and sand wasps adapt their behavior to circumstances, change their occupations when necessary, and are very flexible. A strong spirit of individuality has been observed in fiddler crabs (Uca), which possess the most highly organized nervous apparatus of all the crustaceans. Jocelyn Crane, studying them on the west coast of Panama, has reported their habits of play, curiosity, and their unpredictable activities. She has also described their changes of coloration which are caused not by nervous reflexes, as in cuttlefish, but by hormones in the bloodstream, so that they are indications of the equivalent of changes of "mood" in humans.

Among the most intelligent of nonhuman species are some of those of the genera Mustelidae (which includes weasels, stoats, ermines, badgers, skunks, martens, and otters), Cetacea (whales, dolphins, porpoises) and the suborder Mysticeti (seals and sea lions), and Primates (which include tree-shrews, lemurs, aye-ayes, lorises, monkeys and apes: the first four of these are classified between the insectivores and the monkeys and apes, and are considered to be the most primitive primates).

Much has been written recently about whales. As Justice William O. Douglas wrote in a review of Victor Scheffer's *The Year of the Whale,* the author "makes almost human these amazing denizens of the ocean depths, long known to man but little understood and seldom appreciated for their complex personalities and varied skills." Scheffer describes how the whales not only communicate; they navigate by vibrations beamed over a far greater sound range than that comprehensible to the human ear. They are highly intelligent, gregarious mammals, who long ago left the land for the sea, and in doing so reduced the importance of the eye in favor of new perceptive mechanisms, so that they "hear" rather than see the shapes of objects. The sperm whales are great hunters, engaging in endless battles with the tons of writhing tentacles of the giant squid, the enormous monster of the deep rarely seen by man. Yet these huge mammals can also be gently social. They have been known to buoy an injured comrade so that he does not drown. Their social ties are great, and unfortunately are contributing to their destruction, as the warm-blooded, affectionate instincts forged long ago are no match for the electronic devices that now scout them mercilessly from the air. The sperm whale's head makes up a third of its body. It can detect the presence of an invisible squid in a pressure of one hundred tons to the square foot. The brain lobes concerned with sound and its rapid interpretation have squeezed out and overridden the "small brain" of the primitive mammal—just as in man the "eye brain" has become similarly dominant. If we were to study rather than destroy these highly specialized creatures, they might teach us much. Yet nature seems to have no future plans for the whale. As Scheffer remarked, the chances of survival for the little calf, swimming observantly beside his mother, are diminishing in inverse ratio to the growth of man's monstrous technology and that it is, perhaps, nature's final irony that man himself, for that same reason, may be taking his last look at the sun.

In *The Mind of the Dolphin,* the record of an experiment in interspecies communication in which a young woman and a bottlenose dolphin lived together for a period of a year, mutually exchanging learning and teaching, Dr. John Cunningham Lilly writes:

The large dolphins ... are highly intelligent and have complex, highly abstract communication. ...

A dolphin can be a cognitive equal with a human being. ...

I should like to be able to exchange ideas with a willing sperm whale because the ability and the potential of such a vast computer as his is so far beyond our present theories, beyond even our imagining, that it is an intriguing and challenging subject. ... The sperm whale's brain is so large that he needs only a small fraction of it for use in computations for his survival. He uses the rest of it for functions about which we can only guess ... [it] is computing continuous inner experiences beyond our present understanding. If a sperm whale, for example, wants to see-hear-feel any past experience, his huge computer can re-program it and run it off again.

His huge computer gives him a re-living, as if with a three-dimensional sound-color-taste-emotion-reexperiencing motion picture. He can thus review the experience as it originally happened. He can imagine changing it to do a better job the next time he encounters such an experience. He can set up the model of the way he would like to run it the next time, re-program his computer, run it off, and see how well it works. . . .

A sick dolphin cannot afford to go into a coma. He cannot afford even to fall asleep for periods longer than about six minutes. If he falls asleep longer than this he is in danger, great danger, of dying. Asleep too deeply, his respiration stops. Because of this particular peculiarity and necessity in the dolphin's makeup, a sick dolphin must be attended twenty-four hours a day. One dolphin will do this for another dolphin. Again and again in the Institute we have seen dolphins tend one another twenty-four hours a day until recovery took place, several days or weeks later. . . .

From the time of Aristotle (300 B.C.) it has been observed that dolphins have the ability to mimic sounds. . . .

In addition to its normal underwater sonic communication path, the dolphin can be trained to emit sounds from the blowhole opened in air. By proper rewarding and evocative techniques, such vocal emissions can be changed from the natural pattern. One such group of sounds is said to resemble the human voice. Aspects of these sounds which are physically determinable, specifiable, and demonstrable are the similarities in numbers of bursts of sound emitted by the man and by the dolphin. In 92% of the exchanges the number of bursts emitted by the dolphin equalled plus or minus 1, the number just previously emitted by a man in sequences of 1 to 10 bursts. No other animal (with one exception of unusual humans) can match this performance. . . .

If we put ourselves in the position of the dolphin, who has three sonic emitters as opposed to our one, who is used to transmitting his information to other dolphins underwater, who is forced to speak to us in our medium in air, who is using his nose and not his tongue and mouth for his enunciation, I think we can understand his difficulty in attempting to mimic us and to convince us that this is what he is doing.

The young woman who participated in the experiment, Margaret Howe, wrote among her conclusions:

> Dolphins not only can learn, but enjoy learning, learn fast, and they have learned lots of things we cannot know about. . . . Dolphins can play *with* someone . . . Peter [the dolphin] learned *how* to work during a vocal lesson (as taught by the human) and also made vocal progress. Peter learned how to teach me. Peter learned how to curb his physical energies to allow for my being so "human."

Gavin Maxwell wrote, in the first part of his *Ring of Bright Water:*

> The smaller members of the whale tribe are a feature of every summer at Camusfearna. Sometimes the great whales, the Blue and the Rorquala, pass majestically through the sound. . . .
> Of all sea creatures whales hold for me a particular fascination . . . so highly convoluted are those brains that it has been suggested that were it not for their frustrating limblessness they might well have outstripped man in domination of the earth's surface. . . .
> The American "oceanariums" have allowed their porpoise and dolphin inmates to reveal themselves as highly intelligent, amiable, and playful personalities who evince an unexpected desire to please and cooperate with human beings. They play ball games, come out of the water to greet attendants, retrieve with obvious pleasure ladies' handbags and kindred objects that fall into their tank. They are also capable of unquestionable altruism to one another. Their behavior compares very favorably with that of humans.

Maxwell also notes that dolphins can hear sounds four times higher than the upper limit the human ear can detect and that they possess a highly developed system akin to our only recently discovered radar.

Of course, Maxwell's book is better known for its second

part, in which he described his loving relationship with his otter pet, Mijbil. These excerpts give a very vivid picture of this otter's intelligence:

Mijbil took a keen interest in his surroundings—went wild with joy in the water in the bathroom. Two days later he escaped from the bedroom where he was kept and made straight for the bathroom. "By the time I had caught up with him he was up on the end of the bath fumbling at the chromium taps with his paws. I watched, amazed by this early exhibition of an intelligence I had not yet guessed; in less than a minute he had turned the tap far enough to produce a dribble of water, and, after a moment or two of distraction at his success, achieved the full flow." . . .

He accepted relationship with his owner within a week, came when his name was called, indulged in the principal otter characteristic of perpetual play. He spent hours shuffling a rubber ball around the room like a soccer player, and he could also throw it with a flick of the neck, or lie on his back and juggle it between his paws. Later, marbles became his favorite toys. . . .

"Even during this first fortnight in Basra I learned a lot of Mij's language, a language largely shared, I have discovered, by many other races of otter, though with different variations in usage." The simplest is the call note; it is short, penetrating, but not loud, between a whistle and a chirp. There is a query that sounds like the word "Ha!" in a loud, harsh whisper. He also made a musical bubbling sound interspersed with chirps, but it was the chirp in all its permutations and combinations of high and low, from single notes to continuous chatter, that was his main means of vocal communication. There was also a high, snarling caterwaul, indicating extreme anger. . . .

An otter must find out everything and have a hand in everything; most of all he must know what is inside any man-made container, or beyond any man-made construction. He has an uncanny mechanical sense of how to get things open, in fact a sense of statics and dynamics in general, and has great ingenuity. . . .

"Mijbil displayed a characteristic shared, I believe, by some other animals; that is, to go into a deep sleep, almost a coma, as a voluntary act, independent of exhaustion; it is an escape me-

Intelligence as a Regressive Factor 29

chanism that comes into operation when the animal's inventiveness in the face of adversity has failed to ameliorate its circumstances." . . .

"There was nothing haphazard about the demonstrations he planned; into them all went all the patience and ingenuity of his remarkable brain and all the agility of his muscular little body." . . .

In unfamiliar surroundings he appeared to watch and copy his owner's motions. . . .

After Mijbil was killed in an accident, he was replaced by a female Indian Small-Clawed otter, whose chief difference was that she had hands, unwebbed, without nails, and nearly as mobile as a man's. With them she ate, peeled hard-boiled eggs, arranged her bed, picked her teeth, and played. She seemed to delight in her dexterity. . . .

Her language gave some difficulty at first, some of the same sounds having different meanings, and she had a whole range of (to the owner at first) unfamiliar expressions of greeting, affection, pleasure and casual conversation strongly reminiscent of the human infant.

In *The Rocks Remain,* a sequel to *Ring of Bright Water,* Gavin Maxwell wrote further details of his experiences with three or four subsequent otter pets. Although there were differences in temperament, as among individuals of any species, the general tenor is the same: quick and real intelligence, great agility, affectionate companionship, adaptability, communication, and tireless playfulness.

Maxwell is not the only human to have become so enchanted with otters as to write a book about some otter individuals. Dorothy Gross Wisbeski wrote of her friendship with one, Okee, in these terms:

Okee's little brain must have had a great capacity for creativeness, for he was forever inventing new ways to keep himself wet. With additional strength came the discovery that he could get much wetter much faster if he picked up the bowl and dumped it on himself ... an expression of delight came over his face as he lay on his back pouring water lavishly over every inch of his body....

Okee learned how simple it was to open this kind of door....

He made a game of everything....

He enjoyed an audience ... would put on his best performance when people were there to watch him. He often played a special trick with his toy penguins. With a look of mischief he would swim over and remove one from the soap dish. By squeezing it together with his hands he could expel the air, so that the water filled it when he submerged with it. Armed with this loaded water-pistol he would surface and place it on the edge of the tub. Then by squeezing his hands together with a quick slap he would thoroughly drench the unwary person who happened to be in the line of fire.

The animal let his owner know when he wanted to be let out in the morning by making a noise, as they had shut his door on the outside. He played ball games. He followed the housewife around and took part in everything she did, including climbing a ladder behind her. Anything he discovered that gave him pleasure he never forgot. He learned to go up and down stairs....

Experience proved his keen perception and ability to remember enabled him to initiate action days or weeks after he had noticed something. For example, he watched her fastening cabinet doors with a metal ruler to impede him. Many days later he not only removed the ruler in her absense, but everything from the cabinet....

He had an eloquent "eye language," and his owners also learned to recognize various sounds he made so that it was easy for them to know what he wanted. "Whether he was 'talking' or 'smiling' Okee was the most communicative pet I had ever had."

R. I. Pocock has written of the Oriental Small-Clawed otter:

The abbreviation of the claws of the front foot is accompanied in this otter by extreme delicacy of the sense of touch in this extremity. I have seen one of these animals manipulating and playing with a marble in a manner recalling that of a conjuror juggling with a cricket-ball.

Pocock also noted that various species of this otter have been trained by some of the Asian peoples to catch and bring fish to them. The species is reported to be kept tame and employed by fishermen in Malacca.

The Sea Otter has been described by Ernest P. Walker thus:

It spends the nights in kelp beds to avoid drifting while sleeping. It floats on its back while eating (sea urchins, mollusks, crabs, fish) and uses its chest as a "lunch counter." . . .

This is one of the few mammals that makes use of a tool: while floating on its back, it places a rock on its chest; it then uses the rock as an anvil for breaking the shells of mussels, clams and large sea-snails in order to obtain the soft internal part. . . .

The sea otter is born in an advanced state of development, as its eyes are open and it has a complete set of milk teeth at birth. It nurses for about a year, although it begins to take soft food from its mother a few weeks after birth. The pup is carried, nursed, and groomed on its mother's chest as she swims on her back.

Not only whales and otters, but seals and sea lions too display great intelligence, as will be attested by any child who has watched them perform in circuses, where their acts are of quite a different caliber from those of such trained animals as lions and tigers, and much closer to the human type of intelligence, as is that displayed by the chimpanzees in such performances.

The badger, too, has found friends and biographers among man. Irenäus Eibl-Eibesfelt wrote of a badger that lived willingly and affectionately with a human in spite of the fact that he was completely free and allowed to come and go as he pleased. The owner only offered him care, toys, and occasional supplementary food. He slept mostly during the day, liked to play with his owner in the evening, and ran around at night. He developed enormous skill. If the door was closed, he not only called to get someone to open it, but worked at getting it open himself. When he was successful in getting in, he "scolded" angrily and loudly. He was skillful in opening drawers and cupboards, and liked to get everything out of them. He pulled down the wastepaper basket to get at the paper, which it amused him to tear up, and he removed the lid of the water pot himself if he wished to drink. His attachment to his home was particularly strong. He built his own sleeping place out of moss, hay, and pieces of stolen cloth. He had a very good sense of orientation, and got to know the topography of both barracks (which constituted his owner's dwelling and office, in wooded country) inside out. In the company of humans he showed himself remarkably tame. He followed his owner around step by step, and if he walked too fast made himself noticed by high, clear, vocal complaints. He did this also if he were too cold, when he got stuck in the blackberry brambles, or whenever anything bothered him. When he was a little older, this sound became a deeper complaining grumble. If he found himself in very difficult situations, he cried. Although he was hostile to all other animals, his behavior was very delicate toward his owner. The author then goes into details of his extreme playfulness, covering about eight closely printed pages, and at the end remarks:

The playful experiments with his own body, the curious investigations of the room and its possibilities for future action, the changes from time to time in his usual games, and other signs of an understanding, approached human levels.

Another writer, Ernest Neal, wrote of the badger:

They are capable of travelling long distances, but if food is plentiful they stay within a mile or so of their sets. They are social. Families paid each other visits constantly. They have few enemies, man being the chief one. They are wonderfully clean animals.

Mothers clean the cubs, adults groom themselves. They dig series of small pits for excrement away from the sets. The young are taught to use these pits. They sometimes bury their dead in specially excavated holes away from the sets. One "funeral" was observed, when a sow was burying her mate with the help of another male. It seemed to the observer that the proceedings contained some ritual. . . .

They are noisy creatures when playing, with excited yelps, like puppies . . . they recognize and acknowledge sounds made by their own kind. They indulge in much romping and play, and families stay together.

Elephants, too, show a high degree of intelligence, and to a certain extent make use of a tool, insofar as they have been observed breaking off branches of trees in order to use them to drive away flies.

Many people credit the beaver, remarkable creature as it in any case is, with more sagacity than it actually has. It is not true that it can fell a tree in any desired direction. L. L. Rue observed that one of every five trees a beaver cuts down cannot be used because of where it falls. When a tree becomes hung up in another, the beaver does not know enough to cut out the supporting tree. Sometimes a beaver is killed by the tree it is felling, and trapped beavers are not aided by others of the colony. Nevertheless, they are attractive animals. They are good mates and parents, remaining as a pair until death removes one. They are sociable when feeding, share food, raise their young with great tolerance, and are in general amiable. And even if their skills as engineers have been overrated, persistence often gets their dams built and kept in shape, even if the location is not ideal. Beavers are like people in that some are more intelligent than others, and they make many mistakes. Sometimes their dams are washed away or broken, or placed where more work is needed to complete them than would be the case a little distance away.

Where the beaver shows its intelligence, ingenuity, and industry to best advantage is in the construction of its canals. When desired food trees cannot be made accessible to them by flooding, the beavers may dig canals to bring water near their standing food supplies. They dig as many canals as they need to make the food accessible and transportable, and dig them just deep enough (twelve to eighteen inches) to allow the animal to swim and transport it. They sometimes build a series of small dams above their main dam, forming a series of steps or locks, to enable them to reach more food. They also sometimes tap or cut into a spring hole or brook to supply the needed water to carry out this project. Beavers fully understand the problem of water levels and their control. They have also been known to divert or channel springs to the main pond to maintain a higher water level, or to dig canals across sections of land to save time and distance. If the land is high and a canal would be too much effort, they simply tunnel under it.

George Stansfeld Delaney, under his pseudonym Grey Owl, wrote of his beaver pets that they were gentle, affectionate, and always good-natured and scrupulously clean. They gave little bleats when they saw their foster parents, nibbled fingers, climbed into laps, and fell asleep halfway up a sleeve. Sometimes they climbed into Grey Owl's bed when they were soaking wet and squeezed the water out of their coats on the blankets. To make an indoor lodge, they stole the contents of the woodbox, barricaded an area beneath a bunk, cut a hole in the flooring, and dug a tunnel under a wall. They then plastered the chamber with mud.

We have deliberately quoted examples of intelligence observed in species other than the monkeys and apes, whose adaptability, use of tools, and ability to solve problems are better known.

Intelligence as a Regressive Factor

What do these intelligent species have in common? What is it that has impelled them to develop the use of their brains to supplement their physical capacities?

It will be readily admitted that although man is the dominant form of life at the present time, there are many areas in which he is inferior to other species. His body is not so powerful as some; he is not as fleet as others; his senses are not so acute as those of scores of wild animals. He cannot leap as well as many, nor are his teeth as effective as those of most other creatures. Some have better vision than he, and others are able to scale trees, climb perpendicular surfaces, and perform with ease what to him would be the most acrobatic acts. His skin does not protect him. He needs shelter from the elements.

For all these, and many other, skills and powers that his body does not afford him, he has substituted intelligence. There are those who would say that the sequence of this argument is faulty. They would assert that since the species of ape we call Man developed an enlarged brain, the many other physical strengths became superfluous, were not used, and either became vestigial or disappeared.

However, whether whales, dolphins, seals, otters, badgers, elephants, apes, or man, all are species that in some or many ways are physically regressive. The water mammals, having left the land in early tertiary times and returned to the sea, have lost their limbs and taken on the bodily forms of fish. Otters and beavers too, bound by their dependence on water and adapted to it, would not have the strength to survive if forced to compete physically with other animals. Elephants, like dinosaurs, have become unwieldy by reason of their size. Both beavers and badgers are smaller and less powerful than their ancestors. Beavers, by the way, are descended from the castoroides of the Pleistocene era, monsters weighing 700 lbs. Men, too, have had to find ways to survive with inferior physical equipment.

The consideration of all these species' case histories leads us to the conclusion that intelligence is compensatory rather than determinant. In fact, if they had not developed their brains to compensate for hampering physical or adaptational defects, would not these species have become extinct?

Should we not consider the possibility that man, like all these species, as a consequence of his regressive evolution in terms of body structure (which, without the increase in the power of his brain, would have diminished his capacity for survival) has depended on this enlargement and development of his brain simply to enable him to exist as a viable species? And that therefore the development of brainpower itself should be considered as a symptom and indication of man's regressive physical condition?

THE MODULATING EFFECT OF INTELLIGENCE ON EMOTIONAL DEVELOPMENT

Men are rarely able to decide unanimously on values. What one considers important another may find trivial. Throughout historic times Western man has esteemed intelligence, knowledge, and education as worthy achievements. When any ethnic group has created works of art, literature, or science, but has not been capable of adapting to environmental situations, we nonetheless consider it to be superior to another ethnic group that has adapted to its environment in an optimum fashion but has not produced intellectual works. It would be just as easy to make a case against intelligence, especially when we see it applied in the production of death-dealing devices or used in schemes to defraud fellow men. The bushman commands a knowledge of his habitat that evokes admiration in the visiting anthropologist who, in spite of his erudition, or maybe because of it, could not manage for long in a jungle without the help of the intellectually "inferior" bushman.

If we remove the value we place on intellectual achievement, we can then see it purely as a biological manifestation. We start out with the oversimplification that the neocortex is the seat of intelligence. Actually, although it is the most important factor, other structures of the brain do also take part in the thinking process. Nevertheless, the gradual increase in size and complexity of this part of the brain from the times of prehistoric to modern man roughly parallel his intellectual development.

Although some investigators have found that unmyelinated nerve fibers are capable of conducting impulses, if at a considerably slower rate, in order for the nervous system to function fully it has to surround each individual nerve with a myelin sheath which, among other services, acts as a nutritional support. In the newborn human, this newest acquisition, the neocortex, is the last structure to develop its sheaths (at about the sixth month). Most parts of the brain govern specific functions that are laid down genetically, but this part remains uncommitted for a considerable time, allowing it to store information in the formative years.

An important tool for learning is play. The skills learned in play are stored as information in the neocortex which in turn, having stored this extra information, is facilitated in further discovery and exploration by the child. This produces a self-feeding, ever-widening cycle.

For a child, all learning is play. This is reinforced nowadays by the teaching methods in kindergartens and the lowest school grades. The neocortex starts its functional existence as a *play-cortex*. It is quite likely that it preserves this particular property throughout life. The fact that the mind is capable of the most complicated and abstract reasoning should not detract from recognition of the way the neocortex works. Its primary purpose is the preparation of the human child throughout his prolonged infancy for the requirements of adulthood. The incentive lies in the satisfaction of the child's urge to explore, to be curious, and to master his environment through trial and error.

Experiments carried out with chimpanzees at the Yerkes laboratory show that the need to satisfy curiosity is so great in young animals that they will continue to work in problem-solving experiments, actually beyond the endurance of the experimenters to observe them, with no other reward than the satisfaction of their curiosity and the solution of their problem. This demonstrates that even the budding neocortex of the chimpanzee has an inherent need to be exercised. Failure to exercise this faculty, both in apes and man, creates the unpleasant state of boredom, whereas its exercise produces pleasure.

This satisfaction remains the dominant drive in the adult's pursuit of intellectual activities. An elegant solution to a mathematical problem, the discovery of a new chemical compound, a well-turned phrase, an eloquent speech, a deep insight into another person's responses—all these are the more sophisticated versions of a child's successful attempt to stack one building block on top of the other.

The neocortex, then, (or its emergent manifestation, the intelligence), is the development of the child's playful manipulations of objects into their extensions—adult knowledge. It does not possess the automatized instinctive responses necessary for survival. Although we constantly refer to man's intelligence as the agent which should control his behavior, the reverse is the actual case. Emotions govern our actions, and we use our intelligence to justify our motivations and the consequences of the actions we have taken.

Gradually during the evolution of man, as it does still in the child, the neocortex has taken on the role of making evaluations and judgments. The two-to-three-year-old child of our own time, for example, when playing with a pegboard having variously shaped holes and pegs, will at first try to put the pegs into the holes indiscriminately. He will then find out that this process doesn't work and will experiment until he finds the square peg for the square hole, the triangular peg for the triangular hole, and the round peg for the round hole. In doing so he discovers the quality of squareness of a peg, and recognizes a similar squareness in one of the holes. He has now discovered that if he wants the peg to stand up he has to put a square peg into a square hole. On the basis of this evaluation he will judge future actions, and in subsequent trials he will be able to perform the same task with greater speed and skill. It is the neocortex which coordinates the flow of associations, permitting the ability of making comparisons, which leads to evaluation and finally to judgment.

Retarding mechanisms constitute the basic driving force which has shaped the development of man as a species. We find this retarding principle at work in all facets of his evolution. It applies to his anatomy, his functioning, and by no means least to the method by which his mind operates.

Man differs from other animals in that they have an automatic response for any situation in which they are likely to find themselves. There is no provision for the modulation of their reflexes, and therefore they cannot exert control over their actions. Even in those animals domesticated or "trained" by man, the responses desired are largely obtained by setting up conditioned reflexes over which the animal has no more control than it has over its instinctive responses.

As a result of the growth of the neocortex, when man himself faces a new situation he is able to delay his response to it and thus give himself time to ponder, evaluate, come to a conclusion, and make a decision. He mentally visualizes alternatives and chooses the one which suits him. He can array all the possibilities before his mind's eye in the same way one feeds a flow of information into a computer. Not only does he visualize alternative solutions, but he is able to retain the images of them as though on a recording tape and to replay this tape again and again until the best of them appears obvious. Such inhibitory mechanisms as doubting and other action-delaying powers of thought are of paramount importance in the development of man's character structure. We teach our children how to interpose a delay between the perception of a need and its satisfaction.

("Mommy, I'm hungry." "Sorry, dear, we have to wait until Daddy comes home, and then we shall all have dinner together.")

Action-delaying also enables man to construct in his mind the probable consequence of a series of actions and to prepare his response to it. Thus he commits himself to a future deed which he believes, but is not sure, will be appropriate. In these circumstances he sometimes has to shelve the impression of his immediate reality—or even deliberately neglect it—in the hope that his conclusion will prove to have been correct. Here we see the intricate workings of this type of inhibitory mechanism, which is one of the highest achievements of the neocortex. It requires a quick evaluation of alternatives and their possible consequences that may or may not take place in the future. The time element involved is often incredibly short. In a game of tennis, for instance, a player has barely one second to decide where the stroke that his opponent is in the process of making is likely to drive the ball. In this instant the player coordinates all the movements of his legs, arms,

Intelligence as a Regressive Factor

and the rest of his body on the basis of his judgment, even before the ball has actually been struck. This requires an awareness that a particular thing, not there at the moment, will be there at a later moment, and the expectation of its presence is based on the immediate perception.

Not only is man able to delay mental processes; he can also put out of his mind matters which displease him. Most of us abhor the thought of killing an animal and slicing its carcass to provide us with food, but we are able to eliminate this thought from our minds while we enjoy the main course of our evening meal.

Man can also, and often does, suppress reality by imagining desirable but unattainable goals. Since this faculty creates a high expectation that is unlikely to be fulfilled, it often leads to psychological symptoms.

These various methods of retarding or inhibiting responses create a tension which amplifies the ability to perceive and to think, improving the chances of arriving at the best possible solution.

Without the use of the neocortex, as we see in some brain-damaged people, the individual responds on a purely literal basis. Such a person, instructed to "clean the room," would be at a loss as to what to do. If, however, each specific task is detailed ("Clean the table, clean under the table, wipe the window, dust the chair, empty the ashtray, sweep the carpet," and so on) he would be able to carry it out. Each request has to be specific in order to obtain a specific response, since the elimination of the use of this part of his brain has rendered the individual unable to associate all the ideas comprised in the instruction "Clean the room." In the normal adult the neocortex responds to inferences, innuendos, connotations, implications, nonverbal communication, and suggestions, which makes detailed requests unnecessary.

To come back to our child with the pegboard, the evaluation and judgment he has just made will be etched on his neocortex in the form of associations, and when he is given another game he will be able to infer what action to take without going through his experiment again. In this way each new game broadens his base for evaluative judgment, resulting gradually in man's phenomenal intelligence.

But now we must emphasize again that intelligence only solves problems. It is the paleocortex, the older portion of the brain, that has among its functions the control of the emotions. Therefore it is the development of the paleocortex that determines adaptational capacities and maturity.

This will at least in part explain why extremely intelligent people at times behave in an irrational or immature fashion. Human behavior is dictated by emotional needs which a purely problem-solving intelligence might sometimes reject. We can see an excellent example of this in the paradox of an adviser who can solve the problems of any group or individual in the area of behavior. Yet when he himself has to face a similar situation he behaves according to his emotional needs and not according to his better judgment. A desire to "get even," for example, may override a recognition of the futility of an action.

Giving advice therefore works rarely, if ever, because it is given from the vantage point of an intellectual appreciation of a situation, and does not correspond with the emotional needs of the individual to whom it is given. As a rule, people tend to accept advice only when it corresponds with their emotional needs. When they feel uncertain about a life situation, no advice will be heeded. The *status quo* will be maintained unless or until there is a change of attitude. The intellectual part of our brains approaches human behavior in the same way as any other problem to be solved, and arrives at conclusions which seem logical and sensible but rarely coincide with the operations of emotionally conditioned behavior. This fact actually accounts for the often-given joking advice "Do as I say, don't do as I do!" which is frequently all too apt.

The emotional ripening of modern man proceeds through approximately six stages. The first of these, until the age of about one and a half years, is the stage of extreme dependency. The second, from a year and a half to three years of age, is dominated by the exploration of his own body, available objects, and the environment. The third stage, from three to six, brings a gradual lessening of dependency on the mother, the beginning of social interaction with contemporaries, and the imitation of adult life in games. From six to the mid-twenties, preparation for adult life constitutes the fourth stage. The fifth, from the mid-twenties to the sixties, is the adult stage, and the sixth, from the mid-sixties to death, is the senescent stage.

In primitive man the fourth stage is considerably shorter, leading into the fifth stage at the age of anywhere from eight to thirteen years. In modern times we have carried over a vestige of this in religious confirmation rites. In earlier times of our own era, too, youngsters were apprenticed to crafts and guilds within this earlier age range, and were expected to undertake adult responsibilities from then on. It is only three generations ago that the child labor laws were enacted and these were another expression of the tendency to prolong childhood.

The intellectual development of primitive man lagged behind his emotional maturity. As man acquired greater control over his environment, and childhood became prolonged, evaluative judgment acquired in games-playing grew to greater prominence. Emotional development did not continue into old age, but was cut off in man's middle years, the period of his greatest virility. Coincidentally with this, not surprisingly, the importance and respect given to old age diminished. Increasingly, the pacemaking part of society has shifted further and further toward the younger years, until at present we find adolescent attitudes imposing standards on the whole society, a condition we shall be discussing at greater length later.

In this chapter we have endeavored to show how intelligence has arisen as an overcompensatory mechanism as man's bodily powers diminished. We have also shown that wherever intelligent species appear in nature, these species are also in some way physically regressive, and the means by which the intelligence has developed and how its evaluative function is gradually replacing automatic instinctual responses.

Intelligence may be considered both a cause and an effect of regression, and it is safe to state that where we see intelligence we may expect to find regression.

CHAPTER THREE

Genius

Le genie, c'est l'enfance retrouvée.*
　　　　　—*Baudelaire*

The word itself has an interesting derivation. In its earliest meaning, the *genius* of the Roman house-father and the *iuno* of the house-mother were worshipped. These were not the "souls" of ancestors in our sense of the word, but rather the male and female forms of a family's or clan's powers of continuing itself by reproduction; they were, so to speak, in the custody of the heads of the family or clan for so long as they lived, and passed on at death to the care of the successors.

With the rise of individualism the original meaning was lost and the word came to signify an equivalent of the Greek *daimon*, a sort of personification of an individual's natural desires. Still later it was thought of as a kind of guardian angel, a higher self, and eventually as the essence of a person's character or temper. In this way we speak of the *genius* of a race, meaning not its gifts but its essential nature.

* "Genius is childhood recaptured."

Nowadays, of course, when we use the word *genius* we are referring to "the highest conceivable form of original ability, something altogether extraordinary and beyond even supreme educational prowess, and differing from 'talent,' which is usually distinguished as marked intellectual capacity short only of the inexplicable and unique endowment to which the term 'genius' is confined."

The word itself, therefore, carries some implication and recognition of genius as an essential part of a personality, quite unique, and inherent in the person's genealogy.

Nothing, however, is unique in nature. Whenever we see a property that appears to us remarkable, we may be sure that it is to be found somewhere else in nature, even if in a less obvious form, and a case in point would be the genius.

In evolution a deviant organism, if it does not perish, is apt to have found and developed an overcompensation for the deficiency, and so we see in a single living entity the surprising coexistence of maladaptive features alongside one or more that are superb. A good example would be the whale, with its exceptional capacity for auditory perception on the one hand and its huge, unwieldy body on the other.

In a genius we see exceptional capacity for original and innovative thinking in an individual who frequently harbors deficiencies that are sometimes obvious, sometimes less obvious but nevertheless present. While every genius is not necessarily "mad," yet we often find in him either physical or mental characteristics which function less well than those of his fellows, and the popular concept of the "mad genius" indicates some instinctively felt understanding of this.

As we have mentioned, virus infections have a strong tendency to find their way to the nervous system. In doing so they may damage it to such an extent as to cause death or, in less severe infection, they may incapacitate the invaded organism. But in some rarer cases the damage is slight and its exact nature is as yet undetermined. Our instruments are not now sensitive enough to detect subtle damage to the nerve cells, and we cannot examine living brain tissue without altering it.

For a genius to come by his great gifts he must possess a greater facility than other mortals to utilize his associations. Basically he does not know more than many others, but he is able to use the knowledge he has to better advantage by detecting similarities between diverse objects or thoughts that would escape even his most intelligent colleagues, if his bent is in the physical field, or to perceive fundamental principles, causes, and effects, if it is in the humanities.

This is, of course, a question of degree, because even an average person may perceive such similarities, leading to solutions to problems; but the genius makes totally unexpected connections. A hundred years ago, suppuration in wounds of surgical patients was accepted. It was the Scottish surgeon Joseph Lister who first revealed the relationship between suppuration in a wound and the distant phenomenon of fermentation in wine, and his conviction that bacteria were equally responsible for both was for a long time vehemently resisted by his colleagues.

Nerves are not like telephone wires that lead in an uninterrupted line from point to point, but they are in sections, at the junctures (synapses) of which chemical agents in a gelatinous substance control the impulse passing to the next section.

These interruptions act as a kind of series of dams or locks to prevent the flooding of the entire nervous system by any and every stimulus that reaches any part of it. In an epileptic fit, for example, that is what actually happens. It is possible that when a genius has a flash of insight this also happens, but to a lesser degree. That is, his associations, finding little resistance at the synaptic transmissions, are greatly facilitated. This allows the rapid collection in his neocortex of analogies and comparisons, and a recognition of similarities from which he can then assemble a conclusion which opens up entirely new vistas.

If such minute damage should affect the paleocortex as well as the neocortex, it would release uncontrollable instinctual behavior. A person afflicted in this way is at all times aware of such a possibility. Dreading its consequences, he is inclined to shun human contact. This would add to the reasons for the preference of many geniuses for isolation, and that they often lead reclusive lives. These would also be factors in the unbearable tensions and frequent nervous breakdowns commonly associated with their lives.

Dostoevsky, one of the greatest novelists of all time, is a splendid example; indeed, more than an example, he is almost a personification of what we mean. He suffered from epilepsy, so that we know his brain was flooded from time to time with the uncontrolled rush of perceptions that is a result of the diminished resistance at the nerve synapses. His perceptiveness was so phenomenal that he has been credited with foreseeing, or being a precursor of, the science of psychoanalysis, especially in his *The Brothers Karamazov,* where each of the brothers has been seen as the embodiment of an aspect of a single human personality. He had an aversion to bourgeois civilization and found isolation and escape from it in gambling and in traveling abroad. It has been said that his ideas loomed even larger than his imaginative creation, great as that was. Thomas Mann showed the insight of his own genius when he wrote of Dostoevsky:

I am filled with awe, with a profound, mystic, silence-enjoining awe, in the presence of the religious greatness of the damned, in the presence of genius disease and the disease of genius, of the type of the afflicted and the possessed, in whom saint and criminal are one. . . .

I would find it utterly impossible to jest about Nietzsche and Dostoevsky. . . . "The Pale Criminal"—whenever I read this chapter heading in *Zarathustra,* a morbidly inspired work of genius if ever there was one, the eerily grief-ridden features of Dostoevsky, as we know them from a number of good pictures, stand before me. Moreover, I suspect that they were in the mind of the drunken migrainist of Sils Maria [Nietzsche] when he wrote it; for Dostoevsky's work played a remarkable role in his life . . . he calls him the most profound psychologist in world literature. . . .

Mann goes on to speak of Nietzsche as a Luciferian genius, stimulated by disease, and then quotes the Russian critic Merezhovsky who, in various studies of Dostoevsky, wrote:

The criminal curiosity of his insight. . . . The reader is aghast at his omniscience, his penetration into the conscience of a stranger. We are confronted by our own secret thoughts, which we would not reveal to a friend, not even to ourselves.

Undoubtedly [Mann continues] the subconsciousness and even the consciousness of this titanic creator was permanently burdened with a heavy sense of guilt, a sense of the criminal, and this feeling was by no means of purely hypochondriac nature. It was connected with his infirmity, the "sacred" disease, the pre-eminently mystic disease, epilepsy. . . . The attacks occurred on the average of once a month. . . . He often described them. . . . Two symptoms, according to his description, are characteristic of the falling sickness: the incomparable sense of rapture, of inner enlightenment, of harmony, of highest ecstasy . . . and the state of horrible depression and deep grief that follows it. . . . No matter to what extent the malady menaced Dostoevsky's mental powers, it is certain that his genius is most intimately connected with it and colored by it.

Even more revealingly, Nietzsche himself said, "Exceptional conditions make the artist, all conditions that are profoundly related and interlaced with morbid phenomena; it seems impossible to be an artist and not to be sick."

c

Many people have sought to identify genius and have puzzled as to why it seems to be a one-sided development, apparently at the expense of other faculties. One of the purposes of Hunter College in New York, when its experimental school for gifted children was set up was, in addition to a teacher-training program, to attempt to find out whether genius could be recognized at an early age, and fostered. Hunter's experiences after about fifteen years of educating brilliant children was that high intelligence (as measured by standard IQ and achievement tests) led its possessor into a professional life of teaching, law, science, or literature. It was not a prerequisite of genius. They then experimented with admitting children with very great one-sided gifts, regardless of their general intelligence. It is probably too early to determine results from this experiment, but we understand that such children were hard to educate and the school reverted to admitting the very intelligent and orienting its objectives more to its teacher-training program.

We offer our thought: a damage which causes death or enfeeblement of mind in most, in a few individuals (perhaps determined by the very precise degree of the affliction) will promote the appearance of a very unusual mind—in fact, a genius. The arising of genius in this way is an exact analogy of what we have suggested as a factor in the emergence of a new species in the course of evolution.

CHAPTER FOUR

Ideals, Morals, and Esthetic Appreciation

In recent years, ever since the knowledge of man's derivation from and place in the animal world has been widening and more generally recognized, there has been an outcry from those to whom this idea is anathema. The theme of their protest has been: but look at man's intelligence; his ideals and lofty aims; his efforts toward high morality; his poetry, philosophy, and arts; his esthetic appreciation of beauty, of nature, of the wonders of creation; his divine spark, his soul, his essence as an individual—all these set him apart from the animal world! Even if his origins are to be found there, he has progressed beyond it and is now a race apart.

Even George Gaylord Simpson, whose very materialistic view of man was quoted in our introduction ("Man . . . is a state of matter . . .") expressed this response when he added to the statement the comment:

It is, however, a gross misrepresentation to say that he [man] is *just* an accident or *nothing but* an animal. Among all the myriad forms of matter and of life on the earth, or as far as we know in the universe, man is unique. He happens to represent the highest form of organization of matter and energy that has ever appeared. . . .

and he goes on to say that man plans and has purposes; that plan, purpose, goal, all absent in evolution to this point, enter with the coming of man and are inherent in the new evolution, which is confined to him.

The authors have every sympathy with this viewpoint. We treasure our sense of identity, of the inviolability of our "personhood." We like to think that each of us is, in his or her way, at some core, unique. One of us is inclined to resent the invasion of the innermost springs of motivation that constitutes the profession of the other. We each like to regard ourselves as a whole—a result of many forces and influences, yes—but, as they happen to be arranged in each of us, individual, personal, in some ways private—our own. These may or may not be valid feelings, but in some degree or other most people share them.

When most of us look at a splendid painting—a Rembrandt self-portrait, perhaps—we are awed by its deep insight, its masterly composition, its subtle colors, its brilliant execution; we see it whole; it leaves an indelible impression on our minds and senses; it enriches our lives. But there are others who are not satisfied simply to enjoy the painting. They want to find out the means the painter used to achieve it. They measure the proportions, examine the brush strokes, analyze the pigments. None of these activities detracts from the magnificence of the work of art. They do not change it in any way. It remains a work of art, a unique thing, a phenomenon not to be duplicated, even though they may discover the constituents of its

Ideals, Morals, and Esthetic Appreciation 53

achievement. The same is true of man as a species, and of each individual as, in his way, a masterpiece.

Our endeavor, like that of the man who analyzes the pigment in the Rembrandt, is simply to find out how it was done.

We have just written of man's intelligence and of that special sort of intelligence we call genius. Now we should like to present some thoughts on the other virtues which in the opinion of so many set man apart from the rest of the animal kingdom.

In the first place we must recognize that, with the exception probably of esthetic appreciation, none of the other virtues is unique to man. In the matter of individuality there are as great differences between members of other species as there are between men, and they possess many of the same instincts. Throughout nature, as Professor Kessler observed in 1880, "besides the 'law of Mutual Struggle' there is in nature the 'law of Mutual Aid.'"

Prince Piotr Kropotkin, in his well-known *Mutual Aid, A Factor in Evolution,* wrote:

Two aspects of animal life impressed me most during the journeys which I made in my youth in Eastern Siberia and Northern Manchuria. One of them was the extreme severity of the struggle for existence . . . against an inclement nature . . . and the consequent paucity of life over those vast territories. And the other was that even in those few spots where animal life teemed in abundance, I failed to find—although I was eagerly looking for it—that bitter struggle for the means of existence, among animals belonging to the same species, which was considered by most Darwinists (though not always by Darwin himself) as the dominant characteristic of the struggle for life, and the main factor of evolution.

Kropotkin commented that in some cases the "fittest" are not physically the strongest, or the most cunning, but those who learn to combine so as mutually to support each other for the welfare of the community. He follows these comments with a long listing (with details of the methods) of animals which practice mutual aid, from the unconscious mutual support of microscopic pond-life and other microorganisms, through invertebrates (not only termites, ants, and bees, but also locusts, burying-beetles, vanessae, cicindelae, cicadae, etc.) and on through land crabs, kites, vultures, pelicans, mentioning specifically the numerous hunting associations of birds and the equally innumerable associations for migration and breeding, right up to herding mammals, colonies of all kinds of rodents, societies of musk-oxen, polar foxes, cetaceans, elephants, rhinoceros, marmots, bears, prairie dogs, rabbits, and so on. He quotes the naturalist Brehm, who reported:

> The highly intelligent parrot lives in numerous societies or bands, co-operates on expeditions, posts sentries to watch and warn the band, lives always closely united

and that the practice of life in society enables the parrot to attain a high level of intelligence, and also show mutual attachment, friendship, and grief. Kropotkin then pointed out that association and mutual aid are the rule with mammals, and concluded that in the animal world the vast majority of species live in societies and cooperate.

This built-in cooperation in so many forms of life is regulated for the most part by instinctive responses arising from the operation of the nervous system and, in higher forms of life, the brain. In man these instincts, feelings, and all emotions are released through the oldest part of the brain, the paleocortex, and whether in man or less complex forms of life, they function to preserve the species.

In animals such instinctual responses have built-in controls. It is as though an equivalent of the Ten Commandments were

Ideals, Morals, and Esthetic Appreciation 55

indelibly imprinted in their nervous systems in the form of reflexes, so that in the animal world attack responses do not irreparably harm their own kind. With the rarest exceptions, and then usually for special reasons, no animal except man will kill a member of its own species. The loser in a fight for a mate, or for leadership in a herd, will make a ritual gesture of submission, thus acknowledging the dominance of the winner; this settles the fight. There are many variations of this ritual. In one species the loser may offer his jugular vein; in others (the monkeys and apes) the weaker signals his subordination by offering his rump to the stronger in a gesture imitating the female sexual posture—this may take place between females and immature young as well as between males. Bison have a "passive-avoidance" system in which one individual simply moves out of another's way in a majority of cases. When this does not occur, the preliminaries to a fight begin. The males approach each other, bellowing and pawing the ground, but even encounters that reach this stage usually do not end in a fight. If they should do so, the fight is over when the loser turns his head away from the winner. An animal that retreats without turning its head is pursued until it does, so that in nearly every case the fight is ended by the loser turning at least his head and perhaps his entire flank to his adversary at a distance of only a step or two. Near fights are ended in the same way as fights, with the loser submitting, often at the last moment, by turning away his head. Whatever the signal of the species, it is given and recognized instinctually and acts as an immutable law.

Man's efforts toward moral behavior, his elaborate philosophies designed to promote it, and his customs and laws designed to enforce it, have all arisen out of the basic necessity of cooperation for survival. Personal desires subordinated to the needs of the group, such precepts as "Do unto others as you would they do unto you," are all codifications of this necessity expressed in a kind of folk wisdom.

Originally man's defenses, like those of other animals, functioned through the operation of the paleocortex (the old brain) by means of instincts and emotions, but as his habits began to promote the development of the neocortex (the new brain) and his reasoning capacities emerged, his group living became more complex, and so did his individual interactions within it.

Somewhere along the way some wise man, a tribal elder or shaman perhaps, surely had an opportunity to observe many varieties of behavior in response to an event or condition of tribal life. His neocortex would have formed an evaluative judgment and recognized which one resulted in the greatest benefit to the group, and he would then teach this particular behavior to the children. In time it would have been acknowledged as desirable behavior by the whole tribe and codified as a law or ideal, or considered essential to tribal morality. In the course of time, conditions may have fostered desires to change some parts of the tribe's laws and customs, and a struggle between conservatives and radicals would have ensued, but eventually the law would have been updated, the ideal revised, and the tribal morality or custom modified.

Since instinctive reflex action is stereotyped and has no flexibility to allow for sudden, unexpected changes in threatening situations, the new ability to make evaluative judgments and to discriminate between courses of action was in many ways an immense advance. The ability to consult his memory-bank speedily and choose the most desirable of alternative actions must have enhanced man's hunting prowess, and later enabled him to use his stored knowledge to increase his agricultural skills. As we approach the times of historical man we see the judgmental quality of the neocortex being exercised in dictating norms of conduct. This development was at variance from every known aspect of animal behavior until then.

Ideals, Morals, and Esthetic Appreciation

As a sidelight it is interesting to note that it was in very early prehistoric times that man discovered the process of fermentation of plants and their products. At first he used such distillations to promote religious fervor, for he rightly sensed a feeling of the falling away of the everyday self and the emergence of a consciousness of being possessed by another "spirit." Since the neocortex is the newest and most delicate part of the brain, it is the most susceptible to anesthetics and intoxicants. Therefore instinctual behavior surfaces more readily in a drunken person, as the voice of his reason has been numbed into silence. When, as sometimes happens, that voice of reason has a nagging or reproaching tone, the muting effect of alcohol or other intoxicant is sought out and welcomed. It is unfortunate that alcohol is addictive and, eventually, maiming and even killing, for it seems that people who resort to strong drink have a vague awareness of the effect it has in silencing their reason (social conscience), and that without actually understanding the mechanisms they enjoy the resulting temporary release from their "civilized" nature.

Before it learned to nag, the *raison d'être* of the neocortex was to provide a speedy appraisal of events in nature, evaluate them, and prompt suitable action. However, as it grew in complexity some of its function was refined to evaluate the manifestations of the rest of the brain, and in particular the emotional responses. In other words, it became introspective. It had recognized that actions which tended to the "greatest good of the greatest number," even if they were a disadvantage to some, in the long run served better the interests of the group than would some immediate individual gratification. In this way such actions would have been taught as estimable, even if they were difficult to perform, and there grew (if reluctantly) a recognition that each person's best interest was thus served. And so a groundwork was laid for the appreciation of, and high value set on, ideals, moral concepts, and such "human" phenomena. All philosophies and systems of ethics stem from this basic necessity of man's nature for cooperation to make group life possible.

However, while the gradual enlargement and growth in complexity of the neocortex promoted these reasonable and desirable results, as we have mentioned several times, it is only a problem-solving apparatus. Emotions and feelings, including compassion, are properties of the older, instinctually motivated, paleocortex. It is a quirk of nature that the growth of our reasoning mind which, because of its categorizing and evaluating propensities, consistently seeks to establish order, in so doing has partially blocked instinctual behavior. We see this most clearly exemplified in such codes as the Ten Commandments, in some Oriental ascetic philosophies, and in the downgrading of sensory gratification by several religions, which are all attempts by the neocortex to neutralize the functioning of the paleocortex.

And so we have, along with the desirable results of reason, also its obverse, which is reason promoting solutions logical enough but devoid of modification by the emotions. This has led to such excesses as the Spanish Inquisition, the extermination of one whole class of people by the French revolutionaries and of another by the Russian Bolshevik revolutionaries, and made possible the mind-boggling mass murder of a third of an entire race by the German Hitlerites—all conducted with ever-increasing efficiency and justified by the process of reason as means to a desired end.

We are speaking here, of course, of impersonal violence, and not manifestations of abnormal instinctual behavior such as rioting, mob action, or murder, which we shall mention later.

It upset all the ideas we had of "human" qualities to see intelligent and educated persons participate in, and direct with cold-blooded cruelty, the mass killings that have stunned our

Ideals, Morals, and Esthetic Appreciation 59

imaginations in recent wars and revolutions. Dr. F. Wertheim stated, on the occasion of receiving the E. A. Sutherland Memorial Medal for outstanding contributions to psychiatry:

"On January 25th, 1944, the biggest wartime meeting of German top military leaders took place in Poznan, Poland. These were not only highly trained but also highly educated men, most of whom were not National Socialists. To the over 250 generals and admirals, Himmler outlined his plans for the extermination of civilians, men, women and children, in the occupied Eastern regions. The population was to be cut down by thirty million. The plan was warmly applauded. Only five persons present at the meeting abstained." Eminent German psychiatrists and pediatricians associated with the foremost universities of their country sponsored, planned, and organized the mass extermination of 275,000 patients in their mental hospitals. Dr. Wertheim further stated: "On no occasion did Hitler or the state order the executions. The doctors were merely given the power to use their own discretion, which they did with zeal."

So far as military leaders are concerned, perhaps we may understand better an impersonal attitude toward killing, since this is part of their profession and their function in society, but these were doctors.

Among military men of all nations, of course, we find the same basic attitudes if not always quite the same ruthlessness. Scientists, too, if assigned to work on weaponry, calculate the effectiveness of their products in terms of so many thousands or hundreds of thousands of people killed with the rational impartiality of a manufacturer projecting sales curves on a chart.

Are all these intelligent men crazed killers? Do they harbor a perverted instinct to maim or kill? Far from it. In their private lives they are as gentle and compassionate as—perhaps even more so than—the pacifist who clamors for an end to all wars. Their feelings are aroused at the sight of a hurt animal, an accident to a child, or a neighbor in difficulties, and they will do their best to be helpful or to mitigate the pain. At their offices, though, only their intelligence and reason are called into play, and here they will pursue logical deductions to the bitter end. The soldier to be killed, the civilian to be incinerated, the destruction to be wrought are only some of many factors to be considered in the efficient and reasoned accomplishment of their objectives.

To sum up our discussion, as the neocortex (reason) has taken over many of the functions of the paleocortex (instinct) it has, it is true, engendered idealism, morality, and sensitivity to beauty and arts, but by the same process our built-in instinctual controls have been overridden. In the same way that we are slowly losing some other physical organs such as hair, teeth, or toes, so are we now losing some of those functions of the old brain governing instincts. Our paleocortex is on the way to becoming vestigial, with the result that killing (ranging from individual murder, through mass executions and war, to the wholesale slaughter of a race) within our species has become as much of a unique phenomenon in the animal kingdom as our capacity for evolving abstract principles and ideals.

The development of precisely those virtues, and just those qualities on which man prides himself as making him better than a beast, are the results of the same processes that have led to the most revolting aspects of human behavior, and in terms of the survival of the species, may fairly be called regressive if not downright degenerate.

CHAPTER FIVE

Art as an Indicator

The arts are to society what dreams are to the individual. Arts, myths, all forms of cultural expression, are symbolic projections of the underlying mental states of the society that produces them.

Man has left records of his presence in works of art for more than ten thousand years. The earliest of which we have any knowledge are those of Paleolithic (Stone Age) man, and they are to be found in caves in many places, especially in France and in Spain. The cave paintings are not all alike or of one age. Some were produced by the use of mineral oxides (those of iron gave various shades of red and that of manganese a blue-black), carbonates of iron (giving colors ranging from yellow to orange), and burnt bones (providing the artist with black)—the raw colors were pounded and mixed with fats. Others were merely engraved with sharp flint tools. Probably the best-known are the famous bison frescos in the cave of Altamira, in Spain.

The caves where these paintings and engravings have been

found were not homes but, possibly, sacred spots where ritual practices took place, and probably they were decorated for much the same reason many later churches were ornamented. The numerous representations of animals and hunting episodes seem to show, as might be expected, that the quest for food was the dominant consideration of the men who produced them, and their drawings give us some indication of their desire to propitiate the spirits of the hunted animals.

We have abundant examples of man's artistic activities in the succeeding Neolithic and Bronze ages in Egypt, Crete, and Greece, and in Malta and Gozo we can see the less well-known, marvelously preserved neolithic temples of Tarxien, Mnaidra, Hagiar Qim, and the Hypogeum, an underground temple and necropolis, all about five thousand years old. In this era man still devoted most of his artistic skills to ritual purposes, though toward the end he began to make ornaments for his person and to decorate his household objects. By this time he had become more of an agriculturalist than a hunter, so the natural forces he wished to propitiate were those connected with fertility, and we find him making images, statuettes, idols, of "The Great Goddess," the giver of fertility in the broadest sense of the term. These idols provide evidence of the beginnings of religious beliefs, although such concepts were still very limited in scope, and must still have contained strong elements of magic. Yet the ubiquity of the idols over the area indicates what was man's greatest preoccupation of that period.

Over a span of about a thousand years, as agricultural man began to prosper and gain sufficient respite from the work essential to sustain his existence, he must have pondered the subject of his own mortality. We are made aware of this by the gradual adding of funerary objects, which we find in increasing quantity and of ever greater splendor, along with a progressive complexity of gods, among the relics we have uncovered in the traces of the beginnings of Western civilization and culture in the eastern Mediterranean, dating from about the second millennium before Christ.

It should be mentioned, moreover, that wherever the works of man have been preserved to us, they show approximately the same developments, especially in the early stages, regardless of which part of the globe the men inhabited. In China, for example, bronze artifacts have been molded and chiseled from the earliest days, and many examples have been preserved which reveal their archaic origin. The bronze cauldrons recorded to have been cast for the great Yu, founder of the Hsia Dynasty (2205–1767 B.C.), were said to have been decorated with evil demons of the storm and nature spirits. Although these cauldrons were lost in the troubles which occurred at the close of the Chou Dynasty, their shape was preserved in the cauldron in the courtyard of the royal palace at Peking. Among the most interesting objects of those primitive times in what is now China are the oracle bones, dating back three to four thousand years, which were used as a method of consulting the spirits of ancestors. And the pottery funerary urns of China and Korea of a slightly later time are certainly at least as carefully wrought and as beautiful as their equivalents in the Western world.

It is not our place here, nor is it our intention, to give a history of art. What we wish to point out is how the works of the artist of each era, age, and period give strong evidence of the chief concerns of their time. In the main, it is not from printed books that we visualize and form our estimate of the life, culture, and character of ancient Egypt, Assyria, Greece, or Rome, but from ruined buildings, carved stones, remnants of bronze works, fragments of pottery, painted walls, personal adornments, and household objects dug out of the ground by the excavator's spade. History becomes a living reality through art. It is not the conscious endeavor of the artist to do this, but he is a man of his own time and place, and he has no choice but to express himself in the terms, thoughts, feelings, and ideals of that time and place. To show how valid this is we shall give here briefly, in the most general, over-all terms, the salient features of the arts of succeeding ages.

By the fifth century before Christ, the increased boldness of navigators led to a gradually developing science, especially in the fields of mathematics and astronomy. The growth of wealth, too, bringing that leisure and security which are the prerequisites of research and speculation, gave men the temerity to attempt to find natural explanations for processes and occurrences that had earlier been attributed to supernatural powers. Socrates expressed the spirit of the age when he said to Crito, "Do you then be reasonable, and do not mind whether the teachers of philosophy be good or bad, but think only of Philosophy herself. Try to examine her well and truly. . . ." Reason was the method, knowledge the instrument, and wisdom the ideal. If man made best use of his best capacities, he could know truth. Art in the Greece of this time, reflecting its thoughts and ideals, was anthropocentric, expressed through the person of man; it presumed the perfectability of his reason, his character, his form. In the writings of its thinkers and its dramatists it achieved heights not regained for two thousand years. In the works of such sculptors as Phidias and Praxiteles and of its architects, it developed a perfection of symmetry and rhythm beyond the reach of nature. It evolved the ideal type of human proportions, which to this day remains the standard of perfection.

Following the grandeur of Imperial Rome and its reflection

in the magnificence and luxury of its buildings and the pride of its portrait statuary, we come to the Middle Ages. In the period from about the fifth to the fifteenth centuries A.D. we find, as at no other time, depths, and the all-encompassing influence, of religious experience. Everything that was fresh and vigorous in the people of Europe was drawn out and directed in the service of religion. Religious fervor permeated every aspect of life. It could be perverted into an intensity of persecution or cruelty, into decadent orgies of sophisticated superstition, just as it could respond to eccentric and heretical influences or be devoted to learning and statesmanship. It pervaded the arts. From the whole of this thousand years, with the possible exception of some portraits, it would be hard to find a painting, a statue, a piece of music, or a written work not imbued with a sense of religion; and the towering monuments of the age—the cathedrals, with their soaring lines, lofty spires, devoted embellishments—stand above all as the sign of the hopes and fears, ideals and aspirations, of the total life of medieval man.

A particularly revealing single instance of the artist as a mirror of his times is offered in a long letter written by Petrarch. Until the dawn of the Renaissance in Italy the beauty of mountain scenery was a closed book to the medieval mind. A mountain was a thing to be shunned, an impediment to traffic, a source of danger and fatigue. Even a poet of the eminence of Petrarch found it necessary to excuse his eccentricity in undertaking an unnecessary mountain expedition by quoting the example of Philip of Macedonia, who had ascended Mount Hemus in a similar spirit of enterprise. Nevertheless this letter, which fills ten printed pages and contains much information about the hardships, dangers, and fatigues of the excursion as well as many theoretical reflections, includes no hint of any emotional response to nature in her most majestic moods, no description, no word of esthetic appreciation. And this from the mind and pen of a poet.

Western man emerged from the medieval age and entered the period we call the Renaissance. Although this is a time where the fresh stage of vital energy has commonly been attributed to a recovery of antique culture, yet it was more than simply a revival of learning. Recovered from the confusion consequent on the dissolution of the Roman empire, the Teutonic tribes civilized and assimilated to the previously Latinized races they had conquered, the time was ripe for a continuation and further development of the exploration, invention, discovery, intellectual activity—the humanism—that had taken root in Greece before the rise of Rome. It was a period of liberation, when man strived to reconstitute himself as a free being and when he reasserted his rights to self-emancipation in his political and intellectual life. In the stupendous flowering of all the arts which took place in the Western world at this time—whether in the paintings of Raphael, Leonardo da Vinci, Titian, Rembrandt, Rubens, Velázquez; the sculpture of Michelangelo; or the writings of Dante, Cervantes, Rabelais, Shakespeare, or Erasmus—the spirit of the age was abundantly reflected.

We have given the most obvious examples from the epochs of Western life and art, since these are the ones that spring most readily to the mind of a Western writer and are most readily recognized by a Western reader. Nonetheless, our first statement, that the mind and soul of a society may be perceived by studying the works of its artists, is true of all civilizations and cultures in all times, and could just as well have been illustrated by examples from Far Eastern, Byzantine, Islamic, African, Central American, Indian, or any other art. It is a truism that art is, and has always been, an essential need of humanity. It is as necessary as articulate speech. It is indispensable to civilization. The art of each race gives form to its distinct character and rhythm. It reflects, if it does not actually condition, the whole manner of life of a nation or period. Life and art are inseparably interwoven.

Now let us look at the art of our own times.

In speaking of our own times we of course realize that no culture succeeds another in an abrupt fashion. While the beginnings of the Renaissance were to be found in a reaction against the long period of the bondage of the human spirit to oppressive ecclesiastical and political orthodoxy, the seeds of the modern world are to be found embedded in the period of the Renaissance. But since we must take some point as a beginning, the reaction of painters to the development of photography in the nineteenth century is the most convenient.

In a preceding chapter we have offered the view that the preoccupation of man with intellectual pursuits constitutes a prolongation of the childlike attributes of learning, experimentation, and discovery. The results of the gradual recovery of the freedom of the human intellect from the time of the Renaissance have been gathering momentum ever since. However, as late as December 1770, in a discourse delivered at the Royal Academy in London on the distribution of the prizes, Sir Joshua Reynolds stated the ideals of the artist in these terms: "Instead of endeavoring to amuse mankind with the minute neatness of his imitations, he must endeavor to improve them by the grandeur of his ideas; instead of seeking praise by deceiving the superficial sense of the spectator, he must strive for fame by captivating the imagination...." He also spoke of "intellectual dignity." That Reynolds was aware of the difference between a youthful and a mature approach to art is shown by a comment in his first discourse, on the opening of the Royal Academy in January 1769, when, speaking of his students, he remarked: "At that age it is natural for them to be more captivated with what is brilliant than with what is solid," and he went on to exhort them to diligence, mastery, and solid achievement. Yet less than a hundred years later, influenced by the scientific developments of their time, we find the Impressionists, completely unconcerned with noble ideas, preoccupied with studying and interpreting optics and the nature of light.

To some extent science had entered the tangled skein of forces influencing art from the time of Leonardo da Vinci—who, himself a scientist, understood that as the subject recedes from the eye, subtle changes in illumination and color occur. Rembrandt too studied chiaroscuro, but although Newton first explained the dispersion of light in 1666, the significance of his discovery for painting was not fully recognized until the time of Courbet, Manet, Monet, Renoir, Degas, and their circles in the nineteenth century. It was they, the Impressionists, who, understanding that white light is made up of many colors, and that two or more may blend to form a third, achieved their effects by amassing small patches of different colors to be blended by the eye of the observer, and it was this principle that became a turning point in the practice of art. After them the Neo-Impressionists (Seurat, Pissaro, Cézanne, Van Gogh, Gauguin, Vuillard, Bonnard, and their groups), taking their ideas further—and, in the case of Cézanne, experimenting with spatial relationships as well as color—led to the work of the Fauves and the Expressionists such as Dufy, Vlaminck, Utrillo, Rouault, Derain, and Matisse, whose "serene detached world of forms wherein line, shape and color exist almost independently of the subject. The subject, so to speak, is only a comment on the artistic elements." The drawing is simplified and the emphasis is on the color. The essence of Matisse's work has been summed up as "simplicity, serenity, clarity."

Later Expressionists, such as the German Blue Rider group and the Russian Kandinsky, carried this development into styles of painting that have been described as "rhythmical musical compositions of sweeping curves and flowing lines."

These art movements, all carried over into our century, were accompanied by a conscious drawing of inspiration from the forms of primitive art, leading to the intellectual play of Cubism by such greatly talented painters as Braque and Picasso and by numerous contemporary sculptors. The term "intellectual play" would also describe the straight-line compositions of Mondrian (with their great influence on modern architecture and the subsequent minimal sculptors) and the geometric forms of such painters as Albers, Malevich, and Kupka.

Gone are ideas of ennobling the thoughts and emotions of man. In fact, as C. M. Phillipps mourned in an introduction to an edition of Reynolds' discourses published in 1906, "These, for art, are melancholy days—days divested of all tradition and agreement—which it occupies rather in experimenting on its own methods and processes than in producing definite constructive work. Such experiments, however, are taken very seriously by contemporaries, and all kinds of ingenious, far-fetched tricks are played in paint or marble with as much zeal as if they formed part of a genuine creative movement.... The combined effect of this kind of art and this kind of art criticism on a disinterested stranger would probably be that, far from conceiving of art as a very important and vitally human affair, he would conclude that it was an extremely clever and ingenious kind of juggling, which, however interesting to cliques and coteries, could be of no concern to mankind in general." He also writes of "this tendency to triviality, to which in an experimental age we are liable." That it was, in fact, the reflection of the then-current concerns of mankind did not occur to him. We like to imagine what the good Mr. Phillipps might have had to say of art and art criticism at our present point in time!

Since Cubism we have seen such movements as the Dadaist of the 1920s. Although the artists of this group were extremely gifted, they concentrated their talents and their efforts on mocking the arts, like children thumbing their noses at anything serious. It is true that there were many factors producing the movement, including the historical and the social. Nevertheless it came into being, dominated artistic life for several years, and influenced later movements.

A little later the Surrealists (Tanguy, Dali, Magritte, de Chirico, Max Ernst, Chagall, Miró, Klee, and others) played fantasy games in paint. Although it is a challenge for the artist to paint dream images, he is handicapped by the fact that each dream is the experience of a single individual and depends for its meaning on the events in the private life of that person. The clearer and more detailed its description, the less likely it is to be comprehensible to others. Thus surrealist art inevitably presented feelings so private that communication became difficult. In many ways its esoteric forms and private symbols remind one of the child's universal delight in secret clubs, secret signs, and passwords. In fact, the similarity to childlike characteristics of this form of artistic expression has been remarked by many people. Jacques Dupin notes in an introduction to the works of Miró: "The striking simplicity of his mature works . . . along with the vitality of the color and the ingenuity of his figures and symbols, have established the legend of a man gifted with a child's sensitivity miraculously preserved in all its freshness." And Paul Klee, writing on modern art, states that he considers art an exercise in self-analysis, but realizes that individual effort is not sufficient. The final source of power in the artist, he notes, is given by society, and "modern society has no sense of community... of people for whom and with whom we work." Social disunity and the spiritual separateness of society, he writes, is reflected in the work of its artists.

Then, among the work of the Abstract Impressionists (Tobey, Rothko, de Kooning, Motherwell, Still, and the many others of this school) there is that of such artists as Jackson Pollock, who surrendered any thought either of ennobling concepts or of technical competence, to drip or fling paint on to canvas, or, like Franz Kline, to daub (albeit intriguing) huge brush strokes, taking as much pleasure in the bodily movements of dripping, flinging, and daubing as in the results of their activity. Most parents of children in nursery schools felt their infants could do as well and, indeed, many of them did. We have seen great interest shown in children's art, its unschooled nature being considered a virtue (exhibiting "fresh" seeing) and in such childlike (unschooled) painters as Rousseau, Grandma Moses, or Bombois. It is also perhaps significant that the extremely attractive "mobiles" of Alexander Calder, probably the greatest sculptor of this period, have been commercially adapted for use in children's rooms, games and "fun" rooms, and for attachments onto baby carriages, where they delight infants below six months of age.

In our own time art has become "fun." We have recently come through a cycle of "Pop" art as practiced by such men as Warhol, Jasper Johns, Rauschenberg, Lichtenstein, and Oldenburg. While one cannot deny the admiration one feels for the artist who sees monumental forms in the artifacts and accouterments of our everyday lives, and there is no doubt of the esthetic pleasure given by the work of such artists as Claes Oldenburg, one's enjoyment is of a different category from that experienced in contemplating the works of art produced by all the generations of man until less than a hundred years ago.

If one looks at Oldenburg's sculptures such as *Fagends* or *Soft Toilets,* and especially at his incredibly imaginative drawings of such things as hamburgers, frankfurters, drainpipes, vacuum cleaners, Good Humor bars, baked potatoes, or ironing boards, projected as public monuments, one feels a certain delight—but the expressions that first come to the mind are "How ingenious!" "How clever!" "Indeed, some of these forms are truly monumental ... what fun!" They are essentially the same feelings we have when confronted with the clever and original perceptions of gifted children—their amusing verbal observations or their ingenious constructions. We feel in them the same freshness of vision, almost the sense of wonder that children feel at the myriad forms of nature and of life around them as they meet each for the first time, and the child's ceaseless exploration and experimentation. The esthetic pleasure is undeniable, but how different it is in quality from the flooding into the consciousness of the high ideals, noble thoughts, spiritual values—along with some sense of admiration for the craftsmanship, the composition, the infinite painstaking attention to every detail inspired in us in the contemplation of the art works of earlier times. Claes Oldenburg, in fact, when interviewed late in 1969 by *The New York Times* and asked what monument he would like to leave of himself, remarked: "It could be something with water—water has fun...."

This century has also witnessed the development of an "adult" audience for such art forms as the comic strip; the movie cartoons, ranging from Felix the Cat through Mickey Mouse and Popeye the Sailor to Mr. McGoo; the so-called Hard Edge painters, whose simple arrangements of prismatic colors can be easily comprehended and appreciated by any infant; collages of random materials, and random forms produced by accident, such as *objets trouvés,* driftwood sculpture, and so on. While it cannot be disputed that some of these last possess attractive qualities, they nevertheless fall into the category of the objects a small boy finds irresistible and with which he stuffs his pockets, rather than alongside the more adult concerns of form, content, religious devotion, high ideals, harmony, and serious study of visual values that have occupied the artists of earlier ages.

And while we speak of form and harmony, let us contemplate the dance of our times. From its origins as a ritual of propitiation and worship of the gods, the social dance has (succeeding a licentious period in ancient Rome) progressed through stately and courtly forms such as the pavane, the minuet, the gavotte, the quadrille, and the cotillion, alongside ritualistic and country forms all over the world until, in our century, we have danced the Charleston, the Lindy Hop, the jitterbug and, now, rock-and-roll.

Although we have mentioned some of the greatest writers cursorily in the course of this chapter, we have not given detailed examples from the course of literature as we have from that of painting. It could be done, for in literature there has been a parallel development. The earliest writers recounted the myths which carried the traditions and lore of their people and sagas of folk heroes who reflected their ideals. Then came the works of thinkers and philosophers whose endeavors were to edify man and teach him to live well, and the great milestones of religious writings like the Bible, the works of Confucius, and the Rig Veda. The great epic poems of the beginning of our era, like *Widsith, Beowulf,* the *Nibelungenlied,* the *Chanson de Roland,* were still to a large extent the chronicles of heroes and chiefs, which continued to be written and recounted alongside the religion-influenced writings of the times.

We included the names of the most oustanding authors along with the painters of the Renaissance who, with many others, added their genius to the incalculable cultural wealth of that time. By then, although some of the work was written to entertain, it was also intended to instruct, even if only by holding up a mirror to human follies. It was only in the eighteenth century, with the beginning of the development of the novel form, that written works as ends in themselves and primarily to entertain, began to appear. The decisive turning-point came in our century with the stream-of-consciousness novel, which had much of the same quality of privacy of language and symbols as the surrealist paintings. Since then there has been an outpouring in two streams, one (which might be called the "How To Do It" or the "Did You Know?" stream) catering to the childlike activities and insatiable curiosity of our times, and the other pure entertainment on the lowest level, without the slightest intent to edify, this stream reaching its culmination in the mass-circulation newspapers, which might be described as our daily deluge of drivel. To go into this more deeply would be redundant, as the points we wish to make are abundantly illustrated by the movements in painting.

It is scarcely necessary to insist upon the fallacy of such popular notions as the identification of art with the representation of nature or, worse still, of the beautiful in nature. Art is not representation, but interpretation; and it is not too much to say that art begins where the artist departs from the strict imitation of nature, imposing upon her a rhythm of his own creation.

The emotional urge which spurs men to create art has at different times and in different individuals been caused by different influences, but if one wished to summarize Western experience one could almost do so in the form of a chart, from ancient to modern times, in these terms:

All Adult	MAGIC PROPITIATION IDEAS OF IDEAL BEAUTY, FORM, AND SPLENDOR RELIGIOUS DEVOTION
Turning point	SCIENTIFIC PRINCIPLES
	to
All childlike (ingenious play)	Art has no object but to delight the eye, or the mind through the eye. Exploring of forms and colors without any reference to content Private symbols. Esoteric forms. Art is an end in itself Art is fun.

It may be asked how we determine which are "adult" preoccupations and which are adolescent or childlike. The method we have used is to look at man at the height of his procreative period in each era, and compare his activities at that point in terms of their survival value for himself and his tribe (extended family).

In the most primitive times man was entirely occupied with the absolutely essential matters of obtaining food, defending himself, his mate and offspring, and ensuring the continuation of his species. We may consider this the classic pattern of behavior for the mature animal (including man). Therefore it is natural for prehistoric man to depict the source of his sustenance, the pursuit of which dominated his life, as soon as he found the means of doing so.

Childhood is a period of learning. The child is protected and his essential needs are provided for him. He occupies his time in play, through which he practices skills, finds out about the nature of his surroundings, and experiments with whatever comes to hand. His activities are not purposeful but experimental, and his products are ends in themselves—produced only because it pleases or intrigues the child to produce them. These qualities are all motivating forces in modern art.

As the child grows into adolescence and youth, he is still protected and it is still unnecessary for him to occupy himself with the mature activities of self- and group-support and protection. However, the early playfulness has largely left him. His interests are more experimental and his occupations exploratory, directed toward learning and discovery. For this reason we have classified the work of the Impressionists as a turning point, or adolescent, stage.

It has been said that art not only holds a mirror up to nature, but also that the perceptions of artists are like antennae which sense and pick up some trend of the future, and that it is for this reason it so often takes a long time for the general public to catch up with the ideas or forms of expression of its artists. If this be the case at the present, it certainly appears that all of our artists have sensed the trend which is the subject of this book!

CHAPTER SIX

The Expanding Nursery

HOME

If our theory of progressive infantilization is valid, as we believe it is, then it will in some way or other be apparent in every aspect of our lives, and should certainly be detectable in that fulcrum of our social being, the home, and extend into all phases of pleasure.

The infant's chief sources of pleasure are bodily contact with his mother, and, accessory to the satisfaction of his hunger, the sensual delights of eating and elimination.

It goes without saying that the pleasures of the table have been appreciated throughout recorded times and that they probably predate both the table itself and recorded times. However, it is possible to observe through the ages some quite basic changes in the partaking, or indulging, in this pleasure.

In the earliest days the possibility of eating at all seems to have been regarded very highly, as witnessed by the proliferation of religious rituals at harvest time, which subsequently became our first festivals. Our own Thanksgiving dinner is the most obvious vestige of this phase. Later, when sufficient food for the maintenance of life was taken more for granted, the greatest gustatory pleasure was derived from quantity—the joy of having enough and to spare—the ability to demonstrate wealth and superiority by overeating. The giving of a banquet became a symbol of status, and participating in it a major satisfaction. The pleasures of banqueting probably reached some sort of apogee in Roman times, when it was the practice not only to gorge to capacity but also to have the throat tickled with a feather to induce vomiting and the ability to gorge again. Actually, overeating as a pleasure remained with us until comparatively recent times. We have a mental picture of the fat medieval monk, whose self-denial in other areas left him the possibility of no gratification but that of overeating, and it is hardly surprising that many of our finest liqueurs originated in the herbal concoctions of medieval abbeys. The great actor Charles Laughton left an indelible impression on our memories with his wonderful portrayal of a rotund, gluttonous, sixteenth-century overeater, so that those who saw his performance are hardly able any more to think of Henry VIII of England except in terms of Laughton's portrait of him in that banqueting scene. As late as the eighteenth century, Rowlandson made the gluttony and some of the more swinish table habits of the upper classes the biting target of some of his devastating drawings and prints.

But as the neocortex is in the process of taking over control of our more basic instincts, it is also moving in on our appetites, indulgences, and pleasures. In approximately the last hundred years there has been a progressive decline in the quantities of food eaten. (We are not speaking here of the rather better feeding of the poorer segments of populations as a result of their growing affluence, but solely of eating as a pleasurable diversion.) We are making up for the lesser amounts eaten by the distinctly cerebral pleasure of refining the flavors, elaborating the recipes, experimenting in subtler taste and visual contrasts, and enhancing the food by serving it in more attractive vessels and surrounding it with beautiful glass, china, silverware, napery and flowers. Alongside this trend we are offered more and more complicated gadgets for the preparation and serving of food. The production of utensils for backyard cooking has emerged as a major industry. A proliferation of cookbooks such as we have never before seen attests and contributes to the ever greater interest in the pleasure of eating.

To come to the corollary of our increasingly sophisticated attention to eating, we must expect to find a similar focus of attention on the elimination of the body's waste products, and on that other sensual satisfaction of infancy, the care of the skin.

Trends of this nature, too, have been observable throughout history. In many instances, a group's attainment of a high point in its civilization is paralleled by a low regard for the unadulterated operation of instincts and a sophisticated, intellectually imposed elaboration of culinary and cosmetic arts. This phase has usually immediately preceded the decline or dying out of the culture that indulged in it. We have examples of this, especially in the cosmetic attention given the skin in the cultures of ancient Crete, Egypt, and Rome, where adornment of the eyes, nipples, and nails by painting was the custom, as well as elaborate arrangement of the hair and lavish indulgence in bathing (often in milk), and anointing and perfuming the skin. In the Western world the court of Louis XIV of France also demonstrated these tendencies shortly before the fall of the *ancien régime*. It may be argued that the wealth accumulated by the successes of these cultures was the prime factor in such indulgences, but the fact is that wealth was put to these uses.

In our own time, along with the multiplication of the gadgetry and refinements of cuisine, we are also experiencing a great interest in the bathroom. A larger variety of gadgetry for bathroom use is being produced; the increase in the number of bathrooms in a home has proceeded from one or two to a home through one on each floor to a one-to-one ratio between bathrooms and bedrooms, until now our more luxurious homes have a two-to-one ratio with the introduction of "his" and "her" bathrooms as adjuncts to master bedrooms. In addition, swimming pools, more for the comfort of the skin in hot weather than for exercise, are becoming an increasingly common luxury. In view of all this it is hardly surprising that modern architects are seriously considering plans to redesign bathrooms to make them "more functional" or—to place this trend into the concept of infantilization—more pleasureful.

In more primitive times, the place for defecation was an outhouse, an unpleasant and evil-smelling shed that had to be placed a certain distance from the dwelling. This amenity has not only been brought inside the home and embellished with comforts and luxuries, but is now usually incorporated into the bathroom, that sanctum for the care of the skin, where the application of cosmetics, shaving, and shampooing; bathing, powdering, and oiling; and grooming, deodorizing, and perfuming are also indulged in. Future designers of bathrooms will undoubtedly come up with an even more voluptuous ambiance for the enjoyment of these physical needs and sensual pleasures.

Perhaps it is not without significance that our current artists, as we have mentioned in another chapter, are decorating our walls with images of hamburgers, soups, and toilet seats

COOKERY

To the extent that the art of cookery is a product of an increased refinement of taste as a consequence of affluence and culture, it is, of course, a decadent art. It ministers to indulgence in luxury and to man's progressive inclination to have his appetite tickled. The art reached higher levels, even in earlier times, whenever a particular society flourished and became rich enough to support a comparatively idle class or strong enough to send some of its number beyond its own borders as fighters, administrators, or explorers. In this way the Greeks learned to increase the sumptuousness of their banquets by their contact with Asia. When the Romans emerged from a pristine simplicity, they borrowed the gastronomic achievements of the Greeks. In its own turn Italy, during the Renaissance, became the starting point of the history of modern cooking for the rest of Europe. It was Catherine de' Medici who brought Italian cooks to Paris and introduced there a culinary art that had been unknown in France before.

However, with whatever degree of refinement or skill or lack of these qualities they have displayed in different areas and ages, most men have cooked a large part of their food ever since their Paleolithic progenitors discovered fire. Cooking is, and has been since earliest times, such a general practice that very few people would pause to wonder why we do it. Most, challenged on the subject, would probably say that primitive man took to cooking his food to render it more palatable, easier to chew, or both. But such reasons as these may only be a projection of our present tastes and not at all coincide with the facts. Facile explanations of human behavior all too often obscure fundamental underlying causes which become apparent only when a broad overview is possible.

For example, the French have traditionally found the English cuisine unrefined, and have lifted their palms and eyebrows in horror at its general lack of garnishing sauces and elaborate preparation. They consider the English barbarous cooks. The English, on the other hand, being a seafaring nation and able to procure for themselves fresh foods at all times of the year regardless of season, would consider it an offense to the quality and fine flavor of their meats and produce to disguise them with such enrichments, and prefer to serve them comparatively unadorned, enjoying the distinctive flavors of the basic foods. They contend that the French developed their sauces out of necessity to camouflage inferior meats, and wines because their water was undrinkable.

Any or all of these explanations may be partially true, but the overriding fact of the matter is that, regardless of historical determinants or cultural preferences, all people prepare most of their food in some fashion, and this factor transcends in importance the diversity of the ways and the degrees of felicity with which it is done.

The nearest approaches to the preparation of food we find in nature are mammalian milk; the practice of predigesting and regurgitating food in some other species, especially birds; and the processing of special foods, like honey, by some insects. The only thing that milk, regurgitated food, and honey have in common is that they are all fed only to the infants of the species, since the digestive tracts of the very young are not immediately able to digest the foods of the adult animal. As soon as these infant animals are capable of taking their nourishment straight, so to speak, they are no longer fed the processed food.

Were the "childhood" of these animals to be prolonged as is man's, it is possible that some form of predigestion or breaking down of food by crushing, grinding, dissolving, or heating might become necessary for them too.

While the discovery of cooking by man was quite possibly accidental—a serendipitous by-product of the discovery of fire—the fact that the first charred food he tried was agreeable to him and not thrown away, but eaten, enjoyed, and the process repeated, quite possibly indicates that it answered a physiological need, that in the course of his physical and mental infantilization the cooked foods suited him better than his earlier diet. And so we find in man's social history a progression from the original searing of food to the growth of gastronomy as an art of life, following a trend toward greater elaboration and a degree of intellectualization as opportunity occurred.

Today we see the extremes of this trend in prepackaged, processed, convenience foods, where almost everything is done in advance for the consumer but the actual ingesting. In what way this development differs from the practice of those birds who hunt for, gather, digest, and deliver food to their young by regurgitating it directly into their mouths would be hard to define.

It is perhaps also instructive to dwell on the curious fact that man is the only species in the entire animal kingdom that continues to consume its infant food, milk, in its adult years.

SHELTER

"The making of nests concerns all that appertains to the preparation for the reception of eggs or the newly-born young, and their subsequent care."

Not only birds, but fish, amphibia, reptiles and mammals, and many invertebrates as well make nests, and all make more or less elaborate preparation in advance for the reception of their young. All kinds of material are used in all sorts of locales, depending on conditions of the environment and on the anticipated state of the young upon emergence.

Among the birds, the sparrow hawk builds a nest of sticks in a tree, the stork piles huge platforms of sticks and reeds on chimney tops, the golden eagle builds on high mountain ledges; the kestrel subleases, so to speak, by using the abandoned nests of crows. The brown pelican likes community living among reeds, as does the crane. Flamingos build their homes of mud and the hermit thrush of sticks, both on the ground. Flycatchers, ibises, and cranes prefer the height of trees. The East Indian swift is self-sustaining in the matter of building material, since his nest is made of solidified saliva. The hummingbird of Costa Rica uses moss and spider's web to make a neat abode in the axils of stems, while the Amazonian Japim Hang-nests, as their name implies, weave beautiful habitations out of grasses and suspend them from the branches of trees. The Mexican black-and-yellow-crested cacique makes remarkable edifices, sometimes several feet in length, of strips of palm leaves joined with grass. The reed warbler has learned to support his cup-shaped home with the upright stems of growing reeds, and the palm swift knows how to agglutinate the under surfaces of palm leaves or the grass roofs of huts. The Turkestan remera makes from dried grass and feathers a nest that looks uncommonly like a goatskin bottle. The African social weaver bird is something of a master builder, and his umbrella-shaped roofs of grass cover an under surface honeycombed with numerous feather-lined cavities. The red oven-bird of South America uses clay to make an incredibly modern-looking cavelike dwelling about a foot in diameter, while the nest of the anis of Mexico is a commu-

The Expanding Nursery

nity affair which accommodates all the females of the group, who separate their eggs by layers of leaves.

The woodcock scratches a hollow in the ground. The gopher turtle constructs a maze of burrows in sand dunes. The mole makes his burrow comfortable by lining it with grass, and the harvest mouse weaves the leaves of corn about the stalks.

Butterfish find prefabricated homes for their eggs in the upturned valves of dead oyster shells, and the salamander seeks the moist shadows of small caves.

Some species are inclined to be lazy in the matter of shelter. The guillemots leave their single egg on bare rock ledges projecting from the faces of cliffs rising steeply from the sea. Others, which inhabit sandy wastes, have found that material ideal as a lodgement and for incubating their young.

Every material imaginable is used: grass stems, horsehair, moss, lichen, clay, decayed wood, cow dung, fiber "ropes," feathers, cotton-down, saliva, mud, sticks, decaying vegetable matter, as well as leaves and branches—and every conceivable location, from tree-hollows and branches, sandbanks, burrows, the eaves of houses, rocky ledges, to simple depressions in the ground.

While few other animals have attained the skill in homebuilding displayed by the birds, there are ingenious constructors among the mammals. The harvest mouse rivals most of the birds; the rabbit builds a nest in her burrow and lines it with fur from her own body, as ducks, geese, and swans do with their down. Reptiles mostly content themselves with digging holes in the ground, although the European pond tortoise takes a little more trouble. She prepares the ground by watering it from her bladder and from special anal water sacs, then bores a hole, using her tail as one would a stick and her feet to enlarge it. After she has deposited her eggs, she replaces the soil and beats it down flat. Crocodiles do approximately the same thing, except for the preliminary watering, while alligators build great mounds of decaying leaves mixed with earth about three feet high and as much as eight feet across.

Amphibia furnish notable examples of nest-building and of parental instinct. Some frogs fabricate nests as elaborate as those of the tailor birds, making a funnel of a suitable leaf and then sealing it with a gelatinous envelope.

Among the fish the sticklebacks build nests of weeds, cementing them with a binding material secreted from their kidneys. The gourami of Malaya makes his walls of air bubbles toughened by a kind of saliva. Some carry their young in their mouths, some in a pouch running along the belly, and others attach them to the spongy skin on the under surface of the head, belly, or fins.

Elaborate care for the housing of their eggs and their young is also displayed by insects, as is well known in the cases of the ants, the bees, and the wasps. Some scorpions and some spiders bear their eggs closely packed within silken bags.

Apart from the fact that these details are rather fascinating for their own sakes, we are giving them here to show that the building of homes is common to an infinite variety of species, besides the use of burrows, caves, dens, and lairs by the animals with whose habits we are a little more familiar.

Many of us, if asked why man builds houses, would reply without hesitation "To keep out of the weather" and would probably add that man's hairless, or featherless, condition renders him more vulnerable to the vagaries of the weather than the rest of creation.

It would appear that this is not quite true. Almost all animals build nests or use habitations of one sort or another, so the instinct to build a home must run very deep in nature. The

The Expanding Nursery

single end and purpose of all these nests, however, is the preparation of a protective place for the very young, and thereby the safeguarding of the species. A bachelor bird would probably never build a nest.

Man's need for shelter stems from two facets of his infantilization. The first, with which we shall deal at a little more length in a later chapter (on anatomy), is the fact of his almost hairless body, which certainly affords him less insulation than would a pelt. It does in fact put him in a less advantageous position in respect to the rain, snow or sleet, or heat of day and gloom of night than all other living things—most, if not all, of which accommodate themselves perfectly well to unsheltered lives as soon as they grow out of infancy. The second is that, in his regression to a childlike stage, he has need both psychologically and physically of the comfort and feeling of security of the nest. What is more, as he regresses still further toward the fetal stage he will have ever more need of an enveloping surrounding which will give him the same kind of total protection and security as the womb affords the growing embryo.

After his ancestors left their lives in the open trees, man's first move out of the weather was into all-enclosing caves. He subsequently discovered fire and then was able to duplicate maternal body warmth. With the development of his mental capacities, he has been progressively improving this arrangement until today not only his home, but the place where he works, the stores where he hunts for food, the buildings and arenas where he entertains his mind and exercises his under-used body, are all temperature-controlled in about the same way as an incubator. And the incubator is, after all, the most sophisticated reproduction extant of a womblike physical surrounding.

It may sound a little far-fetched, but the apotheosis of this trend is surely to be found in the space ship. In that capsule there is a total control of every environmental factor. Not only is the temperature controlled to comfortable levels; oxygen is pumped to the astronauts through a type of hose that resembles an umbilical cord and all the nourishment they require is prepared and supplied to them. Actually, the command capsule of a space ship could very well be described as a rocket-propelled crib.

If this last example sounds a little fanciful, the fact remains that man needs shelter. The ape can live without it. There are no other adult living creatures, unless they are in a condition of hibernation, that will die of exposure to the elements, as man sometimes does. The only other creatures in nature that absolutely require temperature control and shelter are the infants and fetuses (eggs, seeds) of other species. Does not this fact alone speak volumes?

CLOTHING

The fact that man clothes himself has a far wider significance than appears at first. As we remarked in the preceding section, it appears that man builds himself a home to protect himself from the weather, but on closer examination one realizes that home-building is a deep-seated instinct in a vast variety of animals, and that the instinct is geared to the needs of the newborn and to insure their survival.

So it is with clothing. If asked why we clothe and adorn ourselves we are inclined to reply, without giving the question too much thought: to keep warm and to make ourselves attractive. In a more Puritan age we might have added: to preserve our modesty. However, as is usually the case, the facile explanation tends to obscure rather than to elucidate the basic motivations.

To put the facile explanations into proper perspective, it

will be well to deal with them first. These days it is hardly necessary to demolish the idea that clothing satisfies the claims of modesty. Many forms of clothing, especially in the Western world, serve rather to call attention to than to cover those parts of the body it would appear that they are made to conceal. Modesty is not innate in man. Among Mohammedan peoples, until recently, a modest woman covered her face. Some Pacific islanders covered their knees, while others dispensed with clothing but considered tattooing essential. In earlier times a Carib woman might leave her hut without a girdle, but not unpainted, and in Samoa the navel was not exposed. And then there is the striking fact that among Western peoples what is permitted at certain times is considered immodest at others. On a beach far more of the person is exposed than would be considered proper on a city street, and a woman will bare more of her body in the evening in a ballroom than would be seemly during the day. It is clear then that modesty is a highly conventional matter, and that, as Westermarck noted, a feeling of shame, far from being a cause for man to cover his body is, on the contrary, a result of this custom.

There is more substance in the explanation of the use of clothing as an adaptation to climate. It is generally supposed that man originated in tropical or subtropical latitudes and spread from them gradually to cooler zones. Naturally, as the temperatures became lower, a new function was acquired by his dress—that of protecting his body. Climate, then, may truly be considered one of the forces which play an important part in the evolution of dress; but one should not attribute too much influence to it. Arabs, who inhabit very hot countries, cover themselves very fully, while Fuegans at the southernmost tip of South America, exposed to all the rigors of an antarctic climate, traditionally had an animal skin attached to the body by cords as their sole covering, and Australian aborigines still refer to a bitterly cold night as a "two dog night," since it takes not one but two dogs huddled beside them in a trench to keep them warm in their totally naked condition on such nights, which are not infrequent in their habitat.

As for the third reason customarily offered for the use of clothing, there is no doubt that dress almost always tends to accentuate rather than to conceal the differences between the sexes, so that it is fair to say that man's covering and adornment serves the desire of men and women to make themselves attractive to each other.

The earliest forms of dress among primitive peoples fall into three classes. The first is the molding of parts of the body itself to locally admired standards. One may place into this category head-deformation, practiced by the ancient Peruvians and some Indian tribes; foot-constricting by the Chinese; tooth-chipping or lip or earlobe distention by some African tribes; and waist-compression in Europe. The second is the application to the body of paints and tattoos and the inflicting on it of ornamental scars. The third is the suspension of foreign materials from, or attachment to, convenient portions of the anatomy. This category is by far the largest and includes ear, nose, and lip ornaments, headdresses, necklaces, armlets, bracelets, anklets, finger and toe rings, and girdles. These last are the most important, as it is from the waist ornament chiefly that what we now consider clothing has developed. Almost all tropical clothing is based on the girdle; to that is added, in temperate and cooler climates, an attachment fastened around the neck, such as the cloak.

Adornment in the form of jewelry has another derivation, since its origin is to a large extent in primitive superstition. The smaller objects with which primitive man decked himself were supposed to exert a protective influence. Either they enabled him to take on the virtues of the object (or, as in the case of the teeth of wild animals, of the whole of which the object was a part) or to act as an amulet, or charm. Even today necklaces and bracelets supporting pendant religious symbols—patron saints, guardian angels—and other amulets or charms recall this derivation. There developed later a decorative elaboration of such practical objects as clasps, brooches, buttons, and buckles, but the origins of jewelry are so far back as to be untraceable more precisely. It is known that Stone Age man wore objects around the neck and that gold was worked to make personal ornaments even before the use of bronze was discovered. Such adornments have been found in the oldest excavations at Ur, and in Egypt and Greece.

However, there is another aspect of clothing to which zoologists and students of animal behavior have recently drawn attention.

Many species, and the higher primates among them, live within a rigidly stratified social order. Among the chimpanzees, for example, as collaborators of R. M. Yerkes observed, only higher-ranking members of groups are copied by the others. The age of an animal is in direct ratio to the position it holds in the ranking order of its society. The investigators took a low-ranking animal from a group of chimpanzees and taught it to remove a banana from a very complicated feeding apparatus. When higher-ranking animals were present they simply took the bananas away from the trained one without making any effort to copy him. But when a high-ranking chimpanzee acquired this particular skill, the lower-ranking animals would watch with great interest and soon acquired the same skill by imitating him.

In this connection the wearing of clothes by humans may well have evolved, not exclusively as a response to the need for warmth, but for role and rank delineation. During the First World War Wolfgang Koehler, a psychologist, was interned on Tenerife in the Canary Islands, where there was a biological station. While there he kept a colony of chimpanzees, allowing them considerable latitude and freedom. He wrote that they picked up scraps of burlap which they found lying about the station and decked themselves out in this cloth. Later Jane Goodall, studying wild chimpanzees near Lake Tanganyika, reported similar thefts of cloth. She wrote that old and greasy cloths from the kitchen were the most sought-after, but some of the apes went off with a good many blankets as well as with shirts and other garments. It is possible that these antics of the chimpanzees were simply playful copying—"aping." But to some extent they do reinforce the idea that human clothing may not have made its appearance solely in response to the needs customarily suggested—to keep warm and to attract—but rather in response to an instinct to delineate role and rank by visible symbols. In the instances reported by both Koehler and Goodall, the chimpanzees were "outranked" by the humans with whom they gradually came into close and almost intimate contact but of whom they were nevertheless afraid. It is possible that they stole clothing in order to acquire the status of the humans.

Thus, while some of the body markings of primitive peoples may have been purely for ornament, in a greater number of cases these "ornaments" actually are symbols of rank, caste, and condition, in a way similar to the stripes, chevrons, and other badges of a modern military uniform. The most obvious of these are the warpaint markings and the tribal symbols, but there are very many others.

The establishment of sumptuary laws and customs of one kind or another regulating the type of apparel that may be worn has been almost universal. Among the Indians of the northeast coast of America, the chief not only lived in the most ornate house in the largest village, but certain types of dress could be worn only by him and individuals of the highest rank. Only heads of lineages were permitted to wear ornaments made of abalone shell or to have their robes trimmed with sea-otter fur. In Tudor England, only men entitled to be addressed as "Lord" were allowed to wear sable. Among the Natchez, breech-clouts dyed black were the prerogative of the highest class of men and the wearing of circlets of swans' feathers in the hair of women. Face and body tattoos marked every notch of rise in the social order.

Crowns, tiaras, and ornaments denoting royal, noble, or clerical status; the great variety of head gear denoting special occupations; the quality of fabrics and intricacy of workmanship denoting degrees of wealth—all play their part in the degree of respect and attention accorded to the wearer. In our own society we may note that when the once-prized mink coat became available to too great a number of women, its status value declined and it was outranked by sable and chinchilla. The man able to provide his wife or mistress with such costly outer garments partakes in the deference accorded a display of rank or wealth when he escorts her, even though he is not the wearer.

Shakespeare recognized and immortalized the importance of clothing in the social order when he included the following lines in the speech he wrote for Polonius as a father advising his son, Laertes:

> Costly thy habit as thy purse can buy,
> But not express'd in fancy; rich, not gaudy:
> For the apparel oft proclaims the man. . . .

In giving this background of history of the use of clothing what we wish to do is to underline the very fundamental part that every kind of accouterment has played in human social life from most primitive times, for only if one realizes this can one give due importance to changes in attitude toward it.

Right through to our own times we find clothing used as insignia of station and status, most remarkably in the ceremonial regalia of royalty, judges' robes, and uniforms of all kinds, but also in less remarkable and in some quite subtle ways. But in our own century, and especially since about 1918, we find a very noticeable accompanying trend in the everyday fashions of both men and women.

Until the beginning of this century, as Margaret Mead has remarked, the aim of every girl was to reach the age when she would be allowed to put her hair up and her skirts down. Now, however, the aim of adult women is to put their hair down and their skirts up! Of course, this remark was made jokingly but, as jokes so often do, it went to the core of the changed situation where, within half a century, the social ideal has altered from the desire of youth to grow up to a desire of the grown-up to remain young.

Today for all people, male and female, rich and poor, leader or follower, old or young, there is no very great differentiation in manner of attire. A millionaire or a president is just as likely to wear slacks, shorts, jeans, or chinos in informal surroundings as any man or boy, or woman or girl, in the nation. Business, school, office, or other working clothes are just as unremarkable, and it is perhaps only in dressing for evening functions that some elaborations and differences based on wealth or caste, though not on age, remain.

We have mentioned elsewhere that behavioral and cultural practices are frequently anticipatory outriders of biological trends. In the matter of clothing the only equivalent of the current almost total lack of assertion of rank or of differentiation by sex that one can find in the animal world is in the litter, and in the world of man in children under three. It is hardly necessary to labor the point.

A THOUGHT ON WOMAN

The prime biological concern of the adult female is the bearing, nurturing, protecting, and training of the young of the species, which involves, as a secondary concern, the care of the home.

Perhaps because biological necessity kept her closer to these functions than did the equivalent biological concerns of the mature male to his, the female of mankind rarely participated in artistic activities (or, indeed, in any activity outside the home) until our own times. Now, however, that intellectual ingenuity has to a large extent freed her physically as she has been freed politically, she is taking part in artistic as well as all other activities.

Throughout the ages women have always privately considered men's activities to be childlike, and have frequently said among themselves: "Men are children—they have to play." Now that she is freer of the bonds of her biological nature she, too, is playing in all fields.

It is not really necessary to document this, as it is so obvious, but just to mention a few outstanding examples:

In painting: Berthe Morisot, Mary Cassatt, Marie Laurencin, Georgia O'Keefe, and Helen Frankenthaler; in drawing, Käthe Kollwitz.

In sculpture: Louise Nevelson and Barbara Hepworth.

In science: Marie Curie, Lise Meitner.

In government: Indira Gandhi, Golda Meir, and Margaret Chase Smith, besides Bernadette Devlin of Northern Ireland and Barbara Castle and other cabinet ministers and leaders of the Labour Party in England.

In literature: It has always been a little easier for women to participate in this field (even if the result of their work was often not accepted unless offered under a male *nom de plume*), since it could be accomplished from the home. Perhaps for this reason the trend here starts to show earlier, with the anonymous eighteenth-century author of *Evelina*. However, the great Victorian writers Charlotte, Emily, and Ann Brontë, George Eliot, Mrs. Gaskell, and a little later Colette, Mary Webb, Virginia Woolf, and Emily Dickinson, led the way to the multitude of women writers of our own time.

There have been isolated examples of women excelling in the arts and, when opportunity arose, in government, throughout history. Among the greatest of these were Sappho in ancient Greece; the Lady Murasaki of Japan, whose *Tales of Genji* is the best known, most widely read and esteemed of all Japanese classics; Elizabeth I of England and Catherine the Great of Russia. However, it is only now that woman is released from the full consequences of her biological functions that we begin to see a universal flowering, not only in the arts but also in medicine, scientific research, government, and business life. It should be borne in mind that it took several thousand years of practice and the honing of skills for the towering talents of the greatest men to emerge. Women have so far enjoyed scarcely a century of political freedom, and less than a generation of biological freedom. Nevertheless the enthusiasm with which they have joined the fray, and the degree of talent they have already shown in so many fields of endeavor, would seem to indicate that it will not take so long as a thousand years for their neocortices similarly to neutralize their more instinctual urges.

Perhaps we should consider the emancipation of women as yet another indication and aspect of the infantilization of man.

CHAPTER SEVEN

Play

Some sophisticated people would rather speak of existential anxiety, but biologists in general and field naturalists in particular are really childlike and enjoy nature like a child playing in a mud puddle after the rain has given way to sunny skies.

—*Ramón Margalef, a field naturalist, in* Perspectives in Ecological Theory

DEVELOPING PATTERNS

On a *Candid Camera* television show a youngster was asked to complete the saying "All work and no play makes Jack a . . ." Unhesitatingly he replied, "A dope," and right he was.

The theory of recapitulation has been rather convincingly discredited. It is no longer believed that a child relives his race history in his physical development from the time of his conception to the time of his birth. But he does relive his cultural history in his play.

One of a child's earliest games is that of throwing down an object from his crib. Sooner or later someone will retrieve it for him, and he will then throw it down again. When he is a little older he may retrieve it himself. Freud called this the "gone" game, and saw it as a dramatization of the infant's effort to master life's predicaments. The baby felt helpless when his mother left the room, and "acted out" this experience in sending away the toy—but the absence of the toy was in his own control; it was he who could decide when to throw it down. Later, when he was able to retrieve it, it was also he himself who could decide when it would come back. To the same end earliest man practiced magical rites in an attempt to influence the forces of nature.

Many observers have described how children regularly employ magical means of mastery by which they produce pleasurable illusions of power. For example, when a small child plays peek-a-boo it is in his own power to see or to shut out the person who is playing with him, and his great pleasure in the game derives largely from this. Almost all the traditional games stem historically from primitive magical or religious rites, and even the creation and great success of a modern game like Monopoly, invented during the depression of the 1930s, illustrates how helplessness in reality generates a game. When a child gets a little older his games show a partial concession to reality, in that they express the idea of doubt as to the efficacy of his power.

Many games have been handed down from one generation to another with a degree of care suggesting that some inherent and fundamental value is felt in them. Homer's children built sand castles. Both Greek and Roman children had dolls, hoops, skipping ropes, hobby-horses, and kites, and played at hopscotch, tug-of-war, pitch and toss, blind-man's buff, hide-and-seek, and kiss in the ring or very similar games. Spontaneous play is the earliest form; participation in traditional games follows. As social institutions games can satisfy a wish for union with an all-powerful being. On this psychological level games may be compared with religious systems with respect to the functioning of rules and leaders. Trophies are concrete symbols of participation in power and may be either awarded or actively secured. Numerous survivals of primitive social institutions and magical practices can be found in many traditional games. The ancient Mexican game of *tlachtli,* rather like football, originated in the fact that the shape of the ball is similar to that of the sun. We have knowledge that the Mayans, sun-worshipers, played a ball game in an elaborate ceremonial in a court in the vicinity of their temple. At Chichen-Itza in the Yucatán a magnificent Mayan ball court still survives. These games could well have been initiated by a priest kicking, throwing, or rolling a ball in the desired direction in an effort to influence the movement of the sun by magic. That the ball was thrown back to him by the populace may have become a practice as an expression of doubt in the efficacy of the rite and the desire to see it performed again and again, overcoming obstacles, winning. In some such way the practice of opposing teams, perhaps representing light against darkness, may have arisen. In any case, it is a more attractive theory than the more usual equating of all team games with war!

In no sense does a traditional game differ in its origin from a rite. The public games of Greece and Rome, which generally included spectacles as well as athletic contests, were connected with religious observances. The earliest formed part of funeral rites, or were instituted in honor of a god or as a thank-offering. The great contests were held near a shrine or sacred place. Not until the fourth century B.C. was the honor of a games event paid to a living man, Lysander. The simpler ball and skipping games, all games played with bat and ball, the first use of playing cards, gambling, the classical games of

Greek antiquity, horse-racing and foot races have all been traced to close kinship or actual identity with religious or primitive rites. Dice games (knuckle-bones), checkers, backgammon, and guessing the number of fingers held out were all played by the ancients. Many primitive peoples perform solemn rites which we know as games: for example, some Eskimo tribes "play" cat's cradle. As late as the fourteenth century, a regular feature of the Easter ritual in one part of Europe was for the bishop to kick a ball at the head of a procession. Perhaps we may parallel this with the American President throwing the ball at the opening game of the season in Washington, D.C. Even in contemporary versions of games there is a marked similarity to ritual in our practice. This is to be noticed especially in such formalities as the playing of the national anthems (prayers) of the competing teams at international matches, the general convocations at the beginning and end of the Olympic Games meets, and the carrying of the flame. The cheerleaders at our own ball games exhorting us to enthusiasm are also performing some sort of invocation, and the mascots of the teams constitute their totems.

With the onset of adolescence comes participation in sports, an elaboration of play that is uniquely human. As with so many of the highly developed cultural achievements of man, resemblances to behavioral patterns of other higher social animals help to indicate the biological as well as the social roots of play and sports. While retaining some of the qualities of play, sports confront the adolescent forcefully with many realistic aspects of social activities, particularly those related to coping with aggression, recognition of leadership qualities, respect for rules (laws), loyalty to team, establishment of place in the "pecking order," identification with admired adults and peers, experience in acting under conditions of stress, acceptance of instruction, perseverance in the face of failure and fatigue, gains in strength and skill, and enhanced self-confidence. An investigator who set out to answer the questions of what play is in itself and what it means to the player asserted that genuine, pure play is one of the main bases of civilization. He did not identify play with sport, but he did maintain that play is a valuable element in sport, so much so that when sport loses this particular ingredient it becomes divorced from culture and has little dignity or worth for mankind. Society has a need to institutionalize certain games into festivals, circuses, parties, and masquerades. Play and games have social value in cementing bonds and promoting a sense of unity.

While the natural function of play is to aid the child and adolescent in preparation physically, psychologically, and socially for life, adult participation in sport reaches its culmination in a professional caste of players, intensively trained, highly paid, and enjoying great prestige, precisely when the sport has all the earmarks of a ritual, or a quasi-religious cult with its priesthood.

We now find modern man reversing this progression. Any adult activity can be, and often is, converted into a game. Take the very wealthy businessman, who no more needs extra money than the amateur gardener needs the produce he grows or the hunter his kill, who continues to collect companies and acquire wealth for the stimulation and fun he obtains in doing so. He is turning the activities of adult life, for which he prepared in his childhood in part through stages of play, games, and sport, back into games and play for its own sake.

PLEASURE

For our purpose we may divide animals into regressive and nonregressive species. The cubs of a lion, for example, a nonregressed animal, appear to be very playful. Their "play," however, fulfills a natural purpose. Being genetically endowed with the reflexes necessary for survival, the baby animal possesses in a rudimentary way the same skills as the adult. It has to practice these skills in order to perfect them. When we, as outsiders, observe the cub perform the activities characteristic of his species in a clumsy fashion, judging animals in our own terms, we assume that it is being playful. However, as the cub grows and achieves mastery of these skills, the apparent "play" falls away.

In regressed species where, as we have seen, a compensatory intelligence has developed, a new factor appears on the scene. Such animals as the otter or the dolphin also possess the skills they will need for life in their genetic makeup, and practice them playfully when young. But as the young of these animals are clumsily exercising the activities they will need for their lives, their budding intelligences seize upon these manifestations and, by experimenting, discover pleasure in them. In these species, play does *not* fall away as mastery is acquired, but continues, and is even elaborated, since it has taken on the quality of pleasure as an end in itself throughout the creature's life. Man comes into this category.

The interaction between the pleasure and the brain's response to it sets up a self-feeding cycle. As the playful animals and man, in the process of their regression, lose some of their anatomical features, their remaining coordinative skills must overcompensate for the deficiencies. This places a greater burden on the young member of the regressed species than on the young of the nonregressed. He has to practice longer—play more—which in turn stimulates his brain.

An unsatisfied need creates a sense of discomfort within the brain. Its fulfillment restores the nervous system to tranquility, and this is experienced as pleasure. Therefore the prolonged play of the regressed animal, as a culminative effect, introduces pleasure as a new factor into its nervous system, so that the nervous system then seeks pleasure for its own sake.

It has been demonstrated that when the brain experiences pleasure it will seek to renew this sensation at the expense of all its other bodily needs—even overriding the most essential instincts for self-preservation. Scientific experimenters have implanted electrodes into the thalamic portion of the brains of cats at a point which produces a sensation of pleasure. These cats were trained in such a way that they could voluntarily press a lever which would send a current to the electrode and thus produce pleasure. In every case the cats continued to press the levers until they keeled over from exhaustion. Their bodies' signals of tiredness could not restrain them.

This remarkable behavior is seen in even sharper focus in human beings, whose considerations for their own health, or even life, are overridden by the desire for the pleasures of smoking, drinking, or drugs.

HOBBIES

Anna Freud wrote that the place of hobbies is halfway between play and work, and that they have certain aspects in common with both activities. Hobbies appear for the first time at the beginning of the latency period, undergo any number of changes of content, but may persist as this specific form of activity throughout life.

We feel that hobbies are rather different from play. Actually they fall into two groups. There are the hobbies of the collector and those of the doer. The collectors really are appeasing the acquisitive spirit that is found throughout the animal kingdom. Many animals, like small boys, are habitually and indiscriminately acquisitive. We do not think that this tendency forms any part of the playful instinct.

The doers come closer. They are involved in the development of special skills which they use in a playful manner, as a pastime or relaxation rather than as a breadwinning activity. Play is a voluntary activity, and has its aim in itself. The very young are protected, not concerned with survival, and so they are at liberty to indulge in play. It is true that their play serves primarily a biological function, but still it is not imposed—it is a free activity. Later, in intelligent species, as it becomes an end in itself purely for pleasure, freedom is of its essence.

Many philosophers have in some way recognized this. Plato said that life must be lived as play. Friedrich Schiller felt that man is completely a man only when he plays, and in our days Sartre has expressed his opinion that "as soon as man apprehends himself as free and wishes to use this freedom . . . then his activity is play."

In work the end is considered more important than the means, but this is not the case in play, which is "aimless." Thus it is that, as Mark Twain immortalized for us, whitewashing a fence may be play when the physical exercise is felt to be pleasant and invigorating, but the activity is considered work when it is aimed at some utilitarian purpose. Play has an intrinsic quality of pleasure—it feels good to play. It can be serious, and taken seriously. As Freud said, "The opposite of play is not being serious, but reality." A person who, for example, always has to come out on top may enjoy neither work nor play. If one is emotionally conflict-free, then work, like play, can be pleasant. As Mark Twain had Tom Sawyer put it, more succinctly: "I turn work into fun."

Play, games, fun, sport, and hobbies are, indeed, more definable as expressions of attitudes than as specific occupations.

PURITANISM

How do we account for man's occasional turning away from his playful nature? The suppression of the slightest sign of frivolity in such periods is conducted with an unrelenting severity that in itself is an indication of how difficult it is for us, at this stage in the development of our species, *not* to play.

We must keep it in mind that any animal in a process of transition harbors old and new patterns side by side. Under stress old patterns re-emerge. Man is a prime example. His over-all trend is toward creating greater comfort, leisure, and freedom for himself, but in times of urgency he resorts to earlier patterns of more mature concern for survival.

When the early settlers in the United States faced the hardships of subduing and extracting a living from harsh nature, they found their salvation in rigorous, Puritan ways of life. Frivolity and pleasures of the flesh were temptations of the devil. Play, even in children, was evil and sinful. As Karl A. Menninger noted in another context, "Once it was held . . . that all play was dangerous and destructive, indeed, even an evidence of depravity. 'The students [of an American school in 1784] shall be indulged with nothing which the world calls play . . . *for those who play when they are young will play when they are old.*' " A struggling, newly established society could not afford the luxury of play. Man's mature business, his survival, was at stake.

When Oliver Cromwell wrested power from the effete Stuarts in England, social life in the country had been in a stage of decadence following the vigorous Elizabethan age. Work and regeneration were necessary. Here too a stern Puritan way of life was imposed.

The Mennonites, the Quakers, and the Scots, who for varying reasons and in different circumstances lead lives based on the more fundamental instincts for self-preservation through work, all discourage frivolity and play. However, when their frugality and diligence are successful in terms of worldly wealth or coping with their special situations, the tendency is for the neocortex to take over again, relaxing the instincts which support a conservative life and encouraging indulgence in pleasure and amenities once more.

TOYS

The child regards the world around him and acts out his experiences of it in play. For him, his toys are images of the objects he observes in the adult world. To him, they are a source of challenge to activities which he attempts to master in a make-believe way. Toys are, in fact, tools for training a child to attain adult skills. In primitive societies they are tools and nothing more. In technologically advanced societies they are also a source of joy and intellectual stimulation.

At the beginning of this chapter we mentioned that in play, games, and sport a growing individual relives his cultural race history, as to a certain extent he relives his physical race history in his bodily growth before birth. A child's use of toys, in a similar way, mirrors the gradually increasing human skills and understanding.

As an infant the first objects he plays with not only help him to hold, to pick up, to throw, to focus on by sight or sound, a variety of things around him, but also impress on his mind the knowledge that he is able to do so. Each child goes through an almost undeviating progression of toys as his strength and skills grow. As the infant becomes a toddler he enjoys the toys he can push ahead or pull along behind him. In the next stage he discovers his powers of coordination and practices them progressively in block-building and then with more complicated construction toys; in tricycle and then bicycle riding. Later come toys challenging his creativity and invention: beads for stringing, raffia for weaving, paints, sewing equipment, and modeling clay—and, all the time, toys (dolls, costumes, kits) to aid his fantasy in playing at adult life.

When he comes to adolescence, however, and begins to participate in sports, in modern times we find an arrest. We now live with the prolongation of such adolescent activities into the middle, or even the late, years of adult life. Sports perform a function for the adolescent. As we have indicated, in his upward development toward adulthood they are training grounds for life. For the adult many sports imitate pursuits essential in the human struggle for survival, but convert them into play. Those organized around opposing teams are modeled on warfare. Fishing, hunting, hiking, mountain climbing all have parallels in food-gathering activities. Sports cars, gadgets, model trains, boats, and so on, are symbolic extensions of the body and duplicate necessary physical skills. An instinct to fight and subdue an enemy has been diluted (or even subverted) into a playful pursuit to win a game. The lion cub plays at wrestling with his litter mates to gain the skill he will need to kill prey. Man wrestles because the physical exercise gives him pleasure and has become an end in itself, even though, on the way up in his evolution, it was a necessary training. While wrestling, boxing, and more limited body-contact sports come closest to the original purpose of the activity, any sport, be it football, track racing, shuffleboard, or tiddlywinks, can give the winner the pleasure of triumph over an enemy, while the loser may shrug off the defeat by reassuring himself that it was only a game anyway!

In all sports an essential element is fantasy. In this respect, too, we find modern adults resorting for pleasure to a mechanism that is a tool in childhood. Witness the fisherman, whose equipment and incidental expenses may amount to several hundreds of dollars, for which he could purchase a truckload of fish; or the amateur gardener who discovers, when figuring his expenses, that each tomato he grows costs him about five times as much as those he could buy in a store. Their fantasies that they are gatherers or growers of food fulfills an atavistic instinct and is an essential part of their pleasure. It would be ludicrous indeed to relate the expense and effort involved to the minimal results obtained on any other terms.

As the child's toys proceed with the stages of his development toward control and mastery, the adult's recede through the stages of childhood. An eight-to-ten-year-old gets a great deal of satisfaction from a finished product that he himself has made. In the adult this satisfaction is obtained in the arts, crafts, or in any form of creative pursuit. On a lower rung, from four to seven, the child has recently acquired muscular aptitudes which he uses riding bicycles, tricycles, kiddycars, climbing jungle-gyms, jumping rope, and so on. In the adult these have become such games of skill as golf, tennis, or bowling. At a stage younger, say from the first year to the fourth, the child is aware of skin and body shapes belonging to others, especially to his mother, and his toys are teddy bears or any kind of toy animals, dolls, and squeezable objects. The adult's equivalents are the enjoyment of the more sensual pleasures such as dining, fine fabrics, furs, or his partner in sexual activities. At this stage, too, the child practices its burgeoning skills in banging, block-building, or digging; this is reflected in adults in such hobbies as carpentry, amateur bricklaying, or crossword puzzles. In his earliest stages, the infant finds pleasure in his body contact with his mother—he does not yet really differentiate between his own body and hers. In the adult similar pleasures are enjoyed in the routines of spas, ocean bathing, mineral baths, massage, sunbathing, and the physical comforts of heating and air-conditioning.

Before leaving this subject, as a footnote we would add that, of all animals, man is the only one who breeds other species for the express purpose of providing companionship, or creatures as living toys. The original aim in domesticating dogs as guardians of home or flocks, or to assist in hunting, has been in part converted into breeding miniature playmates. The same applies to cats, which were taken into houses in the first place to keep down rodents, but which now serve man chiefly as playmates for his children or for his own companionship or pleasure; and to birds like parrots, parakeets, or canaries, which have never had any other real function in a domestic setting than to amuse their owners.

Just as a child will explore the playful possibilities of everything he happens upon, so regressed man converts anything in nature that proves convertible into objects for his pleasure. Not only domestic pets, but also wild animals such as lions, tigers, bears, or elephants are trained to amuse him in circuses and zoos. For that matter, even plants, flowers, shrubs, and ornamental trees are bred for the sole purpose of delighting him in his gardens, parks, and homes. To many an amateur gardener the care of his plants becomes an engrossing hobby, an only slightly more sophisticated version of play with toys.

EQUIPMENT AS TOYS

The automobile is an extension of the human body—it replaces the legs—and as such it functions as a gadget to reduce time and distance. But on a more regressed level the car becomes a symbol either of virility or aggression, or both. When this is the case, the car takes on a different meaning for its owner. Then the highway becomes a proving ground for him, where he will not allow anyone to outrace him; or an arena in which he and his car must be supreme. When the car is fantasied in this way, of course, it becomes a very dangerous toy.

The car is the most obvious example, but there are many others. Some airplane pilots use their planes to achieve an illusion of mastery over their bodies; for some pipe-smokers the pipe is a prop and stimulus for fantasy; and all are making use of their equipment or possessions as "adult toys." For if "play" is considered "an active physical attainment of an illusion of mastery and gratification," then a "toy" is any "material thing through which mastery illusions are achieved."

On a still lower level, incidentally, the car (or other possession) may become a baby doll, carefully nurtured, cleaned, and adorned, for which nothing but the best is good enough. Woe to him who puts a scratch in its paint or mud on its carefully brushed interior!

M. Csikszentmihalyi, the chairman of the department of sociology at Lake Forest University, has mourned, in an article entitled "The Rigors of Play," that in our day "play is not what it used to be.... Most of the changes can be summarized under the headings of increased specialization, quantification, and *reliance on equipment*. [The italics are ours.] Taken together, these changes have turned play into an activity which produces pay-offs, offers satisfactions quite different from those provided by the games of our fathers," and he observes that "fun" is now not the only reason for playing. We play nowadays more as a child does, combining fun with learning.

"Modern bowling, for instance, is the standardized, stereotyped descendant of its rustic ancestors, lawn bowling and the Mediterranean *boccie*. The older forms of the game allowed an individual flexibility of rules, of format, of play that is not possible now. The open-air alleys had a way of integrating the player with his natural environment and with the shifting group of spectators that the cavelike (modern) bowling alley actively discourages.... Automated bowling encourages the player to concentrate on the score, since that is the only variable in an otherwise uniform environment. Hence the overblown emphasis on keeping scores, averages, records..." much as a child at school likes to know his marks or grades and compare them with those of others, or with his own earlier ones, in a competitive spirit which eggs him on to increase his effort.

"Chess used to be a game that brought together two people in an exhilarating abstract battle of wits. All one needed to enjoy it was any beaten-up set, two people, and perhaps some cups of coffee or shots of brandy. Today a player feels hopelessly amateur if he does not possess such necessities as tournament chess clocks, diagram pads (with stamping pads), spiral-bound or loose-leaf score books, perhaps a portable roll-up demonstration board with tripod base and, of course, a quantity of specialized chess books.... The old game pitted two individual men against each other; they might never exchange a word, but while they faced each other they *participated*. Now with the clocks dictating the pace, the buzzers, the scores to chalk up, the various tactics to remember, each player is in the position of playing against an interchangeable dummy in whom he could hardly become interested as a human being."

Most importantly, companionship in games and sport has often been reduced in our time to the technical level only. We no longer play a game of tennis, golf, or bowl, climb, or hike with individuals because we enjoy their company, but we tend to seek out those whose skills are well matched to, and complement, our own. This, too, reflects the essential self-sufficiency of children's play. Children do not need other children when they play, as the involvement is between themselves and the objects with which they are playing. Other children are only included if they are "needed" to act out parts in "pretend" games, or to throw or hit back a ball.

Csikszentmihalyi also notes with regret the development in the last thirty years or so of rock climbing as a sport tending to displace mountain climbing. Although it started in Europe, "rock climbing really came into its own only when it was transplanted to the United States. The layman who sees the line of stalwarts inching their way up sheer Yosemite crags might think of them as mountain climbers, but they are not and they are proud that they are not. The mountain climber, usually surrounded by friends whose company he enjoyed, approached the hills with something akin to reverence. When he climbed he tended to appreciate the mountain in all its geological, aesthetic, historical and even spiritual, dimensions. Therefore he experienced pleasure at many levels. . . . The modern rock climber doesn't think in terms of mountains; his frame of reference, at most, is the rock face; more usually, it is a particular 'pitch' or a specific 'move.' He cares not at all about history, aesthetics or the spirit. He gets no enjoyment from walking, from crossing ice. When he reaches the summit —if he reaches it, the summit is often irrelevant to a rock climb—he rarely spares a glance for the view. Check the gear, eat a bite, and down we go. . . . The new breed of technical rock climbers has quantified each hold on every rock face of the earth, assigning to it a grade from 1 (very easy) to 6.9 (the limit of human possibilities). They have developed fantastically complex equipment for climbing, and this gear has to be cared for constantly and replaced as soon as possible. They have developed the 'ultimate reality piton' made of chrome-molybdenum to hammer into hairline cracks.

"The technical rock climber looks down on the traditional mountaineer, whom he suspects of hypocrisy and phoniness. How can the mountaineer pretend to enjoy climbing, when he takes no advantage of all the specialized skill and quantified knowledge, all the equipment, that the rock climber uses? After all, the rock climber is infinitely better at scaling difficult peaks than the traditional mountaineer can ever hope to be. This proves that the latter is nothing but a bumbling amateur. And that is just the point—rock climbing, like most other forms of play from bridge to skiing, from swimming to walking (or jogging), has become a highly technical activity based on specialized skill, quantification, stereotyped rules, and uniform equipment.

"So play is changing everywhere from ... an activity which helped man to relate to his social and cultural environment ... to extremely specialized activity which affords him greater and greater control over a small, and in itself insignificant, area of experience."

We have quoted at some length from this article because it is so revealing of so many of the points we have been making.

Like playful children, men today are turning into toys not only their sporting equipment but also any object that can conceivably be turned into a "fun" thing. Furniture has been the subject of conversion into all kinds of experimental and amusing forms. The trend started, naturally enough, with nursery furniture, but recent designs have brought play furniture into all parts of the house. Manhattan's Museum of Contemporary Crafts has exhibited a fountain environment to provide beauty and fun for participants who sit inside large plastic bubbles and watch smaller plastic bubbles floating in a trough of gurgling water. A furniture designer exhibited a "reclining space for one," an enclosed wooden receptacle in which a sculptured door opens into a snug, carpeted cubbyhole with fur pillows and a hole in the top for light and air. Its designer said, "When you get inside, it's almost like being in your mother's womb. The more you define space, the more

E

exciting it becomes." In the same exhibition there was a twelve-foot stroboscopially lighted waterfall. The visitor crawled through an access tube into a clear plastic enclosure where he could sit, perfectly dry, while the water cascaded all around him. At another exhibition, called "Spaces," at the Museum of Modern Art, among many such environments was one where anybody who came in was invited to climb into, sit on, or play with a variety of canvas objects.

In case one should feel inclined to write these off as products of American decadence, it is reported that going to bed in Japan these days often requires a good night's sleep in advance. The Japanese have developed a taste for "play beds," which come in a variety of designs. The earliest were twins that shot together at the touch of a button. Then came circular double beds installed on turntables and surrounded by a television set, a refrigerator, a stereo phonograph, and a bar. Now there is a bed which rises and falls three feet. It is called The Seesaw, and makes a very effective playground of the bedroom—especially in its more elaborate version, which not only teeters but also simultaneously flips a center section up and down. There are other versions, but these are surely sufficient to demonstrate that Asian man is in no way behind Western man in his desire to play whenever he has the means and the opportunity.

If we were to imagine that a child were given the capacity for adult reasoning all at once at his young age, let us visualize what would be the nature of his play.

In the first place, the play would have to satisfy his budding dexterity, but the richly endowed neocortex would not be content with the simplicity of the child's game. It would find such stimulation insufficient and would become bored. It would search out obstacles for the sole purpose of adding to the challenge. In this way the original reasons for the play in exploration and the practice for mastery would become overshadowed by the fun of overcoming the self-created obstacles.

The way to keep the neocortex happy is to present it with an apparently insoluble puzzle—in other words, to stump it. This becomes the impetus for the mind to use all its resources, even if it has to put itself under strain. The tension mounts as each possibility is checked and discarded. Every nook and cranny of the memory bank is explored. The perfect solution is finally found. There is an almost explosive sensation of release—the "Eureka" feeling—and this is the essence of neocortical pleasure.

We see this in a rudimentary way in children when they manage to put the right peg into the right hole. A squeal of delight often accompanies their success. This, in fact, is what Csikszentmihalyi has observed and recorded, and what is happening to all adult play activities as the neocortex takes over more and more the functions of instinctual life.

The simple card game of whist, played with great pleasure for many centuries, has ceased to be of sufficient interest. It has branched into contract bridge (by way of auction bridge), blossomed into countless bidding systems, and burst out all over with so many conventions, rules, and technicalities that schools have been established to enable one to learn and practice the game; a vast library of literature is published, both in book form and in the daily press, to study it; duplicate bridge studios, rubber bridge clubs, and a multitude of regional tournaments have been set up so that a player may find appropriately strong competition. A bridge player may spend countless evenings with people he hardly knows, and often with those he would hardly care to know—but if he gets a "good game," manages to figure out the lie of the cards or to solve a percentage play, a squeeze, or a throw-in successfully, his brain has been teased—he is a happy man.

Not only has the splendid old game of chess succumbed to

a proliferation of conventional moves and tournament apparatus as was noted in "The Rigors of Play," but some fiendish brain has devised a way to intensify the stimulation it gives with a three-dimensional version, with which it will surely take the most highly developed neocortex quite a while to catch up—and in the meantime it can get in some practice with that parlor game which was developed to teach logical skills to budding lawyers and is now advertised as being a "brain-bursting" item for rocket experts and one or two of their friends, or with the newly invented three-dimensional version of the erstwhile children's game of tic-tac-toe.

Besides this, our art-minded, affluent, amusement-seeking species has turned to artist-designed and science-oriented playthings that threaten to transform living rooms into sophisticated nurseries. We see displayed in stores and advertised in newspapers kinetic sculpture for the executive desk (touch it and it moves through fascinating geometric patterns); rhombic hexahedrons which may be joined into many shapes and which patrons of the Museum of Modern Art's store seem to find beguiling, as would any block-building baby; a kinetic light box, a motor-operated demonstration of an ocean wave, a motion teaser that is based on Newton's observations, games incorporating concepts of the "new Mathematics," and a kinetic toy employing magnets to set up a spinning movement, all part of a steadily growing trend that is luring grown-up people to toy counters to buy gadgets that fascinate them by their movement, exasperate them by the complexity of putting them together, or impress them by their visual illustration of scientific laws.

Our brains have become so complex that they dominate our lives and change the character of all our activities. Like all complicated mechanisms, they have to be kept occupied. If it is not used, any organ of the body tends to atrophy. This

Play

would eventually apply to the brain too, but the brain does not allow us to permit such an eventuality. It gives immediate notice when it is insufficiently occupied by inflicting on us the discomfort of boredom. Discomfort has to be neutralized. A bored child becomes restless or destructive. A bored adult, becoming restless, will look for new stimulation. If none is found he will tend to find relief in sleep or in the oblivion of intoxication. If man's brain is deprived of stimulation for too long, as in solitary confinement, in isolated outposts, or in shipwrecks, the mind then turns back to itself for the stimulation it needs by dipping into its reserves of memory and producing hallucinations.

Our brains are no longer satisfied by the simple activities that used to occupy us. In the same way that we have complicated our sports with a plethora of unnecessary paraphernalia, and all our games right down to the child's level are diversified and intellectualized, so too all our works and endeavors are embellished with a complexity of gadgetry for its own sake. We face the ultimate paradox that we are in possession of a brain that was formed to help us to exist, and now we have to amuse our brains to keep them working for us.

Although we have arrived at this conclusion by way of our theory of the infantilization of man (paedomorphism), many other writers and thinkers have arrived at similar conclusions by other paths. There seems to be a convergence of thought, aptly expressed by Johan Huizinga in his *Homo Ludens: A Study of the Play Element in Culture:*

A happier age than ours once made bold to call our species by the name of *Homo Sapiens*. In the course of time we have come to realize that we are not so reasonable after all as the Eighteenth Century, with its worship of reason and its naive optimism, thought us; hence modern fashion inclines to designate our species as *Homo Faber:* Man the Maker. But though *faber* may not be quite so dubious as *sapiens* it is, as a name specific of the human being, even less appropriate, seeing that many animals too are makers. There is a third function, however, applicable to both human and animal life, and just as important as reasoning and making— namely, playing. It seems to be that next to *Homo Faber,* and perhaps on the same level as *Homo Sapiens, Homo Ludens,* Man the Player, deserves a place in our nomenclature.

To return to the opening sentence of this chapter—while it is true that all work and no play makes Jack a dull boy, it is equally true that all play and no work perpetuates childhood.

CHAPTER EIGHT

Sex

In the plant and the animal world, sex is basic. Our structure, our instincts, our habits and behavior; our customs and occupations; the colors and perfumes of flowers; the plumage and song of birds; beauty, grace, charm, and our responses to them are all aspects and extensions of our sexual nature and are molded and modified by it. Societies, no matter how complex and civilized they have become, have arisen from and been shaped by the essential needs of the family units that form them. Birth and death are attributes of sex, and it is the mechanism by which nature preserves and diversifies species. It is the all-pervading apparatus of life itself.

When the earliest and lowliest single-celled form of life first combined with another rather than split its own substance into two parts in order to perpetuate its existence, and thus initiated the cycles of birth and death which today are synonymous in our minds with the word *life,* sex made its debut on earth. Since then, it has determined the structure of all but the most primitive life forms and modulated its behavior patterns.

We are in every cell of our bodies, formed as they are of the union of those of our parents and forming as they do those of our children, innately sexual beings. Not only are our bodies the result of a sexual union, but our sexual nature determines the attributes of our personalities and our instinctual drives so far as they are directed to the perpetuation of life—which covers just about everything that we are, think, do, and say. This is true to such an extent that the joking definition of a hen as the best thing an egg can think of to produce another egg is in truth very close to being a statement of fact.

It is clear, then, that if man's nature in any way, whether in his anatomy, his behavior, or his attitudes, undergoes any sort of change or modification, one area where such a change is bound to have some repercussions and to show most clearly is in that most fundamental one of his sexual behavior and attitudes. Not only the basic act of procreation, but also individuals' concepts of themselves, and their attitudes to the other sex, come into this category. So too do the domestic arrangements of their lives and many of their customs and habits. If the changes in man's general behavior toward more youthful or childlike patterns which we have noted in many phases of his life have any deep implications, they will be apparent in the more overtly sexual part of his existence.

The intrinsic purpose of the sexual act is, obviously, to produce offspring. In order to promote procreation, the sex drive has to become so strong as to be irresistible. In animal life, and in much of plant life too, nature found and utilized the expedient of releasing through swelling. To make this possible the genital organs must, at appropriate times, change from a resting state into one of discomfort through swelling. Biologically this is accomplished in animals by an increase of blood supply to them, causing a congestion of the genital tract to a point demanding decongestion. Thus, when hormonal production promotes such a state, an animal has no choice but to seek sexual congress. If it were not for this necessity, propagation would not take place.

The first evidence of man's infantilization that we meet in the sexual sphere is anatomical, and is manifested in the sexual act itself. Man's preferred position, face to face, is a result of the retention of the pelvic flexure from the fetal stage. In all other mammals this fetal flexure is straightened by the time of maturity, with the effect that the female genital tract is pointing backwards. Human beings retain the fetal feature, so that their females' genital tract is pointed forward, and the face-to-face position is therefore more comfortable. But not only does the anatomical configuration incline man to this preference. It is reinforced by the memory of the face-to-face position of the suckling infant to its mother. The animal position—mounting from behind—is actually physiologically more productive. When the sexual act takes place from behind the female, the pool of sperm is deposited in the deepest part of the vaginal tract, allowing the cervix (the entry to the uterus) to be bathed in the seminal pool. As a matter of fact, this position is frequently recommended by gynecologists for women who have difficulty conceiving.

The actions necessary to carry out this process are brought into play automatically. Once initiated, they are no longer subject to will and fall into the category of reflex responses. They are laid down genetically, and not learned, in such a way that when genital congestion leads to intercourse certain specific body movements are promoted. These body movements are built-in, so to speak, and are present even as early as the infancy of the animal—long before they are needed for their biological purpose. Consequently the baby animal sometimes goes through the motions of the sexual act in a more or less playful manner.

In this respect we find a reflection of a theme that reveals itself in many phases of the process of becoming man, one we shall pick up again. Growth and transformation are not harmonious continua. On the contrary, they are marked by a series of retardations, delays, and inhibitions which occur in every stage of development. A child's sexuality, in a budding stage as it is, reaches a preliminary peak at around the age of six. It then goes into a period of latency until the age of puberty. It is just possible that a reason for this may be found in man's ancestry. His earliest forebears reached sexual maturity at the age of about five. Modern man's prolonged childhood has enforced a postponement of readiness for procreation, and thus we have in man a physiological latency period not experienced by other species. Superimposed upon this physiological latency is a cultural latency, variable in length, interrelated and coinciding with the extended period of childhood. In more recent times this stage has come to include adolescence —another marking-time-period.

Animals possess in their genes a model for the reflexes necessary for mating. In the temperate zones the timing for this process had to be just right, since the newborn offspring could not have survived in the harsher seasons. Regardless of the period of gestation, nearly all animals in the Northern Hemisphere give birth in spring, when the climatic conditions and prospects are most favorable. A remnant of this pattern is left to us in the custom of the June wedding, which is calculated to produce birth in the spring, and thus the prehistoric female of the northern zone was ready for the next sexual congress three months later.

Whenever an animal experiences the genital congestion we have referred to, it will have to seek out a mate to find release from the tension through an integrated complex of coordinated muscular movements. Man has converted this particular physiological response from its original purpose—a quick ejaculation through the male organ into the vagina of the female—into an elaborate pattern of actions and responses.

As man has moved along the road toward infantilization, his sexual activity has assumed more and more of the playfulness of the baby animal, and the sensual gratifications of sexual foreplay become more important to the individuals concerned than the end of the procreative act itself. One hardly needs to elaborate on the presence of this phenomenon in our present culture, where the "arts of love-making" are currently being promoted by countless books, manuals, and marriage counselors and, willy-nilly, we find ourselves receiving through the mail invitations to study photographs, illustrated instruction courses, and even home movies designed to teach us to increase our skills in this area of our lives and thereby enhance our pleasures.

Our culture is saturated with sexuality. Yet when we contemplate the all-pervasive, all-permissive, all-encompassing ambiance of sex in which we live, it must cross one's mind that this would not be possible unless sex had lost something of the deep, central, determining force it used to wield in man's life.

It would not be possible so to surround ourselves with sex-in-the-theater, sex-in-advertising, sex-in-literature-and-art, sex-in-mass-media—in fact in every nook and cranny of our culture—had it not lost some of its importance for us.

At first glance it would appear as if the liberalized sexual attitudes, in removing the subject from the forbidden-fruit category, would make it less enticing, but actually it is our infantilization that makes sex less vital and more playful—and it is this change of attitude that allows the liberalized mores.

Our culture has made sex a cerebral rather than a genital exercise. Our advertising professional, like the classical "tease," seduces the buyer by showing lovely girls with banal products, with the implied promise, but no delivery, of sex. Such men are shrewd enough to sense that sexual instinct is in general sufficiently attenuated to permit this ploy. In a more adult society the attractiveness of the female "bait" would so overshadow the product that the product would receive no attention.

Precisely in this most fundamental part of our lives we have come a long way from the purely primal function of sex, which had no other purpose than procreation for our evolutionary ancestors, and we find a multitude of aspects which point up man's tendency in adulthood to reflect the behavior and gratifications of childhood, and even of infancy.

For example, the behavior of men and women who stimulate themselves by chasing each other around the bedroom and the coyness of the prude who indirectly plays the game of "Chase me, and you can have me if you can get me!" both echo children's games. It does not take a great deal of imagination to recognize in oral sexual practices a reversion to the oral gratifications of infancy, or perhaps even further back into our race history to the lower primates who engage in mutual licking of the anogenital regions in greeting. It is easy to see in voyeurism and sexual experimentation the curiosity and exploratory activities of very young children and animals, and in skin eroticism a return to the pleasureful sensations of the infant animal as it is licked clean and fondled by its mother, or of human babies as they are washed, oiled, and powdered. Neither does it stretch credibility too much to recognize in orgies some of the mass activity of the litter, especially in its undifferentiated sexuality (very young litter animals mount their siblings irrespective of sex, and the very young human has no clear idea of sexual differences). The prolongation of the sexual act, too, in some ways recalls the pleasurable sensations experienced by the child as it is handled, petted, and coddled by its mother. It is only in man that the deliberate prolongation of the sex act itself purely for pleasurable sensations is observed, although many animals, of course, practice elaborate courtship and preliminary rituals.

Although the sexual act is governed by reflexes originating in the paleocortex, in man a new factor has been added with the development of the neocortex. Among the functions the neocortex has taken on is the one of evaluating what constitutes appropriate or inappropriate behavior. Since man's social behavior has largely ceased to be instinctual (governed by the paleocortex), his need to maintain his place within his society is now governed by the evaluative judgment of his neocortex. A sense of shame, failure, or embarrassment has replaced the social instinct of animals. While many of the activities of man are necessarily automatic and instinctual (for the capacity of the neocortex would be overloaded were every single action subject to its consideration), the neocortex nevertheless can, and sometimes does, impinge even upon these by an act of will. Whenever it interferes in this way, it hampers the automatic action. Sometimes this is a necessity for the individual; at other times it may serve the purpose of maintaining cultural standards but is not in his best interest.

For example, a person walking down a street swings his arms harmoniously with his stride. If we should, as an experiment, ask him why he swings his arms so high, he would have to think about them. In effect, his neocortex would be forced to participate in what was an automatic act. Should we then step away and watch our man continue down the street, we should see the previously smooth gait become awkward. The intrusion of the neocortex would have spoiled the smooth, rhythmic flow of the paleocortical reflexes.

When we then take into consideration that the neocortex is the repository of the learned social standards of the community and imposes them upon such an involved sequence of instinctual responses as the sexual act, we can readily see that it may cause the utmost havoc.

The standards that societies impose are as many and as varied as the cultures of man. In our own Western civilization not only a sense of what is proper or improper, but also a feeling of success or failure may impede the orderly unfolding of the many stages of the sexual act.

As with the example of the walker's changed gait when he was made conscious of the movements of his arms, so the interference of the evaluative judgment causes varieties of awkwardness and inappropriate responses in the sexual act, and these then reinforce the fear of being a failure in the "sex department" of life, causing it to become a self-fulfilling prophecy.

There are people who feel the need to impose very strict controls upon their instincts. Sometimes this is because they have seen frightening results of uncontrolled instinctual behavior, such as hysteria or violence, in their parents. At others it is because they have been trained to consider a display of excessive emotion unbecoming. Whatever the reason, they fear surrender of neocortical control. Implied in this fear is the possibility of hurting the woman by the violence of the release of the emotions, or that any display of intense emotion would appear childish or ridiculous. For such individuals a build-up of sexual tension could therefore lead to something they feel to be undesirable, and so inhibiting impulses are sent out by their brains to all the muscles which participate in the sexual thrusts, creating a stiffness and discomfort which makes the act unpleasant to them.

Here we see a vivid example of how the neocortex (the development of which is a concomitant of man's prolonged childhood) has the ability to inhibit the proper functioning of an essential instinct of the mature person.

We shall now discuss how it not only exerts this influence but actually is, to a large extent, in the process of taking over the expression of this vital function of man.

Because the onset of sexuality occurs at an early age, strict cortical controls have traditionally been imposed on the young. In the past, parents reinforced these controls by combining them with threats of most fearful consequences— incurable sickness, illegitimate pregnancy, social ostracism, disgrace, shame, and the withdrawal of parental love. Since parents in our times are themselves caught up in a trend of increasing youthfulness, they are less inclined to have restrictive thoughts about sex. But although the traditional cortical controls are now to a large extent being abandoned, this does not imply a return to the free exercise of the instincts.

On the surface, it would seem that the culturally accepted loosening of sexual morality could be thought of in terms of a "back to nature" trend, but this would give an entirely false picture. In the first place, in nature, mating is a seasonal occurrence, and in the second, it serves no other purpose than procreation. The greater sexual freedom man now tolerates actually serves to widen the distance between the fundamental instinct and present practice, for the emphasis has changed.

As we have discussed in the preceding chapter, modern man has shown a tendency to convert everything he uses and does into toys and play; in doing so he has included sex and thus removed it progressively away from the area of instinct. In his unceasing infantile quest for pleasure he has forced the removal of the shackles of many sexual taboos. Earlier, pair bonding served the purpose of protecting the human infant during its prolonged childhood. Although the thought of having children is still present, the primary purpose of pair bonding now is companionship and the pleasure it brings.

This companionship relationship, rather than the role of responsible parent, leads to the current trend toward wiping out the external signs of gender identification and is probably the most conspicuous aspect of the progression toward infantilization. It leads us even further back into early childhood, where sexual differentiation is minimal.

There is one aspect of this phenomenon where the direction of the trend is identical, but the underlying motivations are radically different. In the past, social sex differentiation was largely associated with the premium the economy placed on the superior strength and muscular coordination of the male correlated with the domestic abilities of the female. Since no purpose is served in our society today by these two characteristics, sex differentiation in the division of labor becomes almost meaningless. The modern couple, isolated from its extended family and without domestic help, must be ready and able to take on each other's roles when necessary. Should the husband be absent from the home, there is no one present but the wife to take on such manual tasks as would normally be assigned to him. Should the wife be incapacitated, only the husband is there to care for the children and perform essential household chores. In this respect decreasing sexual differentiation is functional for our society, and does not connote any blurring of masculinity or femininity. Perhaps, in fact, new definitions of these concepts need to be evolved.

To come back to the trend toward nondifferentiation between the sexes that we have in mind here, the various youth movements that have arisen spontaneously around the world since the middle of the twentieth century offer good examples. They seem to oppose any distinctions at all among people. They reject any convention which separates men from women; they advocate egalitarianism in fashions of dress and hair style; and in their mode of living, bachelor boys and bachelor girls claim equal privileges and sexual freedom. They carry their need for homogeneity into the areas of learning by demanding the abolition of grades, honors, scholarships, and even qualification for entrance to colleges, so as to eliminate the gulf between the scholarly and the nonscholarly.

The sexual mores of these youths are largely misunderstood because of exaggerations and even false reports by the mass media. Observers for the media assume that the unconventional mode of attire and behavior of the young connote equally unconventional sexual habits. But stories of wild orgies cater more to sensationalism than reflect actual fact. For these youngsters, being together and offering each other support is more important in most cases than actual sexual experience. This is even more apparent in the so-called pot parties, where the sensory experience of inhaled marijuana outweighs the desire for sex. In fact, Dr. Bruno Bettelheim has declared that drugs, far from being inducements to wild sex, are more accurately to be described as the "instant nurturing mother" our young feel the need for and never had.

In even the more conservative strata of our society, sex-linked accouterments are disappearing. Men and women increasingly are wearing one another's clothing. Their leisure activities tend not to be sex-linked. Furniture related to either sex, like the leather club chair or the boudoir chair, is disappearing. American men use three times as much fragrance-containing preparations as their wives.

The impression arises, as one follows the process of infantilization in man-woman relationships down its path, that one goes past the stage of pair bonding based on romantic love and finally reaches a level where companionship becomes the greatest binding factor. We have called it a Hansel-and-Gretel relationship, like that which bound the two children of the fairy story together against the fear-inspiring world of responsibility, outside pressures, and the machinations of the wicked. One might equally well call it a Babes-in-the-Wood relationship.

Not only among the young, but also among their elders we see on all sides manifestations of a desire for group relationships analogous to those of nursery schools or kindergartens, where children of both sexes are banded together on perfectly equal terms. An increasing number of adults (in years) participate in such intimate group relationships as the sensitivity groups, communal living experiments, and wife-swapping. They seek mutual support in therapeutic communities designed to cure addiction to alcohol, drugs, or overeating. At lower ages we have the groups known as beatniks, hippies, flower children, and so on, with their yearnings for peace, tranquility, and love.

Until recently, we expected certain qualifications from the young, such as giving up childish pursuits and assuming financial responsibility, before we considered them sufficiently socially mature to be ready for marriage. But as the pattern is changing in the direction of infantilization, we notice that economic independence is devalued and postponed as long as possible. Even poverty is preferred by the young to the responsibilities and discipline of wage-earning. At the same time heterosexual relationships are beginning at progressively earlier ages, so that the man-woman relationship is shifting from the adult husband and wife to that of the boy-friend/girl-friend, and even further to a brother-sister tie.

Previously the prerequisite for a young man to enter marriage was his ability to be a provider, and sexual relationships were postponed until this goal was attained. At present the only prerequisite for marriage is mutually agreeable companionship; the husband, who may still be studying, is supported by his parents, his wife's parents, his wife, fellowships, or some combination of these.

This sector of our latest generation does not look upon sex as a means of proving its masculinity or femininity. In fact, sex has lost its central position in its life. Its heroes are no longer the glamorous actress, the *femme fatale,* the rugged "he-man," or the irresistible Don Juan. They admire and follow young people very much like themselves. They have no strong desire to attain adulthood. The sexual sensation *per se* is no longer satisfactory. The feeling is that there must be some other, greater, sensation beyond it. For them the holy grail is the full abandonment of the satiated baby dozing peacefully, snuggled up to its mother's breast.

The unfulfilled need for this nirvana gives rise to a search for a means to achieve it. Partakers of drugs seek relief from tensions, as do children, who have no tolerance for discomfort. The attempt to explore the frontiers of the mind with hallucinatory drugs is "playing" with the mind, and also reveals the intense preoccupation with the self that is characteristic of the baby.

From a purely biological point of view man, in his adaptation to the changing conditions brought about by science and technology—neocortical elaborations—should have accommodated his reproductive apparatus to bringing forth a very limited number of children. The prolonged childhood concomitant with the elaborate protective systems applied to the modern youngster should be a factor in limiting the number of pregnancies. One would therefore expect that the female of the species would become fertile roughly past the first third of her life, then produce in the limited years of her receptive period a correspondingly limited number of infants and, during the last third of her life assume the role of helping the next generation of females with the tasks of procreation and preservation of the home.

Exactly the opposite has taken place. In view of the ongoing and progressive infantilization we have observed, perhaps this is not surprising. We witness the most remarkable fact that at a time when it is of vital importance to the race to limit the numbers of its population, we have the phenomenon of the receding of the onset of menstruation in girls at a rate of four months in every decade (one year in every thirty). Margaret Mead remarked in a lecture before the Society for Adolescent Psychiatry in October 1969 that within the foreseeable future we may have to halt the onset of early puberty by biochemical means, otherwise we shall be in the position of having to put getting married and having children into the primary-school curriculum.

In more primitive societies the females lag behind in the development of their secondary sexual characteristics.

Since, biologically speaking, there is no need for man to prolong his procreative period, of necessity these sexual potentialities have other causes.

It is true that many activities and rituals are practiced in other species to attract a mate and to defend and hold her, as are those of the preliminaries of mating. We commonly use a metaphor from the habits of courtship of birds when we speak of a young couple "billing and cooing." Yet the intense preoccupation of modern man with actual intercourse goes to a degree far beyond the very limited attention his evolutionary ancestors devoted to this activity, and in the elaboration of the attendant foreplay preceding mating his practices exceed by far any comparable preliminaries seen in other mammals or birds. Thus it is not too far-fetched to state that sex in man, as another "first" in the development of mammalians, has become an activity that is an end in itself, to which the procreative aspects are an incidental, if not superfluous, adjunct.

How did this come about?

Let us observe the child-rearing practices of modern man. Practically from the day of its birth the infant experiences extensive and pleasureful physical stimulation: close contact with its mother's body and bathing, oiling, and powdering of the skin. The equivalent is seen in many animals, but in man this stimulation is intensified and prolonged.

To point up the difference of man's handling of his young in this respect and that of our nearest animal relatives, we quote G. J. von Allesch, who has described the process of defecation of the infant ape: "The mother suddenly raised the baby, which otherwise clung to her, by one leg, so that it hung free in mid-air. With the baby thus 'held out,' the feces could drop to the ground without touching the mother. Afterward the baby was brought back to its former position. Often it was set down again before defecation or during the actual process, and sometimes nothing at all happened. It is easy to believe that in this original form of 'holding out' the mother, carrying her baby on her body, recognizes the right moment more easily than can the human mother, whose child is in bed."

By contrast, in the Western world we use diapers for our infants who, in this way, experience a continuous stimulation of their pelvic regions from the warm waste products. Added to this are the frequent diaper changes with bathing and oiling of the genital area. All of this provides an almost continuous stimulation, perhaps bordering on overstimulation, of the nervous system—for the genital region is richly endowed with nerve endings. In its response the nervous system cannot help but alert the endocrine glands, particularly the pituitary, although on a mistaken interpretation of the message, that the organism is ready for procreation. Other investigators have also considered overstimulation a factor in earlier sexual maturation, but have pointed to other causes.

Simmel collected data on the appearance of menstruation in the girls of Karelo, Finland, during the time of the Finnish-Soviet war, and found that the onset of menarche was earlier in girls living in an area affected by war. He considered stress, increasing the hormonal output, another factor in overstimulation bringing about the earlier menstruation. Bennhold-Thomsen believed that what he called urbanization trauma—the increasing influence of environment, intensified rhythm of life, intrusive effects of lights, heavy traffic, accumulation of sounds—the totality of the stimuli of modern city life, to be the cause of earlier puberty. Arvay found that psychological effects acting over a long time increase gonadotropin production in the hypothalamo-hypophyseal system, and that this stimulating hormonal influence results in precocious ovarian activity and early sexual maturity.

With all its sensory stimulations, from diapering to traffic, the Western world may have set into motion a process which brings about sexual maturation earlier and earlier, to a period in a child's life when it is neither anatomically, physiologically, nor socio-economically equipped to assume the role of a parent. It is not surprising, therefore, that many of the features typical of the infant find their way into sex play. The grown human being nowadays would find the meeting of the genital organs for only so long as it takes to deposit the sperm into the recesses of the vagina highly unsatisfactory. Witness the quarrels between husbands and wives, often leading to infidelity and to the break-up of marriages, when physical gratifications derived from the intimacies of sexual exchanges are lacking.

In more recent times the preoccupation with the place of sex in man's life has reached the proportions of a cult. We have mentioned the enormous quantity of literature in this field that is flooding the public. If one glances at some of it, one is struck with the similarity it has with the "How-To-Do-It" manuals and books of instruction designed to improve one's game of golf, skill at the bridge table, or knowledge of the technicalities of mountain climbing: one might liken them to *The Compleat Angler* of sexual accomplishment. In every instance the most careful attention is given to even the minutest details to ensure a thorough knowledge of the field and a successful game. In this stage, sexual gratification has passed from being a result and concomitant of a limited instinctual response to one in which it is calculated to promote pure, unadulterated, and prolonged pleasure, satisfying the needs both of the paleocortex and the neocortex.

What is more, we can already see the beginning of a new stage, for the neocortex is entering the picture to an evergreater degree. Ultimately the result will be a scientific approach, where we shall teach our children about sexual matters in the same way we teach them physics, mathematics, or ancient history. Then the union between two human beings will lose its spontaneity and become a carefully planned and thought-out project. A successful conclusion will have to guarantee, through proper performance, the full satisfaction of the other partner. The fear of failing in this endeavor will not be different from similar apprehension in other social areas. Modern man's fear of not being "good" enough in sex has already become a source of growing anxiety to him. Sex is now in the process of developing into a skill to be learned and practiced in the same way as other games of skill. We must expect to hear a man declare, with the same sense of pride that he might take in having shot a game of golf in the low seventies, that, through his superior performance, he had given his mate, or caused her to have, an "orgasm."

The mechanisms of several sexual perversions are traceable to behavior common to childhood. These are not necessarily explanations of the causes of the perversions, but only the mechanisms which are available to man, largely because of his progressive infantilization, and these mechanisms guide the perversions into specific directions. Sex is an intimate, person-to-person relationship, and therefore its expressions in the "adult" child will echo the intimate experiences he had as an "infant" child.

Sexual deviations from the norm are many, but as time goes by the consensus appears to narrow this category to such a degree that today there are hardly any sexual practices left that are not considered simply an extreme extension of the norm. Nowadays sexual deviations exist largely by definition. It is of interest here that archaic laws exist in the United States, still on the books, explicitly forbidding so-called perversions. But changing social attitudes have converted many such practices into merely titillating variations of the sexual theme.

As we have said, progressive infantilization promotes the appearance of patterns which are easily recognizable as childlike pursuits once the sexual element is removed. All too often men are inclined to confuse the sexual prowess of a Don Juan with masculinity, but on closer examination it is anything but that. To a four-year-old child his playmates are objects, different from toys only by reason of being animated. A pet, such as a puppy, fills the same need. He is not yet fully aware of himself as a real person (a child of this age will often refer to himself in the third person) and so he relates to his contemporaries in some ways as things. The Don Juan does not see the woman he is in the process of seducing as a human being endowed with many and varied characteristics; to him she is a means of achieving pleasurable gratification. Beyond that he has no interest in her. He will probably become annoyed if she asks him whether he loves her.

When this man-child allows himself to be entrapped into a marriage, the flaws in his personality become more apparent. The erstwhile sexual prowess ceases to be a source of satisfaction, since he now realizes that he has involved himself in assuming responsibility for another human being. While he was dating her she was only an object to him, but after the honeymoon she will certainly insist on her prerogatives as being a person and not only a source of sexual pleasure for his amusement. If, to punish him for some act of thoughtlessness, she withholds this one pleasure, he will react in the manner typical of a four-year-old denied some treat. His displeasure will take the form of temper tantrums, sulking, hitting, refusing to eat, or similar behavior. Often the wife who is wise will understand that her angry man-child must be appeased with sex or with special foods.

The preference for a sex partner of the same sex has many roots. Many of them, though, are extensions of the child's pursuits. A good deal of a homosexual's sex play consists of mutual fondling reminiscent of early experiences. Why is it then that such an individual does not seek a biologically more appropriate choice? Many psychologically conditioned factors enter here; probably the most prevalent for men is the need to find a sense of masculine identity when as little boys they have been emotionally overwhelmed by female influences, and the reverse would be true for women. The characteristics of homosexual pair bonding are similar in many ways to relationships existing between five-to-eight-year-old boys, when intense loyalty to each other alternates with physical and verbal abuse.

Watch a five-year-old and his seven-year-old brother playing. At one moment there is perfect harmony, then Bob accidentally knocks Jim's blocks down. Jim is enraged; he hits Bob on the head. Bob is stunned, but then slowly breaks into tears and ends in loud sobs; now Jim is upset about Bob's pain and pats him gently. After a short while Bob quiets down and their play continues as though nothing had happened. If we substitute genital activities for the child's play, we have some of the basic elements of the amatory attitudes of many homosexuals which both invite and inflict cruelty.

Other difficulties which sometimes appear go back even farther than childhood, to remoter periods of man's ancestry. Paleolithic man was a poorly protected animal, an easy mark for attacking carnivores. His capacity to survive was based on the speed of his reactions to mortal threats, but while copulating, both the male and female are in a helpless condition. As with many animals—for whom, of course, this is also true—it is the female who signals her readiness. Only when she has scouted her environment for the absence of danger will she be able to release the inhibitory brakes and "present" herself. The male then responds with the courtship ritual and ends with the act of mating. But the male is the defender of the species, and he may never relax his alertness to respond to possibly harmful interference; so, of necessity, in a natural state, copulation has to be of short duration. The fear of mutilation or death while in this helpless state demands full attention to visual and auditory messages from the surroundings. Elements of this fear have persisted in modern man to this day, and are responsible for premature ejaculation.

Freud attributed this particular malfunction to a male's apprehension about the mysterious cavity, the female sex organ. He formulated a theory that the unconscious mind of the male experienced a dire fantasy of losing his genital organ in the process of mating, and he referred to this symptom as "castration anxiety." But closer examination of this particular sexual disability reveals an atavistic origin in at least some of the individuals who are afflicted with it. Dreams of being chased by wild animals, fears of injury and bleeding to death, sickening sensations or fainting at the sight of injured persons all indicate a factor that goes far beyond the symbolized dread of losing the penis. Of course there are some cases—especially when direct threats have been made, jocularly or otherwise, of such a kind as "If you don't behave I'll cut it off"—when a castration anxiety could indeed be a determining factor.

The increasing influence of the neocortex, with its powers of evaluative and discriminatory judgment, on man's behavior obviously finds its way into the sexual act as well. The mechanism of the act itself is spontaneous and semiautomatic. The rhythmic stimulation leads to a crescendo of impulses until a high pitch is achieved, culminating in an explosive release of the orgasmic discharge. In the male the pulsating sequence empties the seminal fluid. In the female the rhythmic contractions of the pelvic muscles perform both a massaging pressure on the penis to squeeze from it the last drop of sperm and at the same time release a mucus plug covering the opening of the cervix. Any interference with this semiautomatic mechanism will disrupt the sequence. If cultural mores imprint upon a woman's mind the feeling that an undue demonstration of sexual excitement could cast aspersions on her virtue, she will tend to inhibit the flow of nervous impulses to her pelvic organs. Quite often such a reaction results in altering the rhythm of the pelvic thrusts and causes a stifling of orgastic contractions. However, with increasing infantilization, the strength of cultural taboos diminishes. We now have an ambience where, as the woman regresses toward younger attitudes, she is less and less concerned with cultural taboos. Therefore, contrary to the earlier teachings of psychology that only a mature individual may attain the highest form of sexual enjoyment, we now witness the fact—somewhat unacceptable to an orderly mind—that some emotionally immature females can very well enjoy a perfectly satisfying sex life. In some instances it may even be that this is the only thing which brings them pleasure.

Actually this paradox is only apparent. It arose through the cultural prejudices of those earlier psychologists who felt that a good and healthy sex life should be held out as a reward for the emotionally maturing person. In the treatment of those with emotional problems such a view became both an explanation and a bait, especially for female patients. For the male there is less of a problem, since his orgastic discharge depends on the involuntary contraction of muscles, an action over which the neocortex cannot exert any direct control.

What sex will be like when the neocortex assumes full control of this activity is not too difficult to guess. It will be less and less a plain and unadulterated joy, and will turn more and more into a game of skill. The emphasis will then be on performance and less on physical gratification. A man will derive a greater sense of satisfaction from being a "perfect lover" than from the sense of relief secondary to the act itself.

One could summarize the progress of man toward infantilization solely by the record of his sexual habits thus:

Primitive man: Sexual behavior functional.

Medieval man: Romantic love, which equals the puppy love of pubertal youngsters: that is, intense emotion with absence or suppression of sexuality.

Modern man: Emphasis on sexual prowess, which is the equivalent of the boasting of physical feats by ten-to-eleven-year-old boys: extension of "play"—childlike.

Future man (?): Concentration on play and sensation: sterile—infantile.

CHAPTER NINE

The Matter of Courage

Several generations of English schoolchildren were brought up on such poems as the story of Lars Porsena of Clusium, who swore by the nine gods that the great house of Tarquin should suffer no more wrong. It contains the lines

> Then out spake brave Horatius,
>   The Captain of the Gate:
> "To every man upon this earth
>   Death cometh soon or late.
> And how can man die better
>   Than facing fearful odds,
> For the ashes of his fathers,
>   And the temples of his Gods?"

It may be that some members of our latest generation are unmoved by such sentiments, but in spite of the heroics—which did not strike us as at all overblown at that time—most of us who are over thirty felt an inner singing of the blood at these lines, as a chord of response was touched within us by the nobility of Horatius.

Another of the many paradoxes in the ways of man is the great value we place on courage.

We are inclined to despise a person who is cowardly. We teach our children to stand up for themselves and, if necessary, to fight. We assure our sons that they will lose the respect of their peers if they are not ready to assert their rights by force. In our societies we teach them the "manly" arts of self-defense: boxing, fencing, wrestling, riflery. In primitive societies young men are forced to overcome their native fears by trials and initiation rites at puberty. Everywhere the adolescent boy has to prove his manhood, his masculinity, his prowess and strength through bravery to gain acceptance as a man —a male of the species. The gallant, the daring, the Englishman who keeps a "stiff upper lip," the American "he-man" type, the German dueler, the Japanese samurai have been admired ideals.

Yet the cowardly person is what nature intended him to be. Man's anatomy and physiology are geared to precaution in the fear of danger, and to flight in its presence—*not* to standing his ground and fighting. He possesses neither fangs nor claws, neither muscular power nor agility. His upright stance puts his at a disadvantage against a four-legged predator.

Animals who rely on swift flight as a means of self-preservation have reflexes which facilitate just that. It is of utmost importance to an animal on the run that he carry the least possible weight. To this end such an animal in a situation of danger disgorges its latest meal and evacuates the contents of his bowels. The sea urchin goes so far as to jettison its entire stomach as well as the contents (a procedure known as eventration) in such circumstances, growing a new one at a more convenient time. The sea slug unballasts itself of its lower intestine in the same way at such times. In man the vestiges of those reflexes remain with us in the form of psychosomatic afflictions of the digestive tract. In fear some of us become violently nauseated and vomit. Others feel spastic contractions of the colon, leading to diarrhea. This reaction is so commonly understood that humorous allusions to it have found their way into the vernacular. When fear develops into a chronic state of anxiety it can cause severe disabilities to the digestive tract of the susceptible person. These may range from simple indigestion or loss of appetite to spastic or ulcerative colitis. Although there is no longer any conscious, or acknowledged, intention of fleeing, the brain (paleocortex) still sends its messages to the body to prepare for flight.

It is not only in the culture of Western man that this admiration for courage and disgust for cowardice exists. The American Indian traditionally maintains a completely impervious demeanor when experiencing pain. To show himself a coward would violate his most cherished principles of conduct. Fijian fire-walkers unflinchingly step barefoot over red-hot stones. The Japanese until recently ceremonially eviscerated themselves on the threshold of an enemy to avenge an insult, and in the last world war they found no lack of volunteers for the suicidal dive-bombing missions of the *kamikaze* flights. Although they are allowed a little more latitude, on the whole females as well as males are expected to demonstrate their own kind of courage: to bear children in spite of fear; to tend the sick and dying, overcoming squeamishness; to keep up a brave front in the face of loss, uncertainty, and separation.

This universal esteem for a quality which demands a massive denial of every built-in physical and mental instinct for self-preservation must have a very deep-seated significance.

The Matter of Courage

If we look at courage a little more closely we find that it has two faces. There is that courage that is called out by circumstances endangering the preservation of the species, as when adults jeopardize their own lives to save children or to rescue a fellow man from peril. This type of bravery is not unique to man. Most species will go to any lengths to protect and defend their young, and some will aid other adults in emergencies. It is the other kind of courage that is of interest to us here: the courage to achieve a goal which is more desired than the pain of attaining it is feared.

In the rest of nature nothing but self-preservation or a threat to its species will induce an animal to put itself into danger. Yet for the sake of a medal or trophy, for the adulation of a crowd of strangers, for the admiration or respect of his peers, a man will sail an ocean in a flimsy boat or embark on a solo flight over uncharted air routes, risk his life establishing land, sea, or air speed records, fight to the last against overwhelming odds, or hazard death in hostile terrain.

The fact that man will do such things is only understandable if they are viewed as outgrowths of adolescent behavior, or juvenile curiosity and experimentation without adult inhibitions. Many of the "foolish" displays characteristic of adolescence require a great deal of courage to perform, but they are natural at that stage of life when a youth is preparing to challenge an older generation for dominance. They are not "natural" in the mature adult, who has already achieved a dominant status, and who should be concerned with the safeguarding, not the risking, of his life.

The admiration we all feel for such displays is even harder to understand. Does it indicate some semiconscious awareness, or knowledge, that everything in our structure and our instincts cries out against such actions, and that this adds some extra keenness to our perception of the difficulty of overcoming the remnants of those built-in restraints that are still with us?

Perhaps this universal feeling of recognition of the essential self-conquest that valor implies is some last vestige of our instinctual understanding of the proper business of an adult? Or is our admiration for what is intrinsically foolish action yet another indication of the juvenile level to which our emotional reactions have regressed?

CHAPTER TEN

The Element of Pleasure in Being Destructive

When seeking the causes of riots and disturbances, most people are inclined to overlook the fact that a certain physical joy is obtained by destruction. Any mother who has accompanied her child to a park or playground over a period of years will have noticed that before children are old enough to have the skill and coordination necessary to build with blocks, sticks or mud, they take great delight in knocking down what others have built.

If one observes the playing children closely one will notice that the joy has nothing to do with the grief and annoyance caused to the child whose edifice is destroyed. The child who demolishes it does not think at all of the builder. The fascination is solely in causing the pieces to tumble, in watching them fail—perhaps in some sense of power in being the generator of the process. Often an expression of satisfaction comes to his face as he regards the toppled stones or blocks, as though he had accomplished something very rewarding. When it is pointed out to him that the action is naughty—that Sandy or Jill took a lot of time and trouble to make the block castle and is angry or unhappy at its destruction—the child feels very sorry. He had no intention of upsetting Jill or Sandy, but the impulse to push down whatever had been put up was irresistible, and the satisfaction of that impulse brought him a warm feeling of contentment and happiness.

If we transpose this kind of innocent destructiveness into adult life and add to it the influences of the neo(play)cortex that will by then have accrued, it is easier to understand a very basic aspect of riots. There is a touch of Roman-circus atmosphere in all such disorders. Often the first looting perpetrated is of liquor stores, with the inevitable saturnalian results. An unsupervised party for adolescents, no matter how carefully they have been raised, has been known to turn into an orgy of destruction, with the young men swinging from the chandeliers (as though our theory of regression to our arboreal ancestors needed confirmation!) while the girls gleefully egged them on. At ball games spectators of all ages on the slightest pretext will throw bottles into the arena, rip up benches, and send up pleas to kill the umpire (shades of Circus Maximus, the gladiators, the early Christians, and the lions—*plus ça change, plus c'est la même chose*).

The same, in general, applies to student riots. Although there is no doubt (or so one hopes) of the sincerity of the leaders and many of the participants, there are inevitably a large number of me-tooers who delight in breaking furniture, littering floors, and taking potshots at windows. Some members of the college faculties, themselves harboring desires for the plea-

The Element of Pleasure in Being Destructive 149

sures of destruction but obliged to suppress them for obvious reasons, then honor these riotous activities with the gloss of legitimate protest.

The same motivations apply to vandalism in schools and abandoned buildings. In these cases at least, the youngsters are honest enough not to pretend to be fighting for a cause. Moreover, demolition teams razing buildings always find an appreciative audience of sidewalk superintendents.

Undeniably riots and revolutions *are* sparked by legitimate grievances in many instances, but one should not overlook this element of pleasure which is always present, even in the most warranted revolts against intolerable injustice. The old women, *les tricoteuses,* who knitted beside the guillotine during the French Revolution were certainly there to enjoy the spectacle, and indeed in all countries public executions have been attended by large and festive crowds.

Curiously enough, we indignantly scold small boys who pull off the wings of insects, but we as adults watch high-wire artists at a circus and experience a peculiar mixture of feelings whenever one wobbles. We are horrified at the realization that we may perhaps really wish to have the excitement of seeing him fall. The performers, aware of this, risk their lives daily, forgoing the precaution of safety nets, to intensify this excitement.

It is a credit to the authorities of ancient Rome that they recognized this need of the populace and deflected it into comparatively harmless channels—*Panem et circenses,* "bread and circuses."

CHAPTER ELEVEN

Violence

CIVIL STRIFE AND WARFARE
The subject of violence not only preoccupies the attention of all responsible people throughout the world today; it has caused thinkers of all times to seek explanations and remedies —to such an extent that the phrase "man's inhumanity to man" has become a cliché. Considering all the attention to the subject, all the thought expended upon it, and all the efforts that have been made to curb it, it is somewhat remarkable that absolutely no progress has been made. The variety of plans and schemes that have been tried with the aim of restoring tranquility to the communities of man as it existed, and still exists, among the colonies of our ancestral forebears and their other descendants the anthropoid apes, have been so numerous that it is almost a miracle that none of them has borne fruit.

Most of us know that in the two thousand years since the birth of Christ man has fought over two thousand wars. Supranational agencies such as the League of Nations, the

United Nations, power blocs, alliances, peace treaties, pacts —none has stopped international disputes from leading to war. Similarly, religions, political ideologies, legislation, harsh punishment, kindness, and charity have not reduced the crime rate. No type of culture has succeeded in changing this situation. The enemies we blame as the instigators of wars, however we may accuse or disown them, are just as much fellow members of the human race and a product of its development as we are ourselves.

There has been a veritable flood of diverse explanations for this peculiarly human problem, and an equal number of suggested remedies for it. Why does it not seem possible to arrive at a solution that works?

One of the chief roadblocks is that man has a tendency to weigh the factors of any situation in terms of his own values and to justify or rationalize whatever action he has decided to take. The major dilemma is the lack of objective criteria for human behavior. We may all agree that physical assault is a socially undesirable act, but we qualify this judgment immediately by acknowledging that in some circumstances it is unavoidable. The question then arises as to *which* are such circumstances. As an illustration, we have in our legal code the term *justifiable homicide.* Is depriving a fellow human being of life ever justifiable?

There are so many qualifying aspects to every violent action that any remedies suggested must prove controversial. Is a man who kills his mate in a fit of temper a criminal or a psychologically unstable person? In court the prosecutor and the defender use logic and emotional rhetoric to influence the jury in its decision, but whatever the outcome, freedom or jail, we are left with disturbing thoughts: Was the verdict correct? How can we prevent a recurrence of such an act? Is punishment or psychiatric treatment the answer? Should society exact retribution? Is a stern deterrent—capital punishment, for example—the answer? Or should we exercise patience and understanding to restore the offender to society?

We cite here a brief summary of some of the multitude of explanations that have been offered in recent times to account for the sources of violence:

1. The "Killer Ape" theory. There are those who believe that when they made the transition from a herbivorous to a carnivorous diet, man's ancestors extended the newly released instinct to kill prey into killing his own kind. We do not see this as an explanation. If it were so, why is it that no other carnivorous species has taken the same course?

2. In a report to the National Commission on the Causes and Prevention of Violence entitled *Violence in America: Historical and Comparative Perspectives,* Charles Tilly wrote: "The more intense and widespread frustration-induced discontent is among a people, the more intense and widespread collective violence is likely to be." We feel strongly that frustration does not inevitably lead to violence. There are those who are spurred to greater endeavor by it, and some who even manage to achieve overcompensation.

3. In *The Politics of Protest,* another report to the Commission, Jerome H. Skolnick stated that riots "are spontaneous political acts expressing enormous frustration and genuine grievances." Nevertheless in times past there have been occasions when political grievances have been satisfied by other means. In England at the beginning of the thirteenth century the barons gained the Magna Carta from King John by demands based upon respect for ancient custom and law. India's independence was achieved by passive resistance. And riots are not always political acts.

4. Harvey Wheeler, in his essay in *Alternatives to Violence,* said: "Frustrations of our expectations produce hatred, and

this is merely another way of talking about violence." This, surely, is only one aspect of the results of frustrated expectations, which can range from paralyzing apathy to determination to find alternate solutions.

5. A twenty-four-physician committee on violence was formed at Stanford University School of Medicine following the assassination of Robert F. Kennedy. In the April 25, 1969, issue of *Science* it described rioters as "men who have experienced frustration of their rising expectations" and thus see violence against the "system" as justified. While this may apply to the spokesmen of riotous communities, the rank and file frequently join in the rioting because they enjoy it—for the release of their destructive urges.

6. Richard Maxwell Brown, another contributor to *Violence in America,* indicates that in the United States "all too often unyielding and unsympathetic established political and economic power has invited violence by its refusal to heed and redress just grievances . . . and the possessors of power and wealth have been prone to refuse to share their attributes until it has been too late." This is stating the obvious. Possessors of power and wealth have never in the whole course of history, in any country or at any period, been prone to share their attributes, but this proclivity has not invariably caused riots. There have to be other factors.

7. We are more inclined to agree with Morris Janowitz, who commented in the same report that the motivation for the black "commodity riots" of the late 1960s "is clearly not desperation generated by the anticipation of starvation, as in the food riots in India during famine times . . . rather one is struck by the repeated reports of the carnival and happy-day spirit that pervades the early stages of a community riot."

8. In *Alternatives to Violence* Paul D. MacLean says that "man has inherited the basic structure and organization of

three brains"—reptilian, mammalian, and new mammalian —"the two oldest of which are quite similar to those of animals." The new mammalian brain "is a more complicated form of cortex called the neocortex, which is the hallmark of the brains of higher animals, and which culminates in man to become the brain of reading, writing and arithmetic." Beneath this is the old mammalian brain, which is synonymous with the limbic cortex. The reptilian brain "forms the matrix of the brainstem and comprises much of the reticular system, midbrain, and basal ganglia."

The main problem, states Dr. MacLean, is the lack of neural machinery for verbal communication between the new mammalian brain, "a mechanism that is fully capable of dealing with the difficult medical and social problems of our time," and man's animal brains, particularly the reptilian, which "programs certain stereotyped behavior according to instructions based on ancestral learning and ancestral memories."

The reptilian brain, in other words, "seems to play a primary role in instinctually determined functions such as establishing territory, finding shelter, hunting, homing, mating, breeding, forming social hierarchies, selecting leaders, and the like." It is "a slave to precedent," obsessive and compulsive, and "appears to have inadequate machinery for learning to cope with new situations."

Thus "the most explosive issue" in social problem-solving at present, in Dr. MacLean's opinion, is how to control "man's reptilian intolerance and reptilian struggle for territory." While he finds hope in the fact that "in the last two thousand years the layman all on his own has made great strides in domesticating his emotions, social critic Arthur Koestler and Zen Buddhist Alan Watts are quick to point out in *Alternatives to Violence* that any such progressive "socializing" of man that has put down his natural self-interest has not been an unmixed blessing.

While much of what Dr. MacLean has written is indisputable, it does not explain the fact that animals, who have only the reptilian and older mammalian brains, the paleocortex, never riot.

By exclusion, we believe that it is the neocortex, the only part of the brain not possessed by other species, which must be a contributing, if not the causative, factor in man's special behavior in this respect.

So many well-intentioned investigators who have studied outbreaks of violence use the word *frustration* when analyzing the causes of riots, whether of the black ghetto or the student variety. We should remind ourselves here that it is not only in the United States at the present time that such resort to force to achieve ends exists. Any day that we pick up a newspaper we may read of religious clashes in Northern Ireland, strife due to language loyalties in Belgium, countless tribal struggles in Africa, ethnic differences which have lead to wholesale massacres and open warfare in India, ideological contentions leading to forceful oppression behind the Iron Curtain, and so on. To complete the list would be to recount the story of mankind.

It may very well be true that frustration appears as one of the immediate causes in some cases of rampage or savagery, but we cannot help thinking that it is but one of many symptoms, and that as a "cause" it belongs at best in "the last straw" category.

The phenomenon of violence in the human species runs much deeper than the sense of frustration which may trigger local outbreaks. One of the special characteristics that separates man from other animals is his capacity for thought—

Minerva's gift of reason—expressed in the spoken word and in his early art; and among the oldest monuments of thought in early men—those testimonials by which we know of their existence in a given place—are their cave paintings and flint arrowheads.

To a certain extent violence is built-in to life itself. Life is violent. There is a perpetual competition for the means of subsistence. At the most elementary level an organic chemical compound attaches itself to another and, through catalytic action, first breaks it down and then incorporates it into its own structure. This has become the prototype of behavior of all life forms on earth: to grab, to break down, to incorporate the fragments. Fighting may be said to be part of the order, or disorder, of nature.

In the primordial oceans, teeming as they were with the forerunners of living cells, those molecules capable of grasping others were the most favored to survive. They fragmented their victims into primitive building blocks and reconstituted them into their own (the aggressor's) design—the very essence of the behavior of the evolving species of predators. With the passage of time, as life developed into more complex organisms, these primordial chemical properties were kept intact. Single-celled amoebae and paramecia surround their food and absorb it into their own systems. White blood corpuscles behave like predators, ready to devour any microscopic invader of their territory, the bloodstream. Not only human beings and all other animals, but also trees, plants, fish, microorganisms—every living thing, from the single cell to the most complex structure—are all violent.

Even inanimate nature is violent: volcanoes erupt; meteors crash into planetary surfaces; planets, stars, the universe itself, explode, constantly rearranging the elements of matter.

Yet in spite of all this, there is still something different about man's violence. The violence of inanimate matter is governed by its chemical and physical properties, which to a certain extent are self-regulating. The violence of vegetable life in its struggle for light, water, or space (and if one wishes to have an education in vegetable violence, there is none better than a slow-motion movie of the struggle of trees for light in a dense forest, stretching above and around their neighbors if they can, and blocking them out of the sun) is also largely physico-chemically determined. As we come to invertebrates, fish, reptiles, amphibians, and warm-blooded life, the violence is extended from its purely chemical aspects into the instinctive areas of struggle for mates, for the establishment of right to a territory, for defense of life, and for obtaining sustenance. Every higher organism is usually equipped with organs both of attack and of protection or evasion. The variety is endless. On the one hand are teeth, tusks, paws, claws, antlers, electricity, and even poison; on the other shells, hides, scales, and devices for camouflage.

But all these forms of violence in nature have the redeeming feature that they tend to cancel each other out. They are the means by which life maintains a balance between its various forms, each form contributing to the perpetuation and health of the others, in the cycle of mutual dependence which we call the balance of nature.

The problem with man's violence is not so much the fact in itself, but that it upsets this balance and all the restraints and self-regulatory devices and mechanisms that apply in the rest of nature.

We have replaced *instinct,* which tends to accommodate itself to all life, and which in any case has the great advantage that it invariably works, with *laws,* pious hopes, and good intentions that almost never work.

As has often been remarked, violence in man takes many

forms that do not appear elsewhere in nature: wars against his own kind, pursuing fights to death, murder, revolution, riot, cruelty, rape, vengeance. Some of these appear to be *a perversion by the neocortex of the instincts* for self-defense, domination, and the mastery of territory. Most of the wars of early man and ancient historical man can be placed within this framework and therefore are more natural—closer, that is, to the workings of the rest of nature. As Alan Watts observed: "If war must be, give me rather a war to capture an enemy's wealth and territory, based on honest greed, in which I shall be careful not to destroy what I want to possess."

A state is a society occupying a defined territory and directed by some form of government. A successful state grows in wealth, power, and population. Growth means expansion. Expansion means more space. If the land beyond its borders is unoccupied, all that is required is to take possession of it; but if it is the property of another state its occupation will be resisted and there will be war. The anatomy of the state, as of any other organism's structure, corresponds to its function. Since the function of a state is to accommodate the growing needs of its population, any successful state must therefore have its organs of war.

War may be said, then, to be the outcome of the growth of societies, which can never be uniform, but varies with varying conditions of climate, land, race, religion, and condition. No super-state can prevent this diversity or repress the expansion of a vigorous community, and in this sense man's wars in some way follow the laws of nature, except that in the rest of nature the struggle is between species, as between the predator and the prey, while in man it is between groups of his own kind. And, as we have said, nature finds an equilibrium. Man, even if he were to manage to establish a world state which could end international wars, would find himself confronted with their reappearance in the form of civil strife and wars of ideologies. To quote Alan Watts again: "But as civilized wars are fought for principle, so the technological 'conquest of nature' is in fact becoming waged for the purely abstract satisfaction of making money, as distinct from the material and sensuous enjoyment of good food, beautiful women, and elegant surroundings." And as Arthur Koestler says bluntly: "The aggressive, self-assertive tendencies in the emotional life of the human individual are less dangerous to the species than his self-transcending or integrative tendencies. ... The number of victims of individual crimes committed in any period of history is insignificant compared to the masses cheerfully sacrificed *ad majorem gloriam,* in blind devotion to the true religion, dynasty, or political system."

There seems to be no way out. Violence is an attribute of adolescence. In the process of regression man as a species has been for some time in a physical and cultural stage corresponding to adolescence in an individual. Fighting and rioting are outgrowths of the propensity of the adolescent male to belligerency as a by-product of his emergent sexuality, and these adolescent drives have found their way into the values of adult society right up to our day.

However, we do see some signs that our time is one of transition to a more childlike equivalent, and we may hope for future periods that this is so. The advent of cultures geared to childlike attributes might not eliminate cruelty, especially on the impersonal level governed by the neocortex, but might well lead eventually to the passing of organized warfare from the human scene.

CHANGING SOCIETY

All the available evidence supports the conclusion that mature man corresponds anatomically to the perinatal stage of the anthropoid apes, but that his behavior has not regressed at the same speed.

In the course of this work we have referred to our present stage of behavior as adolescent. Of course, there is no such phase as adolescence in the animal world. To make a precise analogy when making comparisons to an animal species one would have to refer to the youthful animal.

Before achieving sexual maturity the litter animal engages in playful mock fights where the possibilities of inflicting harm are limited by the weakness and lack of skill of the cub and parental interference in any excesses. Were one to endow the baby animal with the sexual maturity and strength of the adult and leave his other youthful propensities intact, we should see a radically different picture.

By the time he reaches maturity an animal has absorbed into its being the ingrained, ritualized responses of its species which curb its aggressive impulses short of inflicting death. The litter animal possesses a play-fight instinct, but has not yet developed the instinctive controls. Our hypothesized animal, grown only in its physical attributes but retaining the behavior patterns of its youthful form, would carry its play-fight instinct to limitless extremes, since its species-specific inhibitions would not have had a chance to develop. Add to this a budding intelligence, youthful curiosity and experimentation, but no inhibitions, and there would then be no way to halt a violent action once it had been initiated but the total annihilation of the opponent.

Man, dimly aware of this lack of instinct, has tried to remedy it by laws, both religious and secular. But as we have learned to our sorrow, neocortically imposed rules are no match for instinctually ingrained restraints.

The division between the adolescent and the child is not clear-cut. There are several substages intervening. Even our department stores have discovered that they cannot make a sudden transition from a children's clothing department to a teenager's, and have instituted two intermediary departments which they have variously named "Sub-Teen," "Pre-Teen," "Young Juniors," "Junior Hi," and the like. This is significant, since different groups within the species of man occupy similarly different steps on a down escalator. Again we come up against the apparent paradox that in our days the further down (regressed) the group, the greater its intellectual capacities and achievements and the more pacific its habits. We also see the opposite, where a scholarly, cultured, and peaceful people, forced by circumstances to stand their ground and fight for survival, temporarily reverse the process and move back up a step on the down escalator.

To come back to the thought expressed at the end of the previous part of this chapter, while we see signs of transition in our times, these are not uniform. Just as vegetation does not immediately grow over the whole area of an abandoned piece of ground where a building has been razed, but shows itself piecemeal in spots here and there before it finally covers the site completely, so any historical development or biological trend plants its seeds scattered in space and time; eventually these come together and form the new ground cover. In our time patches here and there of childlike ways begin to show themselves interspersed in a culture which on the whole is still in an adolescent phase.

In a child's life there are stark contrasts, as there are in his moods. One moment he may weep as though his heart would break, and the next moment he may be laughing through his tears. In his world there is a polarization between good and bad. It is perfectly expressed in fairy stories—the good fairy and the evil witch; the pure heroine and the wicked stepmother; the noble hero and the dreadful dragon; the brave warrior and cruel fate—that have so strong and timeless an appeal to children. It is also expressed in modern fables: the Good Guy and the Bad Guy, Cowboys and Indians, Cops and Robbers, which have the same kind of appeal. At the same time some horrifying cruelty is shown in "comic" cartoons and is accepted by children with perfect indifference.

In the absence of genetically ingrained controls the young of any species do not yet possess the means of handling strong emotions. If the young human feels intense grief, anger, or other emotion, he is not able to contain it, and he is forced into "acting out." A frustrated child is unable to internalize the discomfort or to release it by verbal expression. He rids himself of this unbearable tension by an act, like kicking against the floor, which is destructive only symbolically, and which may even hurt the child more than the person who has aroused the emotion. Crying, head-banging, screaming, or other forms of temper tantrums are a child's way of obtaining a denied wish. Not until the child is able to learn to postpone the gratification of a desire is he able to refrain from expressing his frustration in the form of temper. Although in some instances the kicking of the heels, screaming, biting, tearing, and similar acts are symbolic displays of a murderous rage against the parents, more often they are attempts to discharge unbearable tensions that have accumulated in the nervous system. Any emotional overload threatens the capacity of the nervous system to function. To cope with this eventuality the brain possesses safety valves in the form of "acting out," vomiting, fainting, and even epileptic fits.

As man's emotional regression catches up with his anatomical structure and his behavior begins to approximate to a child's reactions rather than an adolescent's, his equivalent of "acting out" behavior is motiveless violence, purposeless vandalism, and impulsive urges toward self-destruction. A grown person with the emotional responses of a child, who finds the stresses of present social and economic life intolerable, may turn to alcohol, tranquilizers, or narcotics, if he has managed to control the urge to "act out."

Today we are seeing this type of behavior as a world-wide phenomenon. Its fundamental character is obscured for us by the tendency of our neocortices to rationalize or justify this immaturity in ideological terms. For example, today's youths are rebelling against conscription, and citing their anti-war principles as the reason. In many cases, though, in truth, fear is the motivation. In previous generations they would have been ashamed to take this course, for no adolescent will admit to fear. A conscientious objector would have had to prove that he was not simply a coward by undertaking very dangerous jobs, like stretcher-bearers removing the wounded from battlefields under fire, since only in this way could he prove that his objection was truly conscientious and not a result of cowardice—not only to the authorities, but, more importantly, to himself. A child, however, does not mind admitting to helplessness or fear, for they are a part of his life.

We may find other examples of the tendency of our new brain to rationalize in the tolerance by the liberal of the looting, arson, and sniping of the extreme militants in the United States, in the name of civil rights, and the dignifying of the wild rampage of the youthful Communist Chinese Red Guards as a cultural revolution. There are countless other examples. In 1966 New York's liberal mayor turned over the power to hire and fire teachers to community pressure groups that had promoted racist violence against white teachers in an experimental Harlem school, and almost all the city's liberal leadership condoned this by remaining silent, thus implicitly justifying the methods which had been used. In 1968 in a Brooklyn school district where the "community control" concept had its inevitable aftermath, teachers were dismissed in violation of due process, inflamed crowds harassed teachers, and racial tensions were escalated beyond control. Again, with the exception of only one or two individuals, the liberal establishment remained silent on the vital issue of academic freedom, and by their silence gave evidence of their mental explanations and justifications of the violence which brought about such a situation.

A normal child appears to be destructive under even favorable circumstances, but the activity is only so in adult eyes. To the child it seems perfectly natural, when he has made the fullest use he is able to of a toy, a book, or, say, a container, to have a final burst of fun with it by tearing it up. This kind of destructiveness is rather for pleasure than with intent to harm—though a child is capable of an almost mindless, impersonal cruelty. On the other hand he has a strong belief in perfect goodness and, to some extent, man's striving toward goodness, peace, idealized societies, may be an expression of his longing to go back to the peaceful simplicity of his protected childhood, and may be at the heart of his ideas of Paradise, Utopia, or Nirvana.

It has generally been recognized that great religious leaders and philosophers have a childlike ingredient in their make-up, without actually pinning down the nature of it. Today we have such ideas being thought and expressed by a far wider segment of the world's populations—significantly, to a large extent led by the young generation.

It is entirely possible that this may be an overt symptom of the evolutionary process that is going on within us, and it may mark a transition from a violent adolescent to a more idealistic and peaceful childlike stage. It may also be part of the increasing trend around the world for people to feel that it is incumbent upon their governments to take care of all problems by way of social security, cradle-to-grave medical care, assistance for the poor, sick, and handicapped, and so forth, as a good parent would.

As the evolutionary regression on its downward trend passes the emotional level of the present three-year-old, aggression will disappear. At that stage organized violence, in whatever shape, will lose its meaning. Future man will be too passive to express dissatisfaction or frustration in destructiveness. It is more likely that he will do so vocally, reflecting the baby's crying or screaming protests in a torrent of well-chosen words, and then insults and invective will be elevated to a fine art. A small advance patch of this type of behavior may be enjoyed in Mediterranean countries today.

CHAPTER TWELVE

Political Life

GOVERNMENT
Traces of racial memories tend to persist embedded deep in folklore, myths, and even in fairy tales. In a less permanent form they also persist to a certain extent in traditional customs, laws, and in ideals and standards that human groups set for themselves.

When man first began to take shape as a separate species his earliest habits were formed by the natural order of the clans or troops of primates from which he descended, and this natural order may still be studied today in the practices of chimpanzees, baboons, and other primates who share mutual ancestry with us. These other higher primates, whose patterns of social life we may observe, have probably maintained the ancestral practices in a comparatively pure form, since their environment has remained essentially the same. Having had no strong impetus to modify their behavior, it probably solidified into ingrained instincts.

The highest apes have different types of societies. One male chimpanzee rules twelve to fifteen females and their progeny, one male gorilla about four females and eight to ten immature young; the East Asian orang-utang also lives in a large polygamous society. On the other hand, the gibbons are organized in monogamous families of father, mother, and up to four offspring who stay with the parents for up to eight years in a very stable territory defended against other gibbon families. Long-tailed monkeys and baboons live in larger units containing several harems. Howling monkeys live in a clan system. All types of social organization are "natural," from the monogamous family to extreme polygamous organization. Curiously enough we find exactly the same range and diversity among the races of man. The African tribal village units of several harems, the extreme monogamy of the Jew, the four wives permitted the Moslem, the polygamous family groupings that until recently were customary in the Orient, all seem to have their parallels in the animal world. The Earl of Shaftesbury (about 1700) seems to have been the first intellectual in the modern period to recognize that nature presents a racial impulse that has regard for others as well as a drive for individual preservation, although Empedocles, in the fifth century before Christ, had some such glimmerings in a poetic way. Espinas (1878) affirmed in *Des Sociétés Animales* that no living being is solitary, but that from the highest to the lowest each is normally immersed in some sort of social life. We have already referred to Kropotkin's *Mutual Aid as a Factor in Evolution* (1880), and Professor William Patten of Dartmouth College in 1920 also outlined conclusions concerning the importance of biological cooperation. Degener contributed a classification of different social levels about 1920, but, as W. C. Allee wrote, "Unfortunately with teutonic vigor and vocabulary he designated the different categories in words as unwieldy as they were exact" and his real contribution tends to be lost, even to scholars. In 1929 W. M. Wheeler, in his book

Social Life among the Insects, showed that the social habit has arisen some twenty-four distinct times in the known major divisions of insects.

Highly organized social hierarchies with dominant leaders and subleaders exist in flocks of birds as well as the herds of larger mammals. Fifty species of birds have been observed by Schjilderup-Ebbe, who became convinced that despotism is a major biological principle. He wrote: "Despotism is the basic idea of the world, indissolubly bound up with all life and existence." However, most flocks are not so hard and fast in their social order as the chickens and white-throated sparrows, which have been classified as fascist, while pigeons, ring-doves, canaries, and parakeets are more democratic.

In herds or hordes of mammals, leadership, with some, rests with an old and experienced female, the males attaching themselves only at the mating season; with others a male is the leader, sometimes a jealous one. Leadership does not always go to the fastest or the strongest. Sometimes the leader acts like a general to stimulate others.

We are brought back to the thought expressed in our first chapter—that nature moves in circles. In this case the circles take the form of a series of loops which from the vantage point of the distant future have the appearance of a spiral. Whether the spiral is ascending or descending depends upon which frame of reference one chooses. If the frame is of anatomical development, for man the spiral is descending, but if we use that of the intellect it is seen as ascending.

Man's prolonged childhood demands a welding between the parents. The interfaces of this welding are sexual urges and mutual dependence for division of labor and for protection against external threats. The monogamous union represents the greatest safeguard for the helpless child. The next loop is precisely the child's prolonged helplessness, which allows the neocortex to remain uncommitted long enough for it to acquire the learning the child will need for survival, which brings us to another loop. Man, in his condition of disadvantage as a result of the change from the tree to the ground habitat, needed his wits to overcompensate for his physical deficiencies. This apparently closes the loop, but on closer inspection we see a never-ending spiral in which, as man himself becomes ever more childlike, his brain is forced to develop more and more to provide the techniques for an artificial environment to protect the increasingly helpless physical state, in turn needing and being the cause of further development of the brain.

Evolution has always appeared to us to follow a straight path, but looked at in this light we see it as a spiral. This optical illusion is not unique. It has been noted that if we take into consideration not only the motion of the earth around its own axis and its orbit around the sun but also the entire motion of the whole solar system toward the constellation Hercules, and so on, a bullet which appears to move in a comparatively "straight" line with respect to the earth, for a certain length of time, in reality follows a trajectory more closely resembling a corkscrew with respect to a vaster system of reference.

Given the fact of the existence of a helpless child who needs shelter, nutriment, and constant care for a lengthy period, nature would have had to endow the human mother with a pouch like the kangaroo's. The size of the baby rendering this impractical, man was forced to find an equivalent. With the womb as a model he found the cave, and later he devised artificial abodes and the crib, and at our present stage has gone so far as to condition his environment.

To accomplish all this he could not help but elaborate on the social organization he inherited from his anthropoid ancestors. When the point is reached at which cooperation in the communal interest is required of individuals a certain amount of regulation becomes necessary, since people on the whole are not inclined to altruism unless it is forced upon them.

The matrix in which government and its institutions developed was the primitive organization for the defense and security of the group. An attribute of our social structure we share with other higher mammals is that all our natural abilities are appropriate to life in a small group. The small group is more malleable, more adaptive to changes in circumstances. There is a greater cohesiveness; there are no individual needs and desires; the group as such has individuality but its members are anonymous. Channels of communication are shorter. There is a greater responsiveness to direction. Each member's needs are secondary to those of the group, so when the sacrifice of an individual for the good of the whole becomes necessary, it presents no problem. An illustration of this in nature is afforded by the baboon troop, two or three of whose members will attack a leopard, and even die in the delaying action, in order to allow the rest time to get away.

A vivid example of such behavior was given by Washburn and de Voe, who observed that a "senate" of several old males led a troop of baboons. They maintained their superiority over the younger and physically stronger animals by sticking together firmly, so that in this way they proved stronger than any individual young male. In one instance one of the three "senators" was an almost toothless old animal and the other two were well past their prime. Once, when a lion was suspected to be hidden in a high-grass area, the baboons stopped, and the young, strong males formed a defensive circle around the weaker animals. But the oldest male pursued the scent alone to find out where exactly the lion was lying. Then, without having been seen by the lion, he returned to the troop and led it, by a wide detour around the lion, to safety. Without exception, the whole troop followed him.

We still have a vestige of this type of behavior within our military organizations. The platoon system allows a small group to develop internal cohesion and loyalty to each other, permitting acts of sacrifice that would rarely find motivation in a larger unit. In a small social group, too, the assignment of roles in the division of labor is clear-cut and allows no misunderstanding. The hunter provides the food; women gather berries and roots, prepare food, tend the young; the experience of the elders, no longer capable of their functions, is put to directing and training the younger members.

As a further extension of the need to care for the helpless child, a trend to care for the aged emerged (in the first place by providing them with a function), which is rare in the animal world. Man lives on to senility because of what has become an ingrained proclivity to care for the helpless. Society today expects of a man not only strength and vigor but also a quality of love and concern which impels him to care for the helpless and dependent child and the aged parent. Here we see the formation of another loop, for the preservation of the aged allows them to become the repositories of the tribal experiences which build up into customs, traditions, laws, and—finally—government.

From the protection of the child and the aged it was but a short step to the care of the sick and disabled, providing another function for the aged and experienced, who could then have become a caste from which the healers, the shamans, and the priests could be drawn. This forms yet another loop in which the chances for survival are enhanced for the injured procreative male and the childbearing female, improving the odds for the survival of the species. In this may be found the origins of the respect and veneration in which the aged were held in ancient societies in historical times, in which age was considered synonymous with wisdom.

It was an equally short step from hunting for food and the defense of territory to the acquisition of territory and the formation of a military caste.

A natural outgrowth of the primitive troop was the strongly patriarchal society, headed by kings, priests, or elite castes. What we know of the earliest Babylonian, Assyrian, Sumerian, Minoan, as well as Far Eastern and other very ancient civilizations, indicates that they all came into this category. By this stage, though, the instinctual responses which guided the group behavior of earliest man had begun to wane. Leaders were obliged to institute laws in their place, and to uphold them by force. Here we see a demonstration of the functions of the neocortex displacing those of the paleocortex as the regressive process which started with the descent from the trees continued its inexorable course. Incidentally, by this time the groups had become very much larger in number and therefore more unwieldy, which also contributed to the diminishing influence of the paleocortex.

The patriarchal societies were succeeded by tribal and national groups led by virile men. Their wars were for power and the conquest of territory. Their administration of domestic matters was authoritarian and firm. With some exceptions here and there, such men held sway until the end of the period we call the Middle Ages.

From this time on we see the gathering momentum of the emergence of individuality and the desires of peoples for greater freedom. From about the time of the Renaissance a more youthful type of society appeared. Leaders encouraged explorers and adventurers, and the lives of peoples were influenced by the results of their discoveries. Journeys were undertaken to the farthest corners of the earth in search of power and wealth, but in the wake of these journeys a yet more youthful world of men came into being. It was a time of colonization, which might be compared to the period of a young man's life when he is grown and wishes to go out into the world and make a life of his own. In doing so, of course, he not only took the ideals and ambitions of his own societies with him and imposed them upon others; he also encouraged in those other societies the rise to leadership of kindred spirits from within them.

In our own time, when man on the whole has regressed as far as a stage of adolescence, we see this reflected also in our governments and political lives, for we are experiencing world-wide episodes of violence and rebellion against any and every kind of authority, which on a personal level are characteristic of this age.

POLITICS

In times past government existed solely as a means of organizing the defense and security of the community. Now, however (at any rate in Western societies), people expect their governments not only to assure their security but also to see that minimum standards of feeding and housing are available for everyone, that medical care is provided, that the young and the elderly are supported, that the indigent are provided with necessities regardless of their own efforts (or lack of them), that citizens are protected not only from external enemies and internal wrongdoers and criminals but also from their own foolishness, so that some of us are demanding government control in such matters as smoking, truth-in-advertising, automobile safety, consumer protection (right down to figuring out the unit price of merchandise, to make it easier to compare values), and so on. We must recognize that the present government-citizen relationship comes very close to a parent-child relationship and is moving away from the cooperation of participating adults that used to be our ideal.

Let us look at this a little more closely. The mechanism we use to set up our government is the political organization. We shudder when we think of our fate in terms of thermonuclear explosion—but do we ever stop to think that over the course of history we have been putting the management of our lives into ever younger and younger hands? That is not to say that our politicians on the whole, though not invariably, have not continued to be drawn from among our older compatriots, but that the methods of selecting them have changed. The earliest great leaders of the type, say, of Moses attained their position by the influence they gained over tribal chiefs who brought their followers with them to his projects—he was "elected" by chiefs, leaders, responsible men. In ancient Greece there was a system of respected wise men leading selected enfranchised citizens. To take a long leap past the kings, church leaders, and generals, who achieved their positions and imposed their governments by force of arms (though even this could not be done finally without the acquiescence and cooperation of lesser leaders) we come to the Magna Carta and the gradual development of democracy. In the process of increasing the franchise until it is now almost universal, we have of necessity lowered the mental age of the electorate. When we use the expression "lowered the mental age," we are using it in the sense that those who analyze modern television audiences use this term. Any mass public has to be addressed in terms of its average intelligence, which is bound to be lower than that of a smaller or selected audience. It follows that the larger the audience, the lower its average level of intellectual commitment is likely to be, and television programmers have somewhat cynically pinned the "mental age" of their mass audiences at about twelve years.

Be that as it may, it is quite clear that any politician or would-be leader must be responsive to the wishes and desires of his electorate in a system of democracy. Universal suffrage having reduced not only the "mental age" but also the chronological age of the electorate, it has come to a point where we have witnessed in the recent past such would-be leaders as Senator Eugene McCarthy and Robert Kennedy frankly appealing to youth, even below voting age, for their following, and at the present in the United States our leaders are busy amending draft laws (which, after all, concern our security) for no good military reason, but to pacify college students.

We find an analogy in the traditional practices of the Iroquois, who were ostensibly ruled by a Council of Sachems, but this appearance did not reflect the facts. The fifty sachem titles were rigidly controlled by the headwomen of the matriarchal lineages that composed the tribe. When a sachem died the headwomen consulted with all the women of their clans before selecting his successor. If he failed to act in accordance with their wishes he would receive up to three warnings, and unless he had fallen in line by the third he was removed and his badge of office given to another man. So even though the women did not rule directly, they had the sole power to appoint and to remove from office, which gave them actual power by indirect means.

The influence of the voices of the young on politicians is not only a local trend. All over the world politicians who should, by definition, be leading the way, setting the pace, are surrendering in matters of policy to youthful revolts. In France a powerful and seemingly stable regime was displaced in the course of pacifying student rebellions. In Communist China policies were modified or influenced by the excesses of the youthful Red Guard. Much of the steam of the temporary "liberalization" movement in Czechoslovakia was generated by college-age youths, and in the United States the stated policies of many "leaders" have been influenced by campus rioters.

Neither should we forget the use that recent dictators and would-be dictators have made of children, recognizing their enormous power in today's world (Mussolini's *Giovinezza*, the *Hitlerjugend*, China's "Red Guard," and many other fascist and Communist youth movements).

If we look at a very generalized, over-all picture of human government, we see primitive societies ruled by respected elders, and find that as societies "modernize" and become influenced by technological developments they change (we see the changes in process in Oriental societies—Japan is a good example), and the more "modern" the society, the younger its influential segment becomes.

THE LIBERAL APPROACH

A child's mind is responsive to a system of stimulation different from that of the adult (it is organized toward significantly other goals). To a young child all concepts are concrete. He does not begin to have the ability to think in abstract terms until he is approximately six to seven years old.

A child believes that he is the center of his universe. When he cries he expects someone to come; when he is hungry he expects to be fed; when he is hurt he expects to be tended. Adult laws of logic do not govern a child's thinking. If he stumbles against a table, he will say "Naughty table," and spank it. At that moment, the child's experience of pain converts an object he knows under other circumstances for what it actually is into a thing capable of feelings and intentions similar to his own. Thus the child's view of the world does not always correspond with external reality—a sad fact that often haunts us in our adult existence.

As the child grows older, little by little the fulfillment of his needs is frustrated. He is obliged to conform to schedules, adhere to discipline, control his impulses. On the other hand, if his every whim is promptly satisfied, the child's infantile feeling of being the center of the universe persists. Naturally, then, his expectations are that whatever agencies surround him are there to serve him, without any need or effort, or any contribution, on his part.

Philanthropists and liberals tend to place themselves in the role of a parent supplying the needs of a helpless child. In doing so they foster the infantilization of the recipients. The recipients, whether they be the poor, the disabled, or victims of discrimination, have one quality in common: in one aspect or another they seem helpless. This helplessness may be real, as in the case of a paralyzed victim of poliomyelitis in an iron lung, or imagined, as in the case of a highly paid worker striking for greater benefits. The latter evokes a feeling that society owes him more than he is getting for his labor, and should take care of him.

There was no truer humanitarian than Bertrand Russell. He declared that an "unbearable pity for the suffering of mankind" was one of the three "overwhelmingly strong" passions that had governed his life. He wrote in his autobiography that "echoes of cries of pain reverberate in my heart . . . I long to alleviate evil, but I cannot, and I too suffer." Yet this great man understood and also wrote that "The opposite pole of love is pure benevolence."

Actually, no matter how helpless a disadvantaged person may be, in reality he does have resources within himself to compensate, or even overcompensate, for his disability. There are artists who in the face of the loss of their hands paint with their feet; athletes who continue to ski on one leg after the amputation of the other; slum children who become industrial magnates. This is a process which takes place throughout evolution, where handicapped animals survive only by compensating and overcompensating, there being no philanthropic organizations in the animal world.

Philanthropic organizations and liberalism as an attitude thus actually deprive the recipients of what would otherwise be their own natural propensity to develop compensatory abilities. What actually occurs is that the givers, in taking on the role of protective parents, induce in the receivers the attitudes of the child whose every whim is satisfied without having to contribute its own efforts.

It is yet another sign of the ongoing process of infantilization that such views as these arouse quite violent objections and resistance when expressed at this stage of man's history, although they are simple statements of biological fact. The current view, shared by both givers and receivers, is that only total, unquestioned, unconditional support is adequate to meet the needs of the handicapped. Any objection, no matter how legitimate, that some contribution of effort should be made by the receiver is met with vehemently emotional protest, as though one were suggesting to a mother that her six-year-old should earn his keep. The mother would recoil with horror and indignation from such a suggestion and consider it inhuman, cruel, and impractical—yet the six-year-old child of a farming family carries out chores assigned to him with joy and pride. In all fairness to the liberal view, however, farm mechanization (itself also a neocortical product) is responsible for producing both child and adult spoiled children on the farm as well as in the city.

Throughout Europe in the Middle Ages, and for a long

time after, among the lower classes, almost as soon as he was weaned, a child was regarded as a small adult who mingled, competed, and worked with mature adults. In the Old Colony of Plymouth in the United States, children were expected to be "little adults" by their eighth birthday. Not too long ago *The New York Times* published a photograph of a six-year-old boy giving his father a helping hand on a farm near Bonn, Germany, where the conditions were difficult, so it is evidently possible for the very young to perform such work ably.

But today the biological point of view of self-help and over-compensation is considered reactionary, while the antibiological view of the liberal of the necessity for total protection and support is considered progressive. This in itself may very well indicate mankind's direction.

POLITICIANS AND LEADERS

Having discussed some aspects of government and political systems, we should now look a little more closely at the politicians—those individuals who make up the organized groups through which government functions. Our politicians, being men and women like the rest of us, have the same genetic-evolutionary background. Not only are they being influenced by ever-younger segments of the population, they themselves, as part of mankind, are becoming more youthful in their physical and mental processes and cultural inclinations. Basically, the only difference between the ruler and the ruled is that the ruler is usually the more intelligent and the more aggressive. As we have already noted, greater intelligence does not connote greater maturity or wisdom, a fact that can be borne out by observation. Intelligence may be equal in individuals of any chronological age, from infancy to advanced years. General observations would lead one to conclude that on the whole pure intelligence is keener in earlier years than later. Maturity and wisdom are composed of other elements: experience, learning, character, attitudes. Max Born, the brilliant physicist, in his later years became concerned by the great ethical issues that grew out of scientific advances and once said: "It is satisfying to have had such clever pupils, but I wish they had shown less cleverness and more wisdom." Toward the end of his life he wrote, in a collection of autobiographical essays: "Intellect distinguishes between the possible and the impossible; reason distinguishes between the sensible and the senseless. Even the possible can be senseless." His concern was a fear of a total decline of civilization's old values, but his remarks illustrate perfectly the distinction we have just made.

It is intelligence, however, that is at a premium at present, largely because of the complexity of our modern life, and, like the rest of us, our politicians and leaders tend to be more intelligent in the same degree. In the same degree, too, increasingly childlike preoccupations dominate their personal lives. One might mention one of our Presidents who installed a horn on his car that imitates the mating call of a bull, so that he might speed through the countryside startling his cows for his private amusement. But even disregarding this rather extreme example, in any suburbia near centers of government or of learned technological institutions, the sight of men of eminence who have spent their days grappling with complex problems of international relationships, nuclear physics, legal definitions, or budgetary projections, relaxing at barbecue parties dressed up in chef's hats and aprons, earnestly competing in such games as touch football, dunking each other fully clothed into swimming pools, or otherwise cavorting at social gatherings is so familiar as not to elicit the slightest comment. Yet these pastimes are radically different from the types of debauchery or drunkenness that in the past were the vices or private pleasures of the great. They are more childlike in essence.

While speaking of the personal attributes of our recent leaders, we should also remember that there have been some with vast followings whose levels of personal behavior have regressed as far as the temper-tantrum stage associated with children below nursery-school age. We all remember the episode of Khrushchev banging his shoe on the table in the solemn halls of the United Nations, and, more frighteningly, of Hitler dancing his jig of triumph at the news of the fall of France.

As we have already pointed out, the attributes required of the shaman from the dawn of man's history indicate that such leadership evolved from the ranks of the disabled and the sick. Those afflicted with hallucinations or visions caused by psychosis, epilepsy, brain tumors, or other damage to the brain tissues were considered to have been in contact with the supernatural, and were held in high esteem. In the light of this, the number of sick leaders, too numerous to mention, who throughout history conducted their offices unopposed and supported by their people, takes on meaning.

To clarify this assertion we shall restrict ourselves to a few modern examples, because their personalities have been more reliably documented than those (such as Nero, Caligula, Ludwig of Bavaria, or George III of England, to name a few) of other times, and only to those held in high esteem.

In a book by a noted psychiatrist, Gandhi is described as a person who suffered from serious conflicts. His strong sexual drives interfered with the idealized concept he had of himself and that he also wished to convey to the world. The writer had close contact with him, and observed elements of cruelty barely concealed by a submissive stance. As with all leaders who feel they have a mission and are capable of influencing their followers at least for a time, Gandhi's ideals did not leave a permanent influence. The country he liberated by nonviolent means used a military machine to stop its neighbors from reclaiming land and fought bloody civil riots. The poor of his country, whom he hoped to relieve from their abject misery and whom he emulated in his ascetic demeanor, are probably as badly off today as they were in colonial times. Martin Luther King, Jr., who tried to model himself and his movement after Gandhi's ideal of nonviolence, was no more successful. Violence followed in his footsteps. This particular tragedy is one which keeps repeating itself, and has done so from ancient times, even before Jesus, the king of peace, founded a religion that in his name, and to perpetuate his glory, spread violence all over the globe.

Dr. Hugh L'Etang, a London physician, in his book *The Pathology of Leadership*, has assembled the significant medical data on many historic figures from pre-World War I to the present, and he has shown how often the shape of destiny has been formed by the illness of powerful leaders.

As also noted by Barbara Tuchman, in her *The Guns of August*, Dr. L'Etang describes the unhealthy state of the significant men of all the great powers: "Ministers and diplomats of this period were weak in the widest sense.... They were weak in body and weak in mind." Military commands on both sides were shot through with ailing, aged, and disabled officers, some of them called back from retirement. Germany's General Ludendorff grew so tense he "could control neither his nerves nor his armies." He collapsed and resigned in 1918. Years later his condition was diagnosed as toxic goiter. After thyroidectomy he said that if the operation had been performed earlier Germany would have won the war.

In the United States President Woodrow Wilson maintained reasonable health until the armistice, but then his deterioration came on so swiftly as to cause international havoc. Always rigid in personality, he grew worse. He suffered an infection of prostate and bladder, and was thought to have had a stroke. He had severe headaches and asthmatic attacks, and was "tired and absent-minded." After a severe stroke in October 1919, the office of the chief of state was virtually brought to a halt, and the presidency sustained by "a self-selected council of three: Mrs. Wilson, Joseph Tumulty (his secretary) and (his doctor) Dr. Cary T. Grayson." Only they could attest to Wilson's incapacity, and none of them would.

Britain's Sir Nevile Henderson, ambassador to Berlin, was operated on for an abdominal cancer in 1938. When he returned to duty shortly afterward, German leaders took advantage of his physical incapacity. "They would keep him waiting all evening at a reception and then grant him an interview in the early hours of the morning."

At the time of the Suez crisis, in 1956, Anthony Eden was desperately sick, and the aged John Foster Dulles was on the point of a physical breakdown.

Franklin Roosevelt was struck down by poliomyelitis in 1921 at the age of thirty-nine. This did not deter him from twice winning the governorship of New York, and going on to be elected four times as President of the United States, even though by the end of his second term his health was visibly deteriorating.

Among a frightening number of sick, aged, or disabled men appointed to high office or heavy responsibilities by Roosevelt were Louis MacHenry Howe, a special assistant, who was an asthmatic invalid, and Harry Hopkins, whose partial gastrectomy exacerbated many other conditions and who spent all his time at Yalta in bed when he was not obliged to be present at the conference. FDR's appointed attorney general died before he could take office; Secretary of the Treasury William Woodin died after one year of service. The Secretary of War, George

Dern, was too ill to attend many cabinet meetings and died of bladder and kidney ailments in 1936. Secretary of the Navy Claude Swanson, appointed in 1933, was hospitalized for high blood pressure the same year, and by 1937 had to be led in and out of meetings, could not stand unsupported, and could not be understood when he spoke. James Forrestal, another Secretary of the Navy and later the first Secretary of Defense, was driven by compulsions and delusions that he was being followed. During a severe depression he fell to his death from a hospital window in 1949.

Dr. L'Etang writes that pathological changes in the arteries were responsible for Roosevelt's death, but not for other signs and symptoms. Loss of weight and cachexia were so evident at Yalta that photographs were suppressed. Long-term "bronchitis" and his heavy smoking habit suggested carcinoma of the lung. A pigmented nevus above his left eyebrow did not appear in photographs taken after 1943. A medical paper was given at a St. Louis meeting in 1949 on treatment of malignant melanoma. All the slides and specimens shown had a serial number, with one exception. This was a section of brain with a large metastatic melanoma, and it bore only a date— April 14, 1945—the day that Roosevelt's body arrived in Washington from Warm Springs.

President Eisenhower was aware of the problems in both the Wilson and Roosevelt administrations and tried to ameliorate the risks of having a disabled President by directing the release to news media of full clinical details on illnesses he suffered while in office and by trying to have machinery designed to run the government at such times.

Less candor was displayed during the short term of John F. Kennedy, although L'Etang sees him as the candidate with the most precarious health. He wore a back brace as a result of a 1937 injury, and he was rejected by the Army in 1941. Although he refused to confirm or deny that he had Addison's disease, his organization did guardedly reveal a "partial adrenal insufficiency." He had been receiving replacement therapy, including cortisone, continuously since 1947. He once told an aide: "The doctors say I've got a sort of slow-motion leukemia, but they tell me I'll probably last until I'm forty-five." Long-term cortisone therapy, even when carefully administered, may trigger strong mood and energy swings.

As Dr. L'Etang pertinently asks, is a predominantly sick leadership the product of a sick society?

Incidentally, the British Foreign Office recently disclosed reports, hitherto secret, by the late Sir Ronald Lindsay, at one time ambassador to Washington. Apart from health, or lack of it, which he was not qualified to judge, he evaluated the personalities and skills of many of the leaders with whom he dealt. He described Roosevelt as a "baffling character" who seemed to have irresistible personal charm, yet his judgment of men was "open to question and most of his intimate advisors appear to be men of second-rate ability. . . . This disadvantage is accentuated by two other qualities in his character. In the first place he appears to be extremely obstinate and to dislike opposition . . . and in the second place his intellectual powers are really only moderate and his knowledge of certain subjects, particularly finance and economics, is superficial."

Sir Ronald characterized Secretary of the Treasury Morgenthau as so "unsure of himself as to become rather suspicious and rather too mercurial in temperament to keep his head in difficulties." Of Bernard Baruch Lindsay wrote: his "commanding characteristic, apart from his undoubted shrewdness, is his vanity . . . upon which politicians of his party have frequently endeavored to play."

What is it that compels a person to seek leadership? Admittedly there are many factors. Sometimes the need to overcome a personal inadequacy drives a man to compensate for his feelings of insufficiency, which may derive from short stature, low social origin, or sexual problems. These are the leaders who become ruthless authoritarians in whatever the field of their activities. They rule alone and with absolute power. On the whole, today's leaders in political organizations, government, or for that matter in large corporations, are blocked from reaching absolute power by the bureaucratic stratification of the very organization they seek to dominate. In order to achieve top status they are obliged to seek alliances and coalitions, and to engage in behind-the-scenes intrigue and bargains or to be adept at consensus politics.

Here we wish to highlight only those motivations that derive from man's infantilization.

When a baby feels uncomfortable, he cries; his mother hurries and brings relief. After a number of such events he senses in his own way the relationship between his vocal exertions and the restoration of his comfort. As the child grows older and the first rudiments of thought begin to occur, he feels that he has the power to summon his mother whenever he feels like it. Magical thinking in the child, as in primitive culture, has this origin. The child retains the memory of the absolute power of his nursing period, and later on in his adult life this is not completely forgotten. Dreams of unlimited power are part of every one of us. Having a genie at our command, possession of a magic wand, knowledge of the magic word—or even identification with Superman—are part of childhood's fantasies.

Those persons who achieve sudden fame or power without mature coping mechanisms often revert to the behavior patterns of the infant. Then we witness the spectacle of the dictator (or even the entertainer whose rise to stardom has brought power and influence) indulging in screaming, temper tantrums, total absorption in the self, refusal to perform a required activity, and inability to accept the logical reasoning of others. These are all reminiscent of the refusal to eat, and similar strategies used by a baby to exercise his power over his mother.

Political leaders are particularly vulnerable to this syndrome. They often feel that all their needs must be satisfied, that by reason of their power there should be no delay in the gratification of any of their desires. Some may fancy women, and feel that every member of his family should enjoy the prerogatives of his power, while others obtain more satisfaction from having a residence in every climate.

It appears that all societies are ruled or led by the deviants. They may be political leaders, philosophers, priests, scientists, artists, or writers. As is the case in evolutionary changes, it is they who determine the future patterns of their group. Their views may be inimical to the so-called "normal" or well-adjusted—indeed, to the "silent majority"—and not even to their advantage, but by their nature having no significant leadership of their own, the normal have little voice in the trend-setting areas of their own lives. This can reach such extremes that a few "creative" stylists can impose world-wide fashions which may be uncomfortable, impractical, and unsuitable, but which are nevertheless bought.

On every level of society the "normals" are ruled by the "deviants." The normals, in truth, are themselves the offspring of deviants of earlier generations, but they are the ones who have compensated and adapted. They have become the hard worker, the responsible citizen, and the moral pillars of the established church, without whom no society could exist. But even religion, that most conservative area of human activity, is stirred and shaken from time to time by charismatic lay reformers or by fanatics in the uniform of the clergy.

We find, then, in leaders of all fields of human endeavor, and especially in politicians, vestiges of the infant's sense of being the center of the world and of its drive to exercise unlimited power. Combined with these are the neocortical abilities which we call intelligence and creativeness, and which are themselves extensions of the childhood phase of learning. Perhaps even the ancient gods, the supreme leaders usually thought of as father figures, may in fact have been extensions of this theme. The accounts of their exploits are marked by the same magical thinking as that of the child, accompanied by an inability to brook competition (siblings), a sense of omnipotence, and willful behavior and temper tantrums. The gods were conceived by man—an infantilized species. Their attributes were therefore extensions of man's deepest consciousness and awareness of himself, and so it is not surprising that they had infantile characteristics.

Truly we are children, led by children.

CHAPTER THIRTEEN

Psychological Factors

INTRODUCTION

Almost every aspect of life presents man with emotional problems to which he finds no ideal solutions. So much so that not one but several professions are entirely devoted to attempts to ameliorate the results of this condition. We live in a society which has need of psychiatrists, psychologists, marriage counselors, labor relations experts, lay therapists, child-guidance clinics, and a host of therapeutic groups ranging from Alcoholics Anonymous and Synanon to sensitivity groups and psychiatry-oriented parlor games.

On the face of it one would judge that the race of man is coming apart at the seams and yet this is, although intensified, not actually a new phenomenon. It has been a part of man's life for almost as long as he has existed as a species. From earliest recorded times man has needed the services of the succession of shamans, seers, priests, prophets, and philosophers who preceded today's multiplicity of specialists, to help him adjust himself to his own nature, to his group, and to the world he lives in.

Today, the difficulties man experiences are highlighted in every state of his life and every phase of his activities. We are aware of problems in child-parent relations, in adolescent behavior, in the areas of marriage and family, in professional and labor relations, and in social life. All these are in addition to problems arising from brain damage caused by accidents and illnesses. Universal as they are, however, on closer view most of the problems can be reduced to a difference between the expectations of societies and man's ability to conform to those expectations.

We should like the reader to imagine a group of human beings all of whom are inhaling a gas which is invisible and odorless and which causes them all to be irritable. Among the people in this group there happens to be a psychologically oriented observer. Can he, his own state of irritation being equal to that of the rest of the group, recognize this to be an abnormal state? He has no point of reference, since every person in his vicinity behaves the same way he does. All his observations are colored by his own nervous irritation. Yet, if he assesses the behavior he witnesses—including his own—as impartially as he can, conjures up memories and reports of earlier patterns of responses, and investigates and considers the records of his ancestors, it will be possible for him to muster a measure of objectivity.

The authors are faced with an equivalent dilemma. Being a part of the over-all evolutionary trend of our species toward youthful behavior, we have to be objective enough to view even the writing of this book as an expression of playfulness. There is no doubt that we have written it with a great deal of relish. The exploration of fresh ideas and the discovery of facts new to us have generated such enthusiasm that we have frequently found ourselves forgetting the rules of politeness. We talked and interrupted each other, eagerly trying to promote the personally discovered insight, just as do children deeply immersed in their games. But in spite of our childlike attitude toward work as fun, we do still retain some elements of mature behavior, probably remnants from the times when coping with the environment left no room for play. We like to think that a better understanding of our species might enhance its chances for survival in spite of its self-destructive tendencies, and to that extent we hope that our playful pursuit contains an element of the proper seriousness of maturity.

THE INDIVIDUAL VIS-À-VIS SOCIETY
All of us are being made aware today of the tremendous increase in the proportion of emotionally troubled people in the population. We are forced to wonder whether this trend does not affect all of us in some way. We all realize that in today's world a great many conditions contribute to this state of affairs. Even for someone without any scientific bent, one look at the headlines of any daily newspaper brings to the attention riots, strikes, rebellions, confrontations, civil wars, guerrilla wars, declared and undeclared international wars, corruption, increased breakup of families, increase in drug use; religious, political, and racial intolerance; murder, rape, robbery, larceny—the list would seem endless.

We have to remind ourselves that all these evils have existed since man became a separate species. Until quite recent times any travel was a hazardous pursuit, as often as not involving being beset by bandits or robbed by innkeepers or traveling companions. Dickens detailed enough of the horrors of life in the streets of the great cities to make our own civic troubles pale in comparison. While the perusal of the newspaper makes us echo Hamlet with the exclamation that the world is out of joint, it might be simply that because today's communications are more efficient we are better informed. In the opening sentence of the preceding paragraph we made reference to the increase in emotional disturbance, but we have to ask ourselves whether this is a correct appraisal.

How do we determine what is an emotional disturbance or what is socially unacceptable? Looked at impartially, it is actually impossible to establish statistics of mental malfunctions. We should have to define our standards, since few could agree on any norm in an ever-changing society. Moreover, at which level should deviations be considered aberrant? Then, who decides what is normal and what abnormal? An individual may view himself as happy and well-adjusted to his way of life, but society at large may not consider him to be so.

The fact of the matter is that we have been handed down a set of precepts, ideals, moral and ethical standards, and "thou shall nots," through religions, philosophies, and laws which reflect man's strivings for a Utopian state. Samuel Butler's name for this state, Erewhon (Nowhere, spelled backward) is actually far more to the point, for the guiding beacon in establishing what is a mental malfunction is the discrepancy between man's actual behavior and his desires for an ideal state, which truly exists only in Erewhon—nowhere.

It may be objected that here and there in the course of history individuals have appeared who have come close to man's highest ideals, but the closer we look at the record the more we wonder how accurate this assertion is. The writers of the Bible probably appraised the situation most vividly both in God's reply to Lot that he would save Sodom and Gomorrah if Lot could find a single just person in either of the cities and in the instruction of Jesus that the person himself without sin should cast the first stone.

It looks as though we are obliged to come to the painful conclusion that normal human behavior more closely approximates the impression we derive from the newspapers than the ideals handed down to us by the well-intentioned.

Since not all of us are robbers, rapists, and the like, we must infer that some of us have better controls than others, and that what we admire as an ideal is actually a capacity to inhibit, delay, and sublimate antisocial responses. Thus we must limit our definition of mental malfunction to a condition which causes severe discomfort to the person who experiences it.

Some of these conditions elude verbal description—the individual feels bad but cannot pinpoint the nature of his discomfort. Others are described as anxiety, feelings of emptiness, causeless sadness, a state of being separate from one's own emotions, loss of sense of reality, obsessive thoughts, compulsive actions, unjustified suspiciousness, and so on.

In the past many psychiatric ailments were considered physical diseases, and were treated as such. A good example is chlorosis (the term implies a pallid complexion), a diminished concentration of hemoglobin in the bloodstream, which was frequently offered as a diagnosis for ailing adolescent females as recently as fifty years ago. Today, girls with the same symptoms carry the psychiatric label "emotionally immature, inadequate persons" who possibly also harbor schizoid traits. Modern medicine has become aware of the emotional origin of many so-called physical diseases, whereas physicians until the recent past considered them to have been caused by unknown physical agents.

We are inclined to think that industrialized societies have a monopoly on mental illness, but we find in fact that they are present in all cultures today and have been throughout the history of man. A. H. Leighton emphasizes that the symptoms of mental illness he encountered in Africa could easily apply to persons of Western origin. He thinks that every society regards mental illness as a part of its culture in the same way as physical illness, although they may use different explanations.

In many ways mental illness is the human brain's particular response to the abnormal situation the brain itself creates. In this respect it runs counter to the very essence of biology—survival. Throughout most of nature there is a tendency for the unfit to be eliminated in processes of trial and error. The core of man's evolution by infantilization is the prolonged protection of the child and, by extension, of the weak and the sick. In this way illness, both mental and physical, is a concomitant of the means by which the species came into being.

How is it, then, that all of us are not sick? Perhaps, in fact, all of us *are* to some extent "sick," but in all natural phenomena there is enough latitude to allow for a wide range we may include in the so-called normal, which extends all the way to the furthest extremes of the "abnormal."

In man's regressed state his nervous system has less tolerance for discomfort. In his early years his needs were taken care of: his hunger was appeased without delay; his skin temperature was carefully regulated; he was groomed and cleaned; any time he wished to be picked up and fondled he had only to hold out his arms.

In Homo sapiens these needs of the child remain close to the surface throughout his life, perhaps with minor modifications. From a social and cultural point of view, this does not have to be objectionable. However, in the attempt to attain this goal, the means used often lead to an undesirable result. For example, there is the person who feels uncomfortable when he assumes responsibilities. They create feelings of anxiety in him, since he anticipates criticism should he make mistakes. It makes perfectly good sense to him to find a mate capable of making decisions and offering directions. Inevitably, however, such a woman will also tend to dominate her spouse and will probably become very critical of him. He then feels cheated. He chose her because he wanted an easy life, and what he gets is one unpleasant scene after another. Let us suppose that in a fit of anger he decides to leave his wife, telling himself that enough is enough and that he now wants freedom. For a while following his separation he has a great feeling of having escaped from prison. But soon he begins to feel lonely. Loneliness is uncomfortable. The solution for this is the search for a new mate. With uncanny certainty he will again fix on the one woman who has a strong character, is purposeful in her daily activities, and gives him the sense of having found the person who will look after him as he desires. As will be obvious to all his friends, but not to himself, he is in for another round. The newly remarried husband finds fault with his wife. "Why do I have to eat at a time when it suits you?" "I am not a schoolboy; I'll come home when I'm good and ready!" And so on. And another suffering housewife wonders why this man of hers, so respected in the business community, is acting like a child.

Now let us look at the case of a person who is considered successful by the standards of his society. He may be a junior executive with a conservative corporation, married, and the father of two children. If you were to ask him to talk about himself or answer a questionnaire, he would say: "I am happily married; I have two lovely children; and I have a good job." He might also list a variety of material objects that he possesses—house, car, boat, membership in a club, friends—to corroborate his feeling of well-being. But were we to say to him: "Look, this is off the record. Are you really as contented as appears on your official questionnaire?" If he could trust us, his reply might be, after some hesitation and head-scratching: "Well, if you pin me down, I guess not. Let's start with my wife. She spends too much; the more I earn the more money goes out; she constantly complains about how much she has to scrimp and that she can't afford to buy the clothes an executive's wife ought to wear. Then there are her aches and pains. She has them only when things don't go her way. And the children ... well, to be honest, I am disappointed in my boy ... he is lazy, fresh, and doesn't want to study. My little girl ... she is sweet, but she is becoming as clothes-conscious as her mother. The job ... it pays well. The company looks out for you—but you feel like a marionette. Woe betide you if you come up with an original idea. And then, the politicking and undercover intrigues. You'd never notice it if you visit our offices. Everybody is charming. You would think that we are 'one big happy family.' In reality, though, we are a pack of well-trained monkeys, smiling when we are supposed to, but inwardly we often get pretty boiled up."

Is this young executive a deviant specimen of his culture? Or is he a typical representative of the modern, urban variety of Homo sapiens? The evidence points overwhelmingly to the latter. What is puzzling then is the striking discrepancy between what he acknowledges in public and what he feels in private.

Examples of such contradictions can be duplicated manyfold. Let us take a closer look at this discrepancy. Society expects certain standards of behavior. They may vary from one human group to another, but there will always be some expectations. Any infraction is met with rebuff, disapproval, and even ostracism. To question the validity of the rules on any basis, even if reasonable, would only bring the reply: "I didn't make the rules." The situation is sometimes reduced to absurdity when the breaking of some rules is secretly admired, but if the culprit is caught the world turns its back on him.

What are these rules? In many instances they are conventions which were found necessary for the cohesion of society at the time they were brought into practice. Each succeeding generation receives them with the same admonitions and is assured that breaking them is subject to punishment. These rules, codified in many forms, become an ideal that parents try to impose on their children even if they themselves have begun to doubt their usefulness. The inner conviction that impels them to maintain this apparent hypocrisy is the fear that without some form of coercion society would disintegrate.

Modern man's actual behavior when he is without the restraint of social obligations is more characteristic of his system of responses than is his publicly displayed demeanor. We do not consider the behavior of a dancing bear in a circus representative of that of its species. We know that its actions are more in accordance with its nature when it is away from the circus surroundings. It may not be a flattering picture, but in many ways we ourselves are trained circus animals who behave in the arena of public life in the manner in which we have been trained, but back in our compounds we relate to our families more in keeping with our true biological make-up.

This discrepancy is the source of a great many feelings of guilt and despair to the more sensitive members of our species. They tend to blame themselves for being "inconsiderate," "petty," "childish," "rude," "harsh . . ." toward the members of their families. The less sensitive shrug their shoulders, having an easy explanation for their domestic problems. They shift the blame onto their mates!

Psychologists term such behavior "immature." This diagnosis implies that such a person acts more or less like a child and that he has not yet assumed the full responsibility of being a mature adult. What do the psychologists mean by "maturity" in our society? They refer to training that begins in childhood. Parents set an example by the way they handle everyday-life situations. The child, like any young animal, imitates what he sees. As he grows older he encounters a succession of "do not" rules, interspersed with a few "do" admonitions. Along the way a young person frequently faces a dilemma, because the teachings of his parents do not always coincide with what they themselves practice. Sooner or later the antiprinciple "do-as-I-say-but-don't-do-as-I-do" subverts the ideals the youngster has been taught, and he then adopts the actual attitudes of his elders and not their preachings.

All of this indicates that maturity is a goal that is desirable for the maintenance of society, but seldom achieved. Why then do psychologists make distinctions between mature and immature behavior?

One of the outstanding features of anthropogenesis—the evolutionary "becoming of man"—has been retardation. This applies not only to biological characteristics, but to thought processes as well. The ability to delay or interrupt responses allows for alternative solutions to any immediate problem. The neocortex needs time to evaluate a situation and to come up with a solution which would go beyond the powers of an instinctual response. In the course of our growth period we acquire "coping mechanisms" by our own experience that go together with the precepts handed down to us from previous generations. We no longer snarl or bare our fangs when an opponent demeans us, albeit in a disguised form. In this connection we should emphasize that the neocortex can recognize even the subtlest insinuation, which it relays to the paleocortex at the same time as it makes its own evaluation of the implied offense. The paleocortex will initiate the instinctive response as though the insinuation were the same as a threat to life. At the same time the neocortex will have made an evaluation and a decision as to which of its coping mechanisms to use. In this way two separate responses may coexist in the mind. (When a person uses such an expression as "I had half a mind to tell him to go to blazes," his statement is actually more accurate than he realizes.) If an opponent attempts, even if extremely subtly, to undermine our self-esteem, it will have one meaning for the neocortex and another for the paleocortex. If the acquired coping mechanisms—a function of the newest part of the brain—are adequate, then the paleocortical responses are inhibited. It is almost as if the neocortex reassures the paleocortex in some such terms as "Take it easy. I can handle this situation."

On the other hand, many individuals have not acquired the skills needed to defend themselves. Some, or any, of many factors may be responsible for such a lack: prolonged illness in early childhood; overly permissive rearing; brutal, demeaning, ridiculing, shaming, or guilt-provoking attitudes on the part of parents or educators are some of them.

Psychologists refer to some of the coping mechanism as "defenses." There is some uncertainty about the value of a defense. In many instances it is poorly structured and creates more havoc, failing in its primary goal of protection. A person may harbor a profound sense of inadequacy, fearing failure in his social or business life. To protect himself against an anticipated sense of devastating embarrassment he erects a fear of, say, traveling. This gets him out of going to any interview, and surely saves him such a painful confrontation, but at what a price! He is rooted to his house, sometimes even to a point where leaving his room makes him anxious.

A satisfactory coping mechanism allows a person to stand his ground against real or imaginary social pressures with a minimum of discomfort. Let us take the type of man who has a joke or wisecrack for every situation. You could not insult him without receiving a stinging comeback. He is sure of himself, since social encounters are not threatening to him; he is at ease even with persons who outrank him. But even such a defense is not without its disadvantages. In his own home he may browbeat his wife and children, since it is difficult for most people to impose limits upon their coping mechanisms.

The presence of such coping mechanisms points to the basic problem of modern man. It would seem at first glance that society, made up as it is of individuals, would reflect the habits and temperaments of those individuals, but it is not quite so. Society appears to be an abstract, but actually it possesses operational qualities of its own. To give an analogy: a child's impulse, since a child is oriented for immediate gratification and does not yet possess the reflexes for survival that its mother has acquired, frequently forces the mother to impose restrictions which check the child's activity, and which it resents. For that matter, the whole of any group (society) has the same relationship to the individuals that compose it as the mother to the child. Cooperation in groups is a basic pattern in nature, and individuals composing them either instinctively or reflexively subordinate some of their personal good for the good of the whole. In the course of this book we have cited, for example, the baboons, whose older males will sacrifice themselves to gain time for the troop. On a lower level there is also such behavior as that of the Portuguese-man-o-war polyp colonies, which may shed individual tentacles to aid the preservation of the whole—or even a single entity, such as a crane-fly, which can detach itself from one of its own legs if necessary to get away from a predator. This is not to equate these various actions to one another, but merely to illustrate that a group, or whole being, has different needs from those of its parts. In human societies, the higher need of the whole group supersedes the needs of its individuals, and is felt as a group conscience.

It is the difference between the demands of society as a whole and the biological and behavioral characteristics of infantilized man that forms the basis of many emotional conflicts. Being emotionally childlike, the individual needs recognition and approval from society, but obtaining these requires adherence to its tenets, which have been imposed by rearing and education. On the other hand, if he could relinquish this need for society's approval, a person would allow his basic impulses to find expression. These might lead him to flee civilization, abandon his responsibilities—even his family—and give himself over to what today is called "his own thing," as all children do. In most cases it is to a large extent a sense of guilt arising from the indoctrinated obligations that prevents such a step being taken, although there are other considerations. Were we to offer a sufficient sum of money to most people and tell them: Here you are—you don't have to endure the daily grind any longer. You need not face your boss every day, or travel the subways, or suffer the discomforts of the crowded city. This money will take you to a beautiful island in the Pacific where all your needs are provided, and you will have no worries! The probable result, after an initial outburst of joy, would be hesitation, doubt, and then reluctance to abandon the familiar surroundings, family, and friends—just as a young child would be desolate at the thought of being taken from his home.

Nevertheless, infantile needs can be accommodated by compromises. From time to time society permits its members to set their responsibilities aside. Holidays and vacations encourage a "take it easy," "have a good time" attitude. Then there are business conventions, fraternity reunions, and such, where traditional morality is allowed to slide and the man-child, away from his home, may be "naughty" and consort with "bad girls" while drinking too much alcohol to neutralize his conscience.

We sense, in some way, that there is something fundamentally wrong with ourselves as individuals and with society. Some of us hide this awareness behind Pollyannaish hopes: If only we return to the fundamental decencies and values! or If we were to find a way to spread the riches of the nation among the poor! or If we truly could distribute health services to every person who needs them. The number of solutions offered is in itself a demonstration of their futility. Man's capacity to delude himself and find solace in fantasies allows him to discuss forever the possibilities of a better existence. Either society promises him a beautiful life in the hereafter or it points in glowing colors to life in the future once he has overcome his shortcomings. As Alexander Pope so concisely put it:

> Hope springs eternal in the human breast;
> Man never is, but always to be blessed.

Thus every decade begins with promises and ends with a sad summary of frustrated hopes.

For any society of creatures to function ideally, its adult members have to be mature individuals who either instinctively or voluntarily subordinate themselves to the needs of the whole.

The societies of man, composed as they are of individuals anatomically fetalized and behaviorally infantilized, are continually on the verge of falling apart, and are therefore obliged to impose ever stronger regulations, which in turn increase the stress on the individuals. In this climate social unrest and personal inner conflicts are inevitable. Man, as a species which has evolved in the way it has, cannot help but harbor symptoms of maladaptation to his life and environment.

It may be objected that now and then there are persons to be found who seem to be remarkably well adjusted, experience a great deal of happiness, and would not wish for any other way of life but their own. Are they exceptions? Not really. Certain environments and a specific type of parents are highly conducive to a child's development of coping mechanisms (defenses) which permit it an easy mastery of the vicissitudes of group living.

What are these specific factors? Strict and fair discipline; a degree of deprivation; security; love—but not necessarily shielding from pain for, as we see in some primitive societies, the experience of pain forces the youngster to discover in himself the resources to deal with life as it is.

By contrast, an overly permissive, nonfrustrating, and nondeprived setting fails to promote the psychological reactions necessary to foster mature attitudes as an adult. It needs to be said, though, that excessive frustration or deprivation may have the opposite effect and produce a thoroughly beaten-down youngster set on an antisocial course.

Can we turn the clock back and advocate greater discipline both in schools and homes? Unfortunately, this step is not in keeping with the present stage of man's biological development and is therefore most unlikely to be taken. As parents are becoming more and more infantilized, they themselves want comforts, easy life, and coddling. How can they then deprive the "real" children of these joys? It is little wonder that parents feel compelled to soften the transition from childhood to adulthood: permissiveness, in all its aspects, is present in all phases of life. The mere suggestion of a more Spartan way for children raises a hue and cry.

A person growing up in such conditions simply has no way to acquire the coping mechanisms so necessary for group living. It is beyond his ability to deal with the slightest pressures, and even less with competitive school situations. Truancy, oblivion through drugs, inner turmoil, destructiveness then become the rule rather than the exception. Although a person exhibiting this type of behavior would have been considered a deviant from the norm only one generation ago, during the nineteen-sixties he became part of a very large subgroup within the adolescent sector of society.

PSYCHOSOMATIC MECHANISMS AND COPING MECHANISMS

To understand the nature of feelings we have to recognize the limitations of language. We do know what a feeling is, but its exact nature and its subtlest gradations can only be indicated by analogy and metaphor and the deep sensibilities of a poet. It is almost impossible to express in words the precise degree of an emotion. How may we grade, for example, the declaration "I am in love" against "I am very much in love" or "I am very deeply in love"? What is the exact difference between "I am angry" and "I am very angry"?

Emotions nevertheless do find channels of expression, beginning with thoughts, then words, which lead to the next higher level of ideas, beliefs, and commitments. Still further along the line are religions and political and personal ideals. All of these inner experiences can be felt with the same intensity as the simplest direct emotions of love, hate, and fear. In the area of optical perception we find a similar gradation in our recognition of primary (red, blue, yellow), secondary (green, orange, purple), and tertiary (brown, etc.) colors. It is just as difficult to express precisely in words what we see, although we are able to distinguish fine differences of shades.

Should we be forced for one reason or another to suppress the expression of an emotion, it may reappear in an altered or disguised form or find its way into an organ system, which then expresses it in its own terms. Unexpressed embarrassment, for example, may find its way to the skin and appear in the form of a blush.

The sense organs which receive stimuli from the outside world respond to fine distinctions in the areas of sight, sound, touch, taste, smell, temperature, and vibration. The inside world of the body sends *its* stimuli (physiological changes) to the neurohormonal apparatus, which reacts with less discrimination and is relatively less efficient. It often over-responds, misunderstands the stimulus, or maintains a state of response long after the stimulus has ceased to exist. When a stimulus, such as a slight, an insult, or an embarrassment, becomes overly painful, to the point of being intolerable, the individual inclines to suppress it. In such a case the nervous system protects itself by shunting the objectionable stimulus away from the centers of recognition to the less sensitive visceral system. In this way, the stomach sometimes becomes the primary sensory organ for registering an injury to the self-esteem. A slight that an individual may or may not at all be aware of consciously will then be acknowledged by an outpouring of a large quantity of gastric secretion. The result, of course, is indigestion. In some individuals who have a predisposition for it, this situation may even lead to a gastric ulcer.

When an animal senses the nearness of a predator and anticipates bodily harm or even death, certain involuntary mechanisms are brought into play which have the purpose of either minimizing the harm or saving the life. Some of these mechanisms are of the order of a faster clotting of the blood, so that the animal will not bleed to death if injured; a faster heartbeat and elevation of blood pressure, to improve circulation, thus pumping more oxygen to the muscles; an increase in muscle tension to allow for quick action, and so on. In animals as well as in man, the paleocortex and the endocrine glands are the agents which put these reflexes into operation. They react the way a triphammer does, always poised for action, and they respond unjudgingly, in a stereotyped way, to certain stimuli. These responses, of course, vary according to species. When a cat feels threatened by a dog it arches its back, bares its claws, and hisses. When even a newly hatched gosling sees only the shadow projected from a two-dimensional cutout of a buzzard, it runs for cover. Man has similar reactions. His neocortex does not have a chance to participate in such an action —or, stated differently, it is not consulted when the alarm is sounded and therefore it does not have the opportunity to evaluate the body response and determine whether it is appropriate. The paleocortex, being nondiscriminatory, reacts in the same way to symbolic stimuli as to actual threat. In man, the symbols of his well-being are his personal goals and his relationships with other people which, when threatened, take the place of the vulnerable body of the animal. Thus a threat to his self-esteem on the one hand, and a physical attack on the other, evoke the same neuro-endocrine responses—but with one important difference. In bodily injury the responses are short-lasting and appropriate. In social harm, which is often of long duration and may be permanent, this mechanism is not only totally useless but often, as judged by the neocortex, inappropriate to the situation and therefore inhibited from being expressed. Being inhibited it cannot find its normal outlet in such motor actions as fleeing or fighting, but remains only in the visceral system, which is not under the control of the neocortex. The muscular apparatus is kept in an inhibited state of tension. Persistence of this excited state in the viscera may result in damage and constitutes the essence of psychosomatic illness.

Patterns of disease assume different characteristics as social values change. Certain psychosomatic disorders appear more frequently during periods of upheaval, others only in one ethnic group and not in another. This is also true of infectious diseases. Many clinicians have noted a clustering of respiratory infections in college students at examination time.

Man is caught in a web of his own making. Often social circumstances do not permit him either to fight or to run. He is in somewhat the position of the artist who painted such an amazing likeness of the devil on his wall that it frightened him just to look at it, so he decided to wear dark glasses in his room. It did not occur to him either to remove his handiwork or to remind himself that it was, after all, his own handiwork that was frightening him. What we have here is a complex procedure in which the neocortex sets up symbolic representations of states or actions, which after all are only abstractions, but which nevertheless become just as vulnerable as if they were flesh and blood. Yet when the paleocortex sets mechanisms into motion for defense, the neocortex evaluates the mechanisms as inappropriate and inhibits them. The result, of course, is an extremely complex confusion.

When modern man faces an unfamiliar situation in which he does not feel sure of himself, his ability to respond to this situation will be impeded by the very anxiety it provokes in him. In normal circumstances a person deals with any complexity piecemeal, one step at a time, each step leading to and aiding in the solution of the next one, until he arrives at the most satisfactory result in the given conditions.

This is another instance where the possession of adequate coping mechanisms spells out the difference between feelings of well-being and illness. It matters little to the child within the man whether or not there is any reality to the threat if he fears, say, the loss of his job at some future date. What is more important is that he be fortified by a sense of security in possessing a suitable coping mechanism that he can avail himself of. It would hardly make any impression upon him and would not help him at all if a trusted friend were to prove to him that his fears were totally unfounded. He feels safer, on the other hand, knowing that he could, for example, start on a campaign of writing letters to potential employers in case such a contingency should arise. This reaction in many ways is not too different from the child's conduct when he uses good behavior to gain the favor of his parents. The child's experience of the success of such maneuvers becomes the basis for similar strategies throughout his life.

This explains why so many people are reluctant to discuss their methods of coping with life since, even to them, they appear childish. They are not in essence different from the person's touching a rabbit's foot every time a crisis occurs. It is only the more sophisticated varieties of such actions which elicit less, or no, embarrassment, and which we tolerate. Basically, however, all these mechanisms represent the tools of the child within us.

Many onlookers, observing squabbles between children—the words they use and the attitudes they take—assume that they are imitating their elders. Suppose, though, that it is the other way around, and that it is the elders who have never lost the behavior patterns they developed in childhood. In that case, the onlooker would have a keener understanding of adult behavior if he simply watched the way children get along with each other.

As a matter of fact, there is hardly any display of unseemly conduct in an adult that does not have its undisguised counterpart in the familiar behavior of the child. The usual contentions about neurotic behavior are derived from the assumption that unresolved conflicts in childhood influence the adult's attitudes to society. But it could just as easily be that man is not maturing emotionally at all, or only to such a minor degree as hardly to constitute a change. For the sake of making group living tolerable he has indeed learned to impose some coping mechanisms upon himself which enable him to keep his childish impulses in check, but he has not outgrown them. The coping mechanisms form a thin veneer, deceptive enough to allow an unaware bystander to be impressed by the admirable poise and pleasant exchanges of people in a social setting. Yet were he to be present when these same people were in the throes of a typical domestic crisis he would find the poise and pleasantness dissolved, revealing bickering, squabbling, and abusive language commonplace in their children.

This is not to say that such a phenomenon is universal. The exceptions, though, are sufficiently rare as to be held up as an ideal illustrating a desirable *modus operandi* between man and woman. This creates an erroneous impression among the more numerous man-children that it is they who are deviant and sets up in them deep feelings of guilt.

The major source of the discordance between man's expectations for himself and his emotional inclinations is rooted in the peculiarity of the manner of his evolutionary development. He is born an infant and becomes a child in his adult years. Only special psychological mechanisms enable him to assume the mature role necessary for the cohesion of society. Unfortunately the façade, being not organic but painfully acquired during the formative years by rearing and education, is a thin veneer, and it cracks easily. This comes to light very vividly in the course of family therapy.

The mechanisms are acquired as the playful child begins to grow older. More is expected of him, and he is frequently admonished to stop playing about and "act his age." Implied in these rebukes is the threat of a withdrawal of love and respect which he senses accurately. To assure himself of a continued supply of affection which a child, biologically helpless, needs as much as food, he accommodates himself to the expectations by modeling his behavior on that of his elders. It needs to be emphasized again that this is a façade he is imposing upon himself to please his parents—and, later, society—but it does not correspond with his natural inclinations. If, as is often the case, the façade of the parents is inadequate, the child experiences confusion as to what actually is expected of him, and he is again up against the contradiction do-as-I-say-don't-do-as-I-do. If, as sometimes happens, the parents' façades are firmly established, the child finds it easy to model himself on their consistent standards.

These façades, as the child acquires them, become his mechanisms in coping with the demands of society. There are as many types of façade as there are individuals, but to illustrate the point, here are a few:

The façade of being intelligent, bright, intellectual. In many cultures the youngster is aware that his display of intelligence draws approval and admiration. In others, admiration is gained by being intelligent but avoiding the display of it; that is, by covering the cover with a second veneer—modesty.

The façade of being aloof and uninvolved. This avoids the possibility of unacceptable inclinations becoming apparent, on the principle of least said soonest mended.

The façade of being grim and cold. The antithesis of the warm, outgoing child is a very extreme mask. The people using this façade believe that being an adult is a serious business.

The façade of showing off or being a clown. These people deliberately exaggerate the childlike tendency to give the impression that it is only a pretense and not the real thing.

It should be emphasized that children will accept a firmly established and consistent façade only when it is accompanied by love, respect, and security for the child. If any of these qualities are missing, the façade becomes brittle, and we then witness simultaneous acceptance of it and rebellion against it. It is obvious that such a division in the character can cause much unhappiness and uncertain identity.

An added complication in Western culture is the tendency to value individuality. This impels a young person to differentiate himself at an early age, before significant emotional adaptive mechanisms will support such individuation. Parents emphasize that the child has a personality of its own. They foster it with a great deal of attention and mental stimulation, which necessarily accelerates the development of his intellectual abilities. While this usually achieves the desired results, sometimes, when excessive, it results in overstimulation which the neocortex not only suffers itself but also transmits to the paleocortex. To keep itself from breaking down the brain uses "shut-off" mechanisms. The neocortex, overstimulated, becomes refractory to new information. Its owner feels dull, becomes sleepy, and cannot concentrate or absorb any further knowledge. When the paleocortex is overstimulated it "freezes" itself on a level of very low reactivity. Such a person becomes "turned-off"—his capacity for experiencing emotions is limited. In clinical terms this is referred to as a schizoid state. Similarly, a sudden surge into awareness of extremely intense emotions, such as murderous rage or violent sexual impulses, may also cause a "freezing" of the paleocortex and a consequent "turned off" state.

In our present generation (and this has happened periodically throughout the history of man) permissiveness, emphasis on development of individuality and intellectual achievement easily open the door to overstimulation. As a consequence, the "freezing" of emotions is not an unusual occurrence, and it leads to a withdrawal into dream worlds, fantasies, and abdication of responsibility. Young people afflicted in such a way search for an antidote, and often find it in submission to the authoritative guidance of radical political systems, in de-emphasis of individuality, anti-intellectualism, or in the quest for the "unfreezing" of their emotions through drugs or by the excitement of dangerous pursuits (such as car racing, parachute jumping, or even criminal activity for the thrill rather than for the gain).

All of this tends to perpetuate a childlike state, and we are then witness to the paradox of extremely intelligent individuals breaking off studies before graduation, rebelling without substantial cause, drifting without goals, or not being able to attain a position in society commensurate with their intellectual gifts.

FAMILY THERAPY

When a family seeks help from a psychiatrist as a group it is usually for one of two reasons. Either one of the children is seriously disturbed and a doctor considers it necessary for the whole family to participate in a change of emotional climate or the parents find their marriage at a point of crisis and believe it to be because of the difficulties they experience in handling their children. Although these seem to be two quite different situations, in the course of therapy one frequently finds that the same basic principles underlie both.

In the first case, with the exception of those cases where his mental illness is a result of organic damage to the nervous system, the young person usually reflects in a more serious degree some pathological conditions which exist in the entire family. In the second case the complaint most often voiced by the parents is that their marriage is disintegrating because of quarrels over responsibility for the children's behavior. (We are all familiar with the sentiment "when the children are good they are 'our children,' but when they behave badly they become 'your son' or 'your daughter.'") Couples who are incompatible for other reasons do not seek family therapy, but consult marriage counselors or individual therapists if they wish to rescue their marriage.

One of the first things we notice about parents' complaints about their children is that those characteristics they object to are usually the ones they dislike in their mates. Of course, this is an indirect complaint about the mate, who senses it and in turn uses the same tactic. (This is called projection.) Thus the children not only become the performers acting out the parents' script, but also often oblige by taking on their roles and fighting out with each other the same battles the parents are fighting. An only child, having no sparring partner, internalizes the conflicts.

If one goes to the very bottom of these frictions, one finds a pattern that is basic to all group animals. Beginning with the litter stage, there is a constant struggle among the individuals to establish rank. Of course, among other animals there is no question of the parents becoming involved in such struggles. Their rank is established. But in the human species, because of the variable degree of emotional maturity, many parents have not differentiated themselves sufficiently from their progeny. They are inclined to compete with them as they would with siblings, and their children, sensing this, respond in kind.

In animals, the determining criteria for rank are strength and those qualities of skill and experience useful to the species for survival. In humans, physical strength is rarely of primary importance today. Various strategies and maneuvers are customarily used to replace it, and the children spot them quickly. When they realize the power gained by the successful use of such means, they too adopt them.

If a martyred parent sets the pace, the highest rank is attained by that member of the family who makes it clear that he suffers the most. (It has been said that a family is an autocracy ruled by its sickest member!) Other families may be dominated by a bully, jokester, hypochondriac, food-faddist, physical health addict, or the possessor of any of a variety of other idiosyncrasies. Whatever it is, the dominant characteristic will determine the strategies used to gain rank or power by the other members of the family. In this climate of emotional immaturity the children will not only compete with each other, but will also join in the fray with their parents, using the same weapons. Who has not heard the child of a chronically "exhausted" mother exclaim, "I can't clean up my room now—I feel too tired!" What is more, if he can convince his elders that he is indeed "tired," he wins the contest.

Sometimes married couples wonder why the happiness of their courtship days has degenerated into tedium and bickering. It is difficult for them to see that in their earlier years their relationship had the earmarks of play. They would seek fun, explore the world together, exchange ideas. But once married they were supposed to face life on a mature, adult level. They find themselves incapable of this and become overwhelmed by the practical routines of everyday life. Actually, couples can be classed into three categories as regards to their response to the daily vicissitudes of marriage.

There are couples of the uneducated, simple type, who accept life as it comes without question and perform their tasks as a matter of course. These couples thus approximate the corresponding responses of the mature animal. Then there are those, more sophisticated and probably more infantilized, who have developed suitable coping mechanisms, and who make their routines enjoyable by elaborating them and converting them into adventure or fun. For these people every meal is a challenge, the daily walk to the stores is an adventure and the rearing of children becomes an exercise in depth psychology.

Psychological Factors

The third category, though, constitutes the majority in our culture. Under the stress of the discomfort of increasing tedium, the superficial veneer which allows for normal interpersonal relations cracks. The primitive behavior of the babies of any group of social animals emerges in the form of a power struggle to establish rank. Each mate marshals his or her credits as to the contributions to the home which they consider deserve especial consideration. The questions of whose parents to visit first, or who should put out the garbage, may appear trivial to an outsider, but such quibbles set the mood that foreshadows general unhappiness.

Everything in our culture conspires to imbue young people with a roseate but entirely unrealistic view of life. From the fairy tales read to them in childhood to the romantic stories that fill their minds, novelists' happy endings, or the glamorous unrealities of early Hollywood movies, they absorb a picture of the world that has no relation to its verities, so that they are totally unprepared for prosaic existence as it unfolds. Lately, the awareness of the prevalence of unhappy marriages has prompted efforts to alleviate the condition. The focus of these attempts has been on sex education in schools in the hope that children better informed in this area will be able to adjust more satisfactorily to marriage later. While sexual enlightenment may be desirable, it has little bearing on the problems, since it does not convey the emotional maturity which is the essential ingredient of a happy union.

The climate in the home of marriages such as we have described must have its effects on the children, and a tendency to perpetuate itself through the generations. It is little wonder that children growing up in such an atmosphere do not find the "adult" world or married life overly attractive. They tend to stabilize themselves in their adolescent period for as long as they can. Their need for dependency and the possible loss of their playmates forces them to legalize their unions, but they have no preparation for mature relationships.

These children show a peculiarly paradoxical mixture of attitudes. They demand to be treated as equals with adults while at the same time they revert to responses they harbored as infants. Since the parents themselves exhibit a similar paradox, only somewhat mitigated by better defenses, discipline remains ineffective. Children cannot train children.

PARENT-CHILD RELATIONS
In our generation we have prided ourselves not only that we love our children, as all generations have, but that, understanding more of a child's needs, we have been careful to omit nothing that might be of benefit to it. We are now facing the paradox that many of these loved children are turning against us, in some cases in quite vicious ways. It does not seem to make sense—yet there are some clues to the puzzle.

A superficial observation of parents handling their children gives an impression of affection, dedication, responsibility, and concern, and we view these qualities as expressions of love. But are they? In the face of the evidence it appears that the children themselves do not think so. What, then, is missing?

If we use an analogy to be seen in the play of children, we find that playing "house" arouses strong emotions in young children. Little girls bestow on their dolls an almost exact equivalent of mother love. The dolls are cuddled, fed, scolded, praised, dressed, cleaned—indeed, loved. Little boys go through the motions of being wage-earners returning from work, even imitating their fathers' mannerisms. But as soon as these children tire of the game, they abandon the previously adored make-believe infant without a second thought. To complete the analogy, the average young mother devotes similar attentions to her live baby—but she, too, tires of the game. She is probably without help; her female relatives live too far away; her husband is at work. The stress of taking care of an infant—a twenty-four-hour-a-day job with no rest period—together with the tasks of looking after her house and the desire she has to prove herself an attentive and loving mate, very soon take their toll. She regresses to childlike patterns, and before long would like to revert to "playing house" as she did when she herself was a child. But now there is a difference. Her infant, unlike her doll, makes its needs known in a most insistent way should she put it aside for a while, and she will either respond to its cries with a great deal of resentment or let it cry and then experience such guilt that she feels she has to overcompensate for her apparent lack of love. She then worries unduly over insignificant changes and constantly telephones her mother, friends, or pediatrician for advice. The child receives a smothering attention which inhibits any emotional maturing. She and her husband lavish toys, treats, and delicacies upon the child in further overcompensation. In doing so they themselves re-experience the pleasures of their own childhood and sometimes even compete with their own small children while playing with them. The offspring instinctually sense the childlike qualities of their parents, and consequently treat them as if they were slightly older children. The parents come to regard their children as younger siblings, and sometimes even show signs of sibling rivalry. It is not unusual for a young father to exclaim petulantly to his wife: "For heaven's sake leave the baby alone—can't you spend some time with me!"

Children growing up in such an atmosphere do not have a sense of security, nor do they respect their parents. This extends, later on, to a lack of respect for all authority. Neither are they able to develop self-respect, and they express the same type of angry resentment toward themselves that they have learned to have for their parents. Thus we have a situation where emotional children are rearing chronological children, with results that are not difficult to predict. The ones who are children because of fewer years despise the children who are their parents. The latter seem to have no joy. Father complains about how hard he works; mother is always exhausted. The amenities that a good income provides, and that the parents hold out as an incentive to their children to work hard and abide by the rules, are not at all attractive. The children will prefer the freedom from responsibility of poverty so long as they can have their playmates. Possessions, in their eyes, have made their parents unhappy. They form their own societies.

Before we leave the subject of parent-child relations insofar as they illustrate infantilization, there is one other revealing characteristic of our species.

When adults devote time to their infants, they often make baby sounds. The babies respond by gurgling or blowing bubbles. There is no other animal that at an adult stage can revert to phases of its infantile stage at will. Animal pups play around each other and also with the parent. The parent animal allows it to do this, but does not reciprocate. That is, the pup plays with the parent, not the parent with the pup. The only exceptions are some of those intelligent species we wrote about earlier who, like man, are in some ways regressive. Most human adults themselves actively play with their young.

A PORTRAIT OF THE MAN-CHILD

A very successful woman executive terminated her marriage after fifteen years of verbal abuse by an ill-tempered husband. She had tolerated the marriage for so long only in order to maintain a stable home for their children. However, when her husband had taken to bragging of the physical attributes of his latest mistress directly to her, she had found herself unable to exercise patience and restraint any longer. Within a short time after her divorce she met an attractive, outgoing, single man—an artist—who appeared to her to be the antithesis of her disgruntled businessman ex-husband. Before long she found herself again the target of abuse. This time the abuse was physical, and when an occasion arose on which he struck her almost savagely, she decided she had made another mistake and left him. She was an attractive as well as a successful woman, and she found no lack of candidates for her favor. When she finally decided to marry again it was to a man, divorced for several years, who was a model of the suave, well-bred, diplomatic gentleman. She was happy to have found a companion who seemed so different from the earlier men in her life, and with whom she thought she could live agreeably. Her disillusionment was painful when she discovered that he, too, was not what he had appeared to be. He reacted with sulking and punitive silence when he did not get his way, and it was only a question of time before her relationship with him became unbearable. By then she was convinced that the fault lay with herself—that there must be something about her that caused men to dislike her. She decided to seek help.

It was then that she became aware that when she felt love, she responded with the kind of affection and devotion that a mother feels for her child. She was totally unaware of the existence of any other form of love. Instinctively she recognized the child in the men she encountered, no matter how good their façades. The responses of her men were predictable. What kind of love can a five-year-old offer? He permits his mother to bestow affection upon him when he feels the need; when he has had enough he pushes her away and pursues other interests. Should his mother wish to show her love for him when he is not in a mood for it, he wriggles away impatiently, indicating that he does not want to be bothered. His relationship with his mother is based on his receiving affection in the same way he receives feeding and other ministrations to the body when he needs them. His capacity for frustration, or for the postponement of gratifying his needs, is limited. Failure to fulfill his wants is met with anger or sulking; he likes to play with his toys, but tires of them after a while; he cannot control his impulses, and when teased by playmates fights back viciously. With minor modifications this is the pattern of the man-child. Outwardly he appears to be a pillar of society, respected for his accomplishments and the position he has attained in his professional setting. Nothing in his demeanor, either in his work environment or in social gatherings, offers the slightest hint of the child lurking behind the façade of the man. Only in the safety of his home will the mask drop. Just as no rank or high office overawes those who serve the holder of it, so no grandiose posturing deceives a wife. She will readily testify what a "big baby" her husband is: he does not tolerate her devoting too much attention to the children ("What about me? Don't I count around the house? I am only the man who works day and night making money for you!" is a typical tirade; he relates to his offspring as if he were one of them). The wife quite correctly sees him as one more child on her hands. Often she has to intervene since the children sense in him not a figure of authority but another sibling, and they argue with him as they do among themselves.

Should the man-child mature in his emotional development from the child to the adolescent, then he will feel that his family acts as a restraint.

An infant's discomfort from the recurrent hunger contractions of its stomach is severe enough for him to cry out in pain. The relief that follows the intake of food is immediate, and in a way it becomes the prototype for the search for instantaneous gratification of all needs in the man-child. It may play an important part in his character formation, leading him to the avoidance of the discomforts entailed in the efforts of earning a living or acquiring a home, and direct him toward marrying a woman solely for the satisfaction of his sexual appetite and his need to have the preparation of his food and other comforts provided.

The jaw muscles are the earliest equipped to function. The eagerness with which the baby seeks the nipple when it is hungry is followed by an equally vigorous rejection of it as soon as the hunger is appeased. It forces back the breast, purses its lips, moves its own head away, or even spits out the surplus milk. This pattern of responses follows man into his adult years, only then we call it impatience or fickleness.

In the first years of its life the baby learns to know about objects by the way they feel to its mouth, for the muscles of its jaw and throat are better coordinated at that stage than those of its limbs and hands. This infant's way of "knowing" a thing is so deeply embedded in the man-child that it is quite consistently mirrored in his language. He accepts praise as if it were good food; insults and criticism are "hard to swallow" or "difficult to digest." A lovely woman, to him, becomes a "tasty dish." In German a connoisseur of women is referred to as a *Feinschmecker* (a gourmet—literally, "one who savors delicacies"). Should you frustrate the man-child, he "chews you to bits" with "biting" sarcasm; he finds you "disgusting," "tasteless," or even "nauseating." If, on the other hand, the man-child loves you, he "eats you up"; he may "devour" you with his eyes; he wants you to be an intrinsic part of his being, as if he could swallow you. But then he fears that perhaps you will swallow him, making him lose his identity—then, however nice you are to him, he ends up by "biting" the hand that "feeds" him.

At the time its milk-teeth are breaking through the gums,

the infant becomes aware of the power of its jaws, and chews with gusto anything that it can get into its mouth. Its anger or displeasure are easily translated into action by the muscles of the jaws. Since pleasure and aggression are such close neighbors, it is little wonder that in later years kissing and biting become so much a part of love-play.

As the fully grown humans themselves are becoming more youthful, and remaining so for longer, they tend to feel a closer kinship to their infants. Excessive indulgence of the very young prevents the learning of how to deal with frustration, so necessary in the acquiring of social controls. This may result in fixating development at the emotional stage of the infant. On the other hand, if the mother, whether through ineptness or lack of interest, fails to satisfy the basic needs of her baby, it will become fitful, negative, and difficult, and these qualities often persist into later years—so a fine balance between indulgence and discipline is necessary to achieve an ideal result.

Were an infant able to put into words the knowledge it gains of the world around it, we should easily recognize its misconceptions. They might seem ludicrous, but just the same they would have an inner consistency, in the way that the language of the emotionally disturbed has. As the man-child acquires coping mechanisms that enable him to adjust to society, his reason slowly eliminates the original methods of interpretation. This process continues throughout life, until those original methods of interpretation become so disguised as to be nearly unrecognizable. The early inchoate experiences, however, are by no means lost. On the contrary, they form the bedrock upon which the man-child later erects his logical structure. How secure this latter becomes depends upon how successfully he has adapted himself to society. The intellectual superstructure of the man-child is never too securely welded to its foundation, and when it topples the "irrational" modes surface.

TESTS

A word about psychological testing. There are some, known as projective tests which allow leeway for the patient's fantasy to emerge. He is shown pictures of dramatic scenes and asked to interpret them. Alternatively, he may view amorphous inkblots, which present a stimulus that is intentionally kept as meaningless or ambiguous as possible. The patient's personal selection of missing elements is brought about by allowing his imagination to fill in the gaps. In this way he provides material for interpretation.

For all that, psychological questionnaires do not quite fulfill their purpose of revealing a person's character. While they may give good results in a statistically significant number of cases, there are many persons who have a variety of personality responses, such as one for society, one for home, and one for "the boys." Each one of these sets of responses may be distinctly different from the others. When such a person interprets the test as he is directed to do, he will probably respond with that part of his personality reserved for the general public, and the result is then quite one-sided. In this instance the defense mechanism reserved for interpersonal relations would be uncovered, while the area of his emotional immaturity may have remained unrevealed.

This, of course, does not apply to psychological tests alone, but to any evaluation, by no matter how experienced a person, whether he be a doctor, a personnel manager, or a dean of admissions. A candidate in such a setting reveals only his methods of coping with accustomed and unaccustomed situations of life and does not give any clue of his basic response patterns, which he customarily reserves for his home. As a matter of fact such investigators as the personnel manager are really only interested in how good and how believable a show a prospective employe can put on. Interestingly enough, the person interviewed, too, has the feeling that he is performing. If he has a good command of this type of defense, he considers himself successful. If, on the other hand, he feels he is not too skillful in this area, he is usually perfectly ready to label himself, and to feel, "phony." Whatever the circumstances, then—medical, commercial, or social—wherever judges or testers attempt to evaluate a person, all they really discover is how well he is able to hide his essentially childlike self.

Why, then, do we subject our fellow men to tests at all? If we think of any other society of primates, there would be no possible reason to test its members as to whether they are emotionally fit for certain tasks. It is understood that every ape, by very reason of the fact that he is fully grown, is mature and completely capable of doing whatever his society expects of him.

This is not the case with man. Experience has shown that many are not emotionally equipped to carry out some of society's tasks, and therefore we are obliged to devise tests in an attempt to eliminate those who are especially unfit for the particular occupation. The fact that we test is an indication of our awareness that man is not emotionally mature in his adult years, as are the fully grown individuals of other species.

CONCLUSIONS

Human behavior has so many facets that no single explanation can do full justice to all of them. No theory by itself, no matter how attractive, can include elucidations of all the interconnected factors, operating as they do on so many levels. Every originator of a new approach (and this includes the authors) has the feeling that he has hit upon the most encom-

Psychological Factors 225

passing answer. But even while he is savoring this "Eureka!" feeling, he realizes that there are other theories that offer a similar range of understanding, although they do not necessarily cover the same areas of the problem. It is as if we had made a study of clouds and were then questioned as to the source of rain. Our explanation would be couched in terms of our specific knowledge—clouds—and it would be correct, but one may readily see that a complete reply could fill several volumes. In a similar way, what we offer toward the understanding of human behavior in terms of the concept of evolution by progressive infantilization provides significant clues, but cannot illuminate every detail of man's relation to other men.

Be that as it may, nearly all founders of psychiatric schools have based their theories on their observations of the fact of the perpetuation of childlike behavior into adult years. As only those cases came to their attention where the childlike behavior was so in conflict with accepted norms that it caused acute discomfort, they considered such symptoms indications of sickness, and treated them as such. The fact that none of the founders of theories of psychiatry could agree upon what is normal offers us some clues for, to a certain extent, they realized that those symptoms they were defining as mental illness are present in all of us in varying degrees.

Freud believed that psychological phenomena could be traced back to an origin in the development of a person during his formative years. He noted sometimes unchanged, sometimes disguised, infantile characteristics perpetuated in the adult. Impressions indelibly incorporated into the being in early years formed the basis of his theory. Freud stressed the fact that some individuals are arrested at one particular stage of their development (fixation). He defined the retreat to that particular stage under pressure, or in response to a threatening situation, as regression. Freud postulated that in *all* individuals character and emotional development are the results of action and reaction between instinctual demands and the demands of reality. He perceived a continuous interplay between man's personality and his environment, between his needs and the manner in which he satisfies them.

In his earlier years Freud stressed the formation of emotional elements during the childhood of an individual which became unconscious by the time adulthood was reached because they were not compatible with adult ways of thinking. He termed this process repression.

Freud and his many followers and successors all stressed that needs and goals may be pushed back to an infantile level through repression.

What if these manifestations of emotional immaturity noted by so many brilliant observers were, in fact, not a result of a process of pushing back but actually one of arrest and retardation? If this is so, what we have on the emotional level is a parallel to the anatomical and physiological retardations described in a later chapter. In this case it would not be that the adult is repressing infantile wishes, but that he remains infantile while, more or less successfully, imposing coping mechanisms upon his still-infantile adaptive responses which are, for the most part, inappropriate for functioning in society.

The difference between both the orthodox and the present-day psychoanalytic views on the one hand and the view we have presented on the other is more one of emphasis than of essence. All agree that what we observe is childlike behavior. While the orthodox believe that man progresses through childhood to maturity, we are suggesting that the norm for man is an arrest at the level of childhood.

Freud's outstanding intuitive ability perceived correctly the infantile nature of neurosis. We feel, though, that he did not go far enough. It is not that the human being matures emotionally into an adult form of the species. Rather, the fully grown Homo sapiens is infantile anatomically, physiologically, and behavioristically. He can function in society only to the extent that he is successful in developing coping mechanisms which mask, but do not actually alter, his basic infantilism.

CHAPTER FOURTEEN

An Aspect of Crowding

This subject has so many faces that a whole book could be written on crowding as a feature of life as a human being, and if the book were to have any pretensions of being comprehensive it would run into several volumes.

Today when one speaks of crowding, the first thought that comes to mind is overpopulation—or, as it has been very vividly termed, people pollution—and the consequent poisoning and partial destruction of our natural environment. The noted French anthropologist Claude Lévi-Strauss, interviewed by *The New York Times,* drew an analogy between this result of overpopulation and the behavior of maggots in a sack of flour. "When the population of these worms increases," he said, "even before they meet, before they become conscious of one another, they secrete certain toxins that kill at a distance—that is, they poison the flour that they are in, and they die." He added: "I think what's happening on a human scale is a little the same sort of thing. We are secreting psychological and moral toxins."

Many laboratory tests have been made demonstrating the "de-naturing" effects of overcrowding on rats. Under the stress of too close proximity to their own kind they mutilate and kill each other, which they do not do in normal conditions; the females abort dead embryos; they become sterile; their sexual behavior becomes aberrant; and so on. The reader is no doubt familiar with some of these tests, as they have been widely reported.

Although there are many interesting theories on the subject, it is thought that overpopulation may be the cause of the mass suicide marches of the highly prolific lemming, and a generation of research has shown a great variety of measurable ills resulting from the crowding together of laboratory animals. For example, Dr. John Calhoun of the National Institute of Mental Health has found that the sex act—generally surrounded with intricate courtship rituals by most animals—becomes a nervous, quick, and brutal obsession; among males, homosexuality becomes common, although it is virtually unknown in almost every mammalian species in a free state; males brutalize females, actions which also are unknown in the free, uncrowded state; females lose their capacity to build nests and to care for their litters; mothers kill and maim their young; individuals of both sexes withdraw from their societies and emerge from hiding only when the others are asleep.

Even though these studies largely refer to the reactions of laboratory rats and mice, a growing number of investigators in all parts of the world agree that they hold clues to some of the aberrations of man.

Thirty to forty years ago, in the days of the New Deal and of heightened social conscience, the image that first came to mind on the mention of the word "crowding" tended to be of slums, poverty, and the necessity of ameliorating the conditions of humanity's masses. This same image would probably be the second to arise in our minds today when considering this subject, although it would now be transmuted into terms of Negro ghettos, the help necessary for other underprivileged segments of populations, and the problems of aiding underdeveloped countries.

Fifty to a hundred years ago, crowding would have been thought of in economic terms: of the needs of industry for a concentration of labor necessary to fill its needs and of the convenience of individuals to live near a source of employment.

On the other hand, were one a botanist or a zoologist in any of these or any other periods, he would have thought of crowding in completely opposite terms, acutely aware as he was that almost all living forms need a certain amount of space for their very existence. It is in the nature of most species of animals to acquire and defend a personal territory, while plants struggle for air and light. Birds may be heard emitting the most strident threats at any infringement of an area they have staked as their own, and they defend their territory very actively. Chipmunks drive away any others who encroach within a radius of so much as fifty yards of their "property." Many animals make their home grounds known by marking it out clearly with urine, feces, or by means of a deposit from specialized scent glands. Most animals, including man, have need of a certain "personal territory." It has been demonstrated that for man there is a certain area in his immediate vicinity into which he does not readily tolerate intrusion. If another person encroaches into this space the "invaded" person will either step back, become hostile, or feel acutely uncomfortable. Research on this "body buffer zone" in violent

An Aspect of Crowding

prisoners convinced psychiatrist Augustus Kinzel, of Columbia University's College of Physicians and Surgeons, that much urban violence is a result of sensitivity to the physical closeness of other people.

Robert Ardrey has written that animals have an instinct to control their numbers, so that the size of their populations has a relationship to a given territory. He has cited the work of C. M. Breeder, Jr., who in 1932 demonstrated that guppies not only maintain their numbers, but also the proportion of males to females at a biologically desirable level within a given area. Surplus young were eaten to attain this end. Ardrey also mentioned the more recent work of Adam Watson, who was able to prove that available territory is a factor in determining the number of healthy male grouse able to breed within it. In this case a desirable population density is maintained by imposing bachelorhood on those males who have not yet acquired a territory by the very simple mechanism of female sexual unresponsiveness to an unpropertied male. Eliot Howard observed, as early as 1920, that this also holds true in countless species of finches, buntings, warblers, lapwings, and woodpeckers, and Ardrey has asserted that the same mechanism is the means of controlling the numbers of more than half-a-dozen species of African antelopes. In other species, he writes, where the territorial compulsion is absent, the overcrowding of animal populations is prevented by other instinctual means, such as parental neglect of offspring in the wildebeeste, rank order in feeding among lions (the young last), and periodic epidemics of convulsions, or seizures causing death, among the snowshoe hare and the meadow vole even when they are apparently healthy and well-fed. Man, as the functions of his paleocortex are in process of being submerged by those of his reasoning neocortex, appears not to have this self-regulatory instinct.

Konrad Lorenz suggested that the reason for the need for "personal territory" lies in the danger in nature that if an animal species settles too closely in one part of an available biotope it will exhaust all its sources of nutrition. Starving can thus be obviated by a mutual repulsion effecting their spacing out. In plain terms crowding, in nature, is antibiological.

Many social or herd animals, used as they are to the propinquity of their neighbors, nevertheless struggle to obtain and defend individual territories. A well-known example is provided by the sea lions, whose bulls occupy small but viciously defended areas when they go ashore. Baboons live in groups, but whenever a troop stops its march and the animals seat themselves, it is seen that each individual is allocated a certain space, and that the amount of space allowed it depends upon its rank. In fact, rank has become associated with the acquisition of territory in many social animals.

All these and many other considerations of the phenomenon of crowding are vastly interesting, and are of urgent concern to specialists in many fields and to man in general. But it is another, and a largely overlooked, aspect of the subject which interests us here.

In the course of their travels the authors found themselves, a couple of years ago, sitting on the beach at Repulse Bay in Hongkong. Repulse Bay is one of the world's beauty spots, and the beach was crowded, although it is at some distance from the teeming multitudes of the city. We were conversing with a group of local Chinese while idly looking out over the lovely bay, and casually expressed the view that although it was a joy to see them, it was strange that none of the lush green islands in the bay had any sign of habitation; neither had their shores any bathers on the beaches, in spite of the enormous pressure of population in Hongkong and Kowloon. A young schoolteacher replied, and what she said surprised us. She said: "We Chinese like to live close together. When one of our people becomes very rich, he does not isolate himself on a large estate as your very rich do, but he brings in more of his relatives and invites them to live with him."

At that time we accepted her remark, passed it off as another interesting quirk of the varieties of human tastes one finds around the world, and went on to the next thing. Since we have been engaged in this work, however, the memory of the conversation has come back, and we find ourselves looking at our own surroundings with new eyes.

Very few of us have not been irked at some time or other by the oppressive crowding of our city life. We have been unable to reach a beach on a fine weekend because of the congestion of traffic on the roads leading to it, or, if we reached it, unable to enjoy its amenities because its car parks were full and we had to drive on. We have been deterred from playing golf or tennis because of the lines of people waiting to tee off, or inability to obtain a court. We have been unable to obtain services in a store because salesclerks, harried by a superfluity of customers, have become negligent, short-tempered, and rude. We are unable to enroll our children in schools we think would be good for them because of lengthy waiting lists, or attend plays we think we should enjoy on a day that would be convenient. Why do we tolerate these inconveniences? There is actually no need to do so. If one gets into a car and drives across the country, avoiding the superhighways where possible, the chief impression is of space—vast, incredible, almost limitless space. Soon after leaving the seaboards or the shores of the Great Lakes and their cancerous megalopolises, one finds forests, hills, mountains, deserts, dunes, and plains, vast as oceans, with a few cities and towns dotted over them like islands in the Pacific, and almost as sparsely. Why do not more of us betake ourselves from the cities that may be our death to the beauties and natural surroundings of the emptier spaces?

Not only do we not do so but, on the contrary, there is a counter movement. Far more people migrate from the country to the cities than the other way around. A city-dweller, if he acquires the means, may decide to "spread out" a little in a suburban district, or even a little further into those areas of affluence that have become known as Exurbia, but he will rarely pick himself up lock, stock, and barrel and take himself into the real "country." The countryman, on the other hand, blaming the hardships and difficulties of wresting a living from the soil, in growing numbers moves to the cities. Is his stated motivation honest? Does he not, in truth, find the "natural" environment of the countryside monotonous and have a hankering for the amenities, comforts—yes, and the crowds —of the cities? Does he not, like the Chinese, actually prefer to be surrounded by other people?

Even within the cities—where there are, after all, variations in the density of crowding—we see manifestations that seem at first incredible. One is aware of the overcrowding of the poor in slum districts. Yet if a well-intentioned city council decides to raze the buildings in such a district in order to build improved dwellings, what is the inevitable result? There is usually an uproar, a spate of legal suits to enjoin the authorities from proceeding, declarations of attachment to the neighborhood on sentimental or business grounds, and a general impression that the population, in being dispersed, is being abused. Were one to suggest that it might be healthier and pleasanter to get up a little earlier in the morning to walk part of the way to work, rather than to endure the inhuman crowding, the dirty and odoriferous atmosphere, and the short tempers and uncivilized manners of the hordes of rush-hour subway travelers, he would be regarded with a stare of incredulity as though he had taken leave of his senses. It seems that a patron of the subway and public bus systems of any of the great cities (and in Tokyo, New York, London, and Paris alone there are about thirty million of them) actually prefers the daily scrimmage to the use of his legs on the less congested surface of the city streets.

Our cities are witness to the overcrowding of the rich as well as the poor. The rents or purchase prices of apartments in most luxury high-rise buildings would be more than adequate to buy or lease spacious homes in uncongested areas. Yet there is always a shortage of such apartments where, in spite of luxurious lobbies and expensive furnishings, the actual space available is cramping and the convenience minimal. It would seem that the rich, as well as the poor, prefer the penalties of crowding to the discomfort of isolation.

This strange truth is also apparent in resort areas and in places of entertainment. Whether the resort be as expensive and exclusive as the Hamptons on Long Island or the Rivieras of France and Italy or as inexpensive and accessible as Coney Island in the United States and Blackpool in England, they are all crowded. Presumably, if man did not enjoy being part of a crowd, he would shun those places. They are holiday places. Nobody forces him to go to them. Yet he goes. And the same is true of places of entertainment. Who wants to go to a nightclub or a discothèque that is not crowded? Who enjoys eating in a half-empty restaurant, no matter how good the food? Why do the young by the thousands migrate to such events as the 1969 Woodstock Festival at danger if not to life, at least to health and limb, or congregate in "hippy" communities? What is the attraction of the cult of the guru if it is not the losing of the self in a larger unit: one big family—mankind—the universe?

It is true that we are living on an overpopulated planet, and that the sheer number of people is a greater threat to the survival of our species than almost any other factor, but there are actually still very many underpopulated areas in the world. Why don't we spread out? No matter how many practical reasons, or rationalizations, are offered for not doing so, it is clear that we could if we really wanted to. Yet we do not. Apparently all people, not only the Chinese, prefer to live where other people are.

From time to time some explanations have been offered. Zoologists have noted that mammalian territories are a little different from those of birds, in that they are not so closely tied to food requirements, so that for some the home range is for safety—it affords a place that is familiar and in which the creature can hide. W. H. Burt wrote of territoriality and the "home range" concept as applied to mammals, and it has been suggested that this concept, extended from the lower orders of mammals to the hominoid level, might help to explain why some archeological sites show signs of having been occupied for thousands of years. Why should primitive people, not tied to a location by the needs of agriculture, have concentrated in crowded communities when the whole world was open for their habitation?

Why, indeed, do displaced persons' camps in today's disturbed world, uncomfortable and lacking in amenities as they are, have a habit of perpetuating themselves long after their function has been served?

As noted earlier, there are cycles in the lives of animal species. They tend to become sterile, sick, and to die off in large numbers when they become too prolific and are crowded, thus reducing their populations and adjusting their numbers by natural processes. It is, therefore, antibiological to crowd. Why does man do it? A major concern of most mature animals is to obtain and defend some personal space—more or less depending upon its species and its rank within the species. Only the very young are comfortable in, and prefer, the crowding of the nest, the burrow, or the lair, and are not disturbed by the body-closeness of their litter mates.

While man has no "memory-in-the-flesh" of a litter unless he happens to be the product of a multiple birth, is it not perhaps the comfort of the child's close body contact with his mother, the closeness and fondling of his infant years, the familiarity and lack of stress of parental surroundings in infancy that is being sought in our driving need for the company of a crowd? Does this need, antibiological as it is, not have, among other and more superficial causes, its fundamental *raison d'être* in the infantilization of our species?

CHAPTER FIFTEEN

Cultural Trends: The "Normal" and the "Deviant"

We have devoted much of this work to the behavior of the "deviant" in the awareness that it is through the "deviant" that new trends arise. Yet the largest numbers of any species are the "normal." It is they who, by their conservatism, maintain its stability, since by definition conservatism tends to the maintenance of established norms and makes it easier for every new generation to perpetuate standards previously set up. It is quite obvious that the bulk of any species must be conservative, for otherwise there would be no species.

The "normal" sector of a species population is not only the largest, but also the most characteristic at any given time. Unfortunately, though, in the same way that the "good" child is taken for granted in the home and in the classroom and much more attention given to the "bad" child, writers, sociologists, politicians, and even historians are inclined to concern themselves so exclusively with the "deviants," that one may lose sight of the fact that the "normals" even exist.

Actually, the difference between the two groups is not so great. Anatomically all men have traveled approximately the same route to arrive at their present form. The differences are to be found in behavior, and it is for the reason that behavioral variations so often portend deeper changes that so much more attention is paid to the deviants than their numbers would warrant. It is also true that the chroniclers of any period or place, whether writers, scientists, historians, or disseminators of news, are themselves among the deviant and naturally have a sense of kinship with them. It is, therefore, not to be wondered at that they should find the activities of a small group of trend-setters more interesting and congenial than the routines of the "solid citizen," and it is probably for this reason that so little has been written of the "normal" representatives of any society, and that they are so infrequently studied or described scientifically.

Students of all the social sciences in their years of training acquire a generalized overview, in terms of a specific theory, as to what constitutes normal behavior. Instructors seem tacitly to assume that the student knows what is normal, since it is seldom a subject for classroom discussion, and the student is rarely required to define it. This task is left to philosophy. In truth, it is probably one of the more difficult exercises to define normality, since varying values enter the picture, but nevertheless we recognize it in an instinctive way.

In the wake of the world-wide episodes of unrest, disaffection, and outright rebellion that have characterized the youthful sectors of many populations in recent years, some studies have now been made in the United States in an effort to establish "normal" adolescent behavior, largely to have a basis for determining how "deviant" the deviant is.

In a small private college in Chicago the normal young male of an average eighteen years of age was described as a mildly compulsive personality, not crippling but enough so to decrease spontaneity. He has a capacity for deep, close, human relationships; a paucity of interests; mild anxiety related to possible failure; and is marked by passivity. He is stable, but lacks creativity and ambition. The cost of the stability is rigidity and compulsiveness, which reduce creativity and upward mobility. Within the general population of the United States this group is relatively silent. It is goal-directed, aims to do its jobs well, and those who are included in it carry on their lives quietly in simple comfort, marry, raise families, and eventually retire on pensions and social security. They express satisfaction with their home environments.

Another study asserted that misunderstanding and confusion about the behavior of youth is to a large extent due to the lack of studies of normal adolescents. These investigators felt that too many of our psychiatric theories about adolescence derive from the treatment of disturbed patients, so that consequent generalizations and hypotheses from sick to relatively well populations may often be fallacious. However, they concluded that considerable disturbance in mental health is normal in the late adolescent, noting at the same time that a comparison of superior or average rating had a greater proportion of females, while the moderately severe to severely impaired ratings had a greater proportion of males.

A third study showed that "normal" students made an effort to study subjects they disliked, even though they had little curiosity about any matter not encompassed in the school curriculum. They were not motivated for cultural or nonassigned scientific topics, or toward special achievement. The males preferred sport and the females music and social activities. Their relationship with their parents was one of mutual respect and relative equality. They maintained good relationships with their siblings. Their families were supportive, but they provided quite a large degree of autonomy. This study showed the "normals" as possessing initiative, self-sufficiency, and an ease at resolving conflicts. They had many friends, were outgoing, had well-defined educational and career objectives, and were goal-directed.

Another investigator held that there are three perspectives for normality: normality as health (absence of signs and symptoms), normality as utopian (harmonious blending of elements of the mental apparatus which culminates in optimal functioning), normality as average (statistically applying the bell-shaped-curve principle to psychological data with both extremes of the curve implying deviance).

At a forum in Topeka, Kansas, the normal were described as particularly stable in terms of jobs and residence, as not looking for more interesting or challenging work or higher salaries, and as noncompetitive. It was remarked that there is very little that is esthetic or imaginative in their homes or in the way they dress; that they are not colorful, not rebellious, not very aggressive; that they are realistic, autonomous, and competent. Their mothers are not emotionally demanding and do not complain about husbands who are poor providers. Their leadership comes from within their own group.

Having digested these various descriptions, we are not greatly enlightened. Just the same, we have to establish some norms in order to understand where the center of gravity lies in today's population, so as to be able to identify both the bearer of that core of evolution which remains comparatively stationary and the other sector which is deviant and which will carry evolutionary regression to its inexorable end.

If we rescue genetically deficient children from early death and enable them to reach their mating stage, eventually the "normal" core will be reduced in relation to the "deviant" segment until it too becomes deviant. Then we shall have a total population so suffused with abnormalities (by today's definitions) that as a consequence the process of regression will be accelerated.

It is quite possible that we are now on the threshold of such a development. The so-called advanced societies are beginning to show a far greater stratification in terms of deviance from their cultural norms than the "backward" societies. Any nation that improves its medical services is thus inviting deviance. We see an interesting development in the U.S.S.R. There, the cultural ideal was a process of equalization. Workers and intellectuals were supposed to be alike in the eyes of a paternalistic government. But as their medical care has improved and genetically inferior individuals survive, overcompensation in the area of intellect has taken place. At present we see the same disruptive force of a large segment of youth, many of whom in earlier days would have died in infancy, threaten the conservative core of the state in the same way as in the U.S. In this respect it is not without interest that a so-called Kremlinologist recently warned the United States Senate to remember that the present conservative government of the U.S.S.R. consists of "mediocre men." (We should have termed them "normals.") It seems apparent that the more "backward" nations in the Communist orbit will be able to carry on the egalitarian philosophy for the time being, while the Soviet hierarchy has been, and will continue to be, harassed and challenged by its deviant intellectuals.

Of course, the "backward" nations, too, will be subject to disruption as soon as the initial struggles for economic survival give way to moderate prosperity and its attendant improved medical care, which opens the way for a rapid increase in the number of deviants.

Deviants find a greater kinship with each other, even across the borders of national boundaries, than they do with the normals of their own nation. The West has been falsely accused of exporting its brand of culture to the Iron Curtain countries. In reality the rock groups and the earlier jazz are subcultures that are considerably deviant from the American and British Protestant cultures and the ethic on which they are based. The subcultures erode the core cultures of their own countries in exactly the way they act on the Iron Curtain countries. The obvious success of jazz, and later rock, as unasked-for cultural exports, suggested to the State Department and to British authorities (both strongholds of the Protestant work ethic) some belated action to support the trend for political-propaganda purposes. It is quite possible that the deviants will prove to be a more effective international leveling force than any government-inspired programs.

As in any ongoing trend in any area, infantilization likewise produces its own counter trends. In this case the counter trends take two directions: toward greater maturity and toward the rejection of deviance.

The counter trend toward greater maturity is spotty and found more in individual cases than in group behavior. Such people have a sense of responsibility to the community and are to be found in nonsalaried positions volunteering their services for the public good. A group of atomic scientists, for example, banded together and, through their own bulletins, alerted the public to the dangers of some of the applications of their own researches.

Among larger groups the Mennonites and the Amish, for example, form mature and stable societies. They respect their elders, live by the authority of the Bible's laws together with their own enlightened conscience, and stress the sanctity of human life and of man's word. They have no hierarchy, but are guided by responsible elders and pursue holiness in societies pledged to primitive discipline. They lead hardy and useful lives, refuse to bear arms or take oaths. They reject technology and nearly all the neocortical elaborations of modern life. Although their young are as playful as any others, their adults do not play games. It is quite possible, though, that these societies will not survive for much longer. Although they have existed ever since Conrad Grebel first founded his group of Swiss Brethren based on the principles of the Dutch reformer Menno Simons in Zürich in 1525, in recent times rapid changes and the departure of the group's young have weakened these communities.

Another "antineocortical" wave was the Zionist movement of the nineteenth century. The ghetto Jews of Europe, dreaming of a return to their homeland, did not think of it in terms of biblical study or of religious values. They dreamed in terms of a "return to the land," of farming and agricultural communes, and they expressed desires to re-create a Jewish peasantry.

At that time, too, from the most industrialized country of all—from England, the home of the industrial revolution—came a stream of people desiring to get away from "civilized" life and return to a life closer to nature. They emigrated mostly to the vast open spaces of Kenya, Uganda, Tanganyika, and similar territories, toward the end of the last century.

Some of this urge still exists in England. It is largely confined to the comparatively leisured (those who still have just a little capital left) and impels them to break away from the mechanized, urban, deviant world of their homeland, to become sheep-farmers in Australia, or to seek new horizons in Canada and Africa. In England, too, one sees a comparatively large number of men retreating from modern life in solitary round-the-world sailing in small boats. The unprecedented acclaim given to Sir Francis Chichester in the 1960s is an indication that his exploit struck some responsive chord in the whole "normal" population. For all that, for the time being the English working classes give no signs of such counter trends, their only desire being to participate ever more fully in the delights of prosperity and modern convenience.

In the United States, as well, there is a great growth in membership in "back to nature" groups and a proliferation of camping, hiking, and boating clubs, and in this country also it appears to be largely the upper-middle (professional and intellectual) segment that prefers the rough outdoors, the wide open spaces, or the farm for its refreshment and renewal. While much of this is made possible by, and could be attributed to, greater affluence, people who could spend their superfluous means on citybound pleasures or in urbanized resorts like Miami nevertheless in increasing numbers choose to revert to a contact with nature.

All these counter trends notwithstanding, the more significant movements are to be found among the "deviants." The great groundswell of the popular movement known as the hippies exists under one name or another over much of the world today. Its adherents manifest a flight from responsibility, a pacific character, and a Peter Pan-like refusal to grow up. This is also expressed in their almost ritual use of drugs, their desire not to be involved in the world's affairs, their aim of self-gratification rather than devotion to wider causes—the exaltation of the self over society—all of which contain elements of the qualities of childhood, as does the reluctance to be washed and groomed. Some show characteristics of even further regression, to infancy rather than to childhood, in such rather attractive traits as peacefulness, loving and noncompetitive attitudes, and in a yearning for closeness—"snuggling-up"—rather than more aggressive sex.

The hippies are a minority movement, but minority movements have often in the past transformed the conservative societies in which they arose. In fact, it is in the nature of change that it is invariably brought about from small beginnings.

In the course of human history there has been a progressive shift in placing the importance within the human group from the old to middle age to youth.

In ancient times all respect was given to the old. Their virtues—dignity, wisdom, experience, and calm—were the most venerated, and it was the aim of youth to achieve the serenity, knowledge, and authority of the old. A white head or a gray beard commanded reverence.

In the Middle Ages the ideal virtues were those of the virility, power, decisiveness, and vigor of man's middle years; a little later the qualities of younger men, such as adventurousness, daring, gallantry, and beauty, were more esteemed.

In our own times we have seen a cultural development take shape with an emphasis on the values of late adolescence. Our fashions, economic lives, entertainment, and family orientation are all influenced by the attitudes and preferences of the teenager, and it is entirely possible that the present practices of the deviant young point the direction future norms will follow.

In actuality the economic and social systems of the Western world are still geared to the so-called Protestant ethic—the work ethic—and to producing and consuming. On the whole we are still so persuaded of the virtue of work for its own sake that we find it hard to accept the renunciation by the young of this value. It is a powerful influence. Wherever this ethic has taken root in non-Protestant countries, it has tended to undermine indigenous cultures, as it has done in Japan and as it is in the process of doing as it slowly seeps into the lives of other Asian peoples and into South America.

On the other hand, nothing is ever fixed, final, or frozen about any particular form of economic organization. The ancient Greeks considered work demeaning. In their eyes it was a fit occupation only for slaves. And it may well be that in the Western world we are in a period of transition toward a fundamental change in the philosophy of work.

While the technologically backward countries are catching up, those that are technologically advanced are in the process of breaking the very foundations upon which they were built. While still adhering morally to the principles of hard work, in actuality the working day and week are being shortened, and an increasing amount of work is being shunted to robot machines. Thus the Western world is heading toward a different kind of economy, involving the growing elimination of the human element in the area of production, an increasing percentage of the work force engaged in service industries, and a fundamental change in the philosophy of work.

The trend of deviants to renounce their mother culture is world-wide. A sociologist from Tulane University wrote that his studies showed the emergence of a new ideology among the young, which he called "privatism." He maintained that the new emphasis on the personal is both altruistic and selfish, because it acknowledges the privileges of private existence as rights to all men, but tends to become self-indulgent at its logical extreme. He defined personalism as the "whole ideology" that includes "student withdrawal from institutions into the self" and the rejection of "meaning or authority outside the self."

Even in such a traditionally disciplined and law-abiding country as Germany, a leading sociologist writes:

Discipline, orderliness, subservience, cleanliness, industriousness, precision, and all the other virtues ascribed by many to the Germans as an echo of past splendor, have already given way to a much less rigid set of values, among which economic success, a high income, the holiday trip, and the new car play a much larger part than the virtues of the past. Younger people especially display little of the much praised and much scorned respect for authority, and less of the disciplined virtues that for their fathers were allegedly sacred. A world of highly individual values has emerged, which puts the experienced happiness of the individual in first place and increasingly lets the so-called whole slip from sight.

Less than thirty years since anthropologist Ruth Benedict wrote her famous study of Japanese culture, in which she noted that old age is favored there with maximum freedom and indulgence, a Japanese gerontologist from Shukutoku College, addressing a congress on gerontology in Washington, D.C., reported that the old are no longer accorded unconditional respect in Japan. He said that, on the contrary, they are more likely to feel insecure socially, economically, and psychologically and that many experience great loneliness, frustration, and family tension.

At the same congress a sociologist of Punjab University,

India, reported that also in his country aging persons have become more vulnerable as a result of increasing industrialization and urbanization. In the past, he pointed out, the senior person represented his family and caste in community affairs. The aged monopolized the leadership roles in the social structure. But the family system is being rudely shaken and caste ties are weakening as the individual is emerging as the focal unit in the Indian social system.

The authoritarian Communist party of Poland also caters to its young population. The state-appointed management of a new department store was reported by a correspondent of *The New York Times* to be "youthful, [it] doesn't seem to trust anyone over thirty; older people aren't exactly barred . . . but they are not made particularly welcome either."

Yet another example of the new power and influence of the deviant young was given when in January 1970 the President of the Philippines rebuffed his police for handling a crowd of student rioters roughly, and the president of the University of the Philippines stated that he would personally lead any future student demonstrations.

During the period of recorded history, which is the period of modern man, there has been an ebb and flow of adolescent and childlike (as defined in this work) patterns, both in the same culture and in parallel cultures. The ancient Israelites probably exhibited a greater degree of regression (or civilization; however one wishes to view it) when they formulated the ideal:

They shall beat their swords into ploughshares, and their spears into pruninghooks: nation shall not lift up sword against nation, neither shall they learn war any more. [Isaiah 2:4]

than the Romans, at that time at the height of their national vigor, who embodied their philosophy in the terms *"Si vis pacem para bellum.* [If you desire peace prepare for war.]"

In this churning back and forth, in the long run the childlike pattern is overtaking the adolescent pattern.

In our society, because of the prolongation of childhood in the course of the extension of education, an individual caught up in this trend retains the dependent qualities of the child to such an extent that a transition to an adult mode of living is no longer possible for him. He is not prepared for it. By contrast, in primitive societies children enjoy complete liberty for a shorter time and then they undergo rapid, if sometimes extremely brutal, initiation rites which sever them totally from their childhood.

Concomitant with the prolongation of childhood, there is a gradual elimination of the influence of the elderly at the other end of life. In the field of astrophysics and related space science and technology one is considered old at the age of thirty, and in the job market generally employment becomes more difficult to obtain over the age of forty, whereas in the past the opposite was the case and maturity and experience were sought. Until recently nobody became a president of a large corporation until he reached a ripe age—at about sixty to sixty-five. Now this is a compulsory retirement age in many organizations. These practices have the effect of forcing the elderly into premature retirement, contributing to their need for nursing homes, or isolating them into communities reserved for the aged, and are the obverse side of the phenomenon of progressive infantilization.

An experimenter at the Yerkes Primate Center observed that a group of young monkeys which had been removed from contact with more mature monkeys were more intensely juvenile and played a great deal more than a similar group in which the older animals remained present. When a single adult male was placed in the group of juveniles, most of the liveliness was dampened.

In the macaque culture the aged animals contribute an active role in their societies. The oldest female is the center of a great deal of attention. Her daughters remain close to her even after they have babies of their own. She has a great deal of prestige. The old males, too, are well-accepted members of the troop. The "generation gap" is another feature of human society that is not found in macaque society, where the young males—reasonably capable fighters—have well-defined functions. As the troop moves along in the wild, they take positions at its front, sides, and rear, ready to fight off enemies.

Human beings, in removing their elders from the roles of society's counselors and prototypes, force them into an infantilized old age with no function but to amuse themselves as best they can. The cruise boat and the resort retirement community provide luxury-filled nurseries for a second childhood.

Just as in the mature stage there are still a few individuals who reject infantilized society and flee it for a more adult existence, so there are among the aged some who reject this "golden age" of enforced idleness and take up second careers or public service. They are, however, a very small minority in the over-all trend to infantilization.

This leisure is thought of as a result of improved technology—but, basically, the technology and the leisure are both the results of man's infantilization.

Looking back over the material we have presented to this point, we feel that we can now paraphrase Carl Rogers, whom we quoted in our foreword, and say: How does it happen that the deeper we go into man's behavior as a social animal, the more we find of evolution?

There is a parallel between our "normals" and the hypothetical valley goats of our second chapter. They are the mainstays of their species. They pass on their genes from generation to generation undamaged, and only infinitely slowly bow to modifications by natural selection over long spans of time. Our "deviants" may be compared to our mountain goats, forced by their sickness, their handicaps, and their consequently different behavior into new ways. Each plays his part. Without the normal there would be no species. Without the deviant there would be no variety, and no rapid change.

This pattern is not confined to man, or even to living things. Life itself may be viewed as a deviant form of inanimate nature. For that matter, our planet Earth is deviant. It seems that there is not another in our solar system that supports life, and that the odds against there being one like it in any other are very long.

Our book to this point is the record of our observations. The results of our efforts to determine whether or not anatomical and physiological forces underlie and support the contentions we have made are presented in the second part.

PART II

CHAPTER SIXTEEN

Regressive Evolution

"Il faut reculer pour mieux sauter." *

—*a French adage*

INTRODUCTION
Among all natural systems living matter is distinguished by the fact that, in spite of the very significant changes it has undergone, it has kept a way of recording in its organization a tremendous amount of information reflecting its history.

The general rule of evolution has been a progress from the most simple forms by degrees to more and more complex ones. Nature, however, recognizes no rules. Any and every mechanism that is possible is attempted and used. It is only because those attempts which are successful are the sole survivors, and the rest die out, that it looks as though nature were an intelligent force with the production of those forms which have survived in view. Things look perfect only to those who see what remains after a sometimes vastly wasteful process of elimination has continued through an almost incomprehen-

* To jump higher one must step back.

sible passage of time. The truth is that evolution does not always proceed from the more simple to the more complex, and man is a case in point.

Such sapiens-like forms as Swanscombe and Fontéchevade man preceded the time of the appearance of such forms as Neanderthal, whose structure was more primitive. The sapiens type of man is actually not more complex than presapiens types. Evolutionary change has occurred, but with respect to our thinner skull bones or the absence of ridges above the eye socket (*supraorbital tori*), for example, the changes have progressed from the more complex to the simpler.

When we speak of man's evolution as regressive, we do not mean that it is degenerate. It is evolutionary just the same, but the means to achieve the changes are regressive in form or—to put it another way—progressive to younger and younger phases, through a series of arrests in development.

The difficulty here is one of language, because the concept we are attempting to convey is that we are going forward by going backward. To state this a little more precisely: By going backward anatomically we are increasing our capacity for learning and becoming intellectually more advanced.

Geneticists from 1900 onward all but eliminated behavior as an essential element in evolution. They maintained that whatever behavior an animal displays depends upon its gene structure. In the most extreme view it was stated that evolutionary changes arise without any relationship to behavior. In this view evolution is considered the result of random mutations producing a variety of gametes (reproductive cells) which combine in a fertilized egg (zygote) to produce an animal based on the transmitted information residing in the genes. For those holding such an opinion, therefore, adaptational changes are of no consequence in the modification of species. It is simply a matter of the mutation of genes at an uneven rate, creating possibilities for individual genes which differ from each other to combine and thus produce variant forms.

In a typical random mutation based on this theory there would be no direction. Besides this, some mutations would revert to the original state, so that the features of the species would oscillate back and forth along a base line.

Today's consensus is that random mutations obviously do occur and are a factor in evolution, but that this factor is overshadowed by nonrandom solutions. Natural selection, for one, is nonrandom. It favors the reproductive success of the best adapted group. It is anti-chance. The only reasonable conclusion we can come to is that evolution is determined by the cumulative total of many factors.

In this chapter we intend to show:

1. *The Fact:* Man's anatomy is the outcome of a prolonged process of regression.

2. *The Mechanism:* This regression has been achieved by the retarding functions of hormones.

3. *The Cause:* The trigger which sets this process in motion is the mutant effects of recurrent virus epidemics.

4. *The Result:* In spite of similarities between various hominid species and races of early man, each appears to have arisen comparatively abruptly, and Homo sapiens even more abruptly than his precursors.

5. *The History:* The main ideas which led to the concept of infantilization.

THE FACT: ANATOMIC CONFIRMATION

Our thoughts and opinions are shaped by our nature, or (to put it more bluntly) we think what we think because we are what we are. It is inevitable that we should think of ourselves as evolution's crowning achievement, since we ourselves are our own standard. The statues of classical Greece appeal to our sense of esthetics. They please our eyes, and we look upon them as the ultimate perfection for human proportions. Neanderthal man appears to us to have been an ugly brute. Were we to encounter a Neanderthaler today, we should recoil in fear. But we never stop to think of the impression *we* may make on the sensibilities of our distant progeny. From the vantage point of whatever shape or size he has by then assumed, he may consider even the best of us grotesque and misshapen.

It is probably our increase in size over the ages that has deluded us into thinking that we are progressing physically, although growth of itself is an attribute of childhood and immaturity. Actually, modern man's anatomical development stops at an earlier stage than did Neanderthal man's, and still earlier than that of the apes. If we were to place specimens of all three on a staircase or ladder, we should find the apes at the top of the stairs, displaying anatomical developments which have continued uninterrupted into his adult years. Neanderthal man would stand halfway down the staircase, with the development of several parts of his anatomy interrupted, and modern man near the bottom of it, with still more uncompleted features.

Many components of modern man's body remain behind at what is an embryonic stage in our evolutionary predecessors. Therefore the amazing similarity between the modern fully grown human adult and the fetus of the chimpanzee shortly prior to birth (first pointed out by the Dutch anatomist Bolk in 1926 and subsequently verified by many investigators) is not surprising. This marked resemblance may strike some of us as a gruesome thought, but it is nevertheless an amply documented fact. Karl Lorenz in 1954 described it with a term used elsewhere in biology—*neoteny,* "a developmental inhibition permanently retaining the characteristics of youth."

Regressive Evolution

As a matter of fact, the great T. H. Huxley as early as 1863 drew attention to the fact that the structural differences which separate man from the great apes are not so great as those which separate the great apes from the monkeys, and this observation has subsequently been fully confirmed. According to his son and biographer, Leonard Huxley, he even went so far as to say that he thought "transmutation may take place without transition," thereby anticipating the findings we are about to describe in this chapter.

Ashley Montagu writes in his very comprehensive *Introduction to Physical Anthropology:* "The developmental mechanism by which availability of time for learning was ensured [in the development of man] appears to have been achieved by means of a process which caused a retention or persistence of the fetal or juvenile plasticity of ancestral forms in the later postnatal developmental stages of the individual. The process in which young features of the ancestor are retained in the mature stages of the descendant is known as neoteny."

L. Bolk pointed out the following features of adult man's anatomy which are retentions of earlier fetal phases:

- Retention of cranial flexure (described below)
- Long slender neck
- Forward position of foramen magnum (an opening in the occipital bone through which the spinal cord passes from the brain)
- Orbits under cranial cavity
- Flatness of face
- Retarded closure of cranial sutures
- Large volume of brain
- Small face and large braincase
- Roundheadedness
- Small teeth

Late eruption of teeth
Absence of brow ridges
Absence of cranial crests
Thinness of skull bones
Globular form of skull
Hairlessness of body
Lack of pigment in some groups
Thin nails
Nonrotation of big toe
Incomplete rotation of thumb
Prolonged dependency
Prolonged growth period

In the fetus of all mammals and most vertebrates the axis of the head forms a right angle with that of the trunk, the cranial flexure. In all mammals except man, a rotation of the head occurs during the later stages of development, so that the head assumes an orientation that is continuous with the direction of the backbone as, for example, in an adult dog. Man, on the other hand, retains the cranial flexure, his face pointing in a direction at right angles to the axis of his body. The line of sight of both dog and man is horizontal, but the dog's body is also horizontal while that of man is vertical. In the adult great apes the position of the body is in between, being oblique, and the axis of the head is also intermediate, the foramen magnum being situated more posteriorly than it is in either the fetal ape or in man. *It thus transpires that man's erect posture is due to the retention of a fetal condition* which in other mammals is limited only to their intrauterine state.

Similarly the pubic flexure, which includes the sex organs and the rectum, is directed forward in the embryo. In all other mammals these structures rotate until they become parallel with the spine, but in adult man the embryonic orientation is retained, with the result that the aperture of the vagina is directed ventrally. The human mode of copulation is therefore associated with the neotenous condition of the pubic region of the body.

Man's flat-facedness is also a fetal character, and it is interesting to note that since this characteristic (called *orthognathy*) is limited to the early fetal stages in apes, the fetal developmental stage at which neotenous mutations occurred in man's ancestors must have been an early one.

This feature is of particular importance, for a muzzle separates the eyes. When the muzzle is not formed and the face remains flat, the two eyes remain on the same plane and their fields of vision overlap. This makes it possible for both eyes to focus on a single object, and the development of this power of accurate vision has played a very great role in the evolution of man.

The sutures of the braincase remain open in man until all growth has been completed, long after the brain has achieved its maximum growth. While in apes the sutures begin to close within the first few years of life, in man they do not generally commence to close before the end of the twenty-third year.

In this connection, Albrecht Peiper has pointed out that the human hand was arrested at a stage in his race history corresponding to the lizardlike reptiles. An ape's hand passes through this phase and develops further. "Thus a passing stage in the genetic development of the ape became a final stage for man. . . . Man is, so to speak, a primate fetus that has attained its sexual maturity."

Bolk formed his theory on observations that many of the features which differentiate man from ape (there are about eighty) actually appear during the individual development of the primate fetus, but are lost again in the ape because of progressive differentiation—what is a passing stage in the ape becomes a final stage for man. For this reason the fetuses of the monkeys and the newly born of the anthropoids have a distinctly human appearance, not because the apes descended from a human-looking ancestor but because man retains this feature of fetal development. In their individual development, however, the other primates still go through a final stage which man no longer experiences. "Physically man is thus a sexually mature primate fetus."

There is a bone in the hand of the anthropoid called the *os centrale* (central bone). In man this bone fuses while he is still in an embryonic stage, while in the ape it remains as a separate bone and continues to grow. This is one of the many examples of fetal arrest and accelerated growth processes in man relative to nonhuman primates cited in a standard work on living primates by J. R. and P. H. Napier. Others are the early descent of the testes, the fusion of the sternebrae (breast bones), the early closure of the premaxillary suture (upper jaw), and the early development of a mastoid process. Such retardations (or, as Bolk termed them, fetalizations) are an important source of human specializations, although not the only ones.

A. H. Schultz, at the Cold Spring Harbor symposium in 1950, drew attention to other alterations in growth rates that are generally regarded as retardations. These include the retention of the fetal position of the head on the vertebral column, the lack of forward growth of the orbits (cavities of the skull which hold the eyeballs) and of the face, and the lack of rotation of the great toe.

Besides these fetalizations our anatomical structure is also diminished by those losses which have occurred as a result of disuse atrophy. The gradual loss of the mobility of our toes, while primarily a neotenous feature, is reinforced by disuse, since we no longer use them to hold on to branches. The gradual loss of our teeth may be due to an ongoing disuse atrophy as a result of our change of diet to cooked or otherwise soft foods, but these considerations probably merely reinforce the progressive infantilization.

The deciduous teeth of the great apes are more like those of adult man than they are like those of adult apes, so that it is not surprising to find, for example, that the deciduous teeth of the australopithecines resemble more closely the permanent teeth of man than they do those of adult australopithecines.

In the long-delayed eruption of both the deciduous and the permanent teeth in man we again observe a neotenous trait— the prolongation until several months after birth of the fetal toothless state.

It was Spuhler who showed in 1954 that the deciduous teeth of the australopithecines are more like the deciduous teeth of modern man, but the permanent teeth are more like those of the apes. In almost all the traits (such as the globular form of the skull, the comparative thinness of the skull bones, the absence of brow ridges, the absence of crests, the form of the teeth, and the relative size and form of the brain) in which juvenile members of these fossil forms differ from the living apes and their own adult forms, they most closely resemble modern man. The almost complete loss of body hair is also more likely to be a fetalization than atrophy as a result of disuse.

The ancestors of all mammals were extremely small creatures. They needed protection against loss of body warmth, especially when, adapted to a warm or temperate climate, they wandered northward into colder regions. There are two ways an animal can reduce its body's loss of heat. One is by growing larger, so that there is less surface area in proportion to its bulk, and the other is by developing some kind of insulation.

Warm-blooded mammals living in arctic seas, for example

the whales, evolved a thick layer of fat under their skin as well as great size. While the mammals which stayed on land did indeed greatly increase in size, such vast bulk as the whale's would have been an impediment in the nonbuoyant atmosphere. Hair became the solution (as feathers did for birds). There is a small muscle attached to each single hair. When this muscle is relaxed the hair lies flat and the pelt is thin, allowing body heat to dissipate more easily. But when the muscle contracts the fur is raised, permitting air to enter between the hairs and make a thicker layer of insulation to hold back the body heat.

All land mammals except man are able to adjust the density of their coat according to the climate of their habitat. That modern man is an exception is probably also due to the process of infantilization. About a month before its birth, a chimpanzee fetus has a hair distribution closely resembling that of a human child. It has a thick crop on its skull, while the rest of its body is covered with short fine hair which in man is called lanugo hair (baby hair). Man is born at this stage, but the chimpanzee loses this hair before it is born, and grows the pelt characteristic of its species while it is still within the uterus. Thus the lack of body hair is one more example of the retention of an embryonic feature in man's anatomical make-up.

The growth (increase in size) and development (increase in complexity) of the human brain is also a neotenous phenomenon. That is, man preserves something akin to the rate of growth and development characteristic of the fetal brain, or preserves and improves on the rate of growth and development of the infant ape-brain long after the latter has ceased to grow.

One of the consequences of the prolonged dependency period of man is that it involves a rather long nursing period, and it is presumed that the unique everted mucous membraneous lips of man have evolved as an adaptation to the prolonged suckling period of the human infant. Just as the cheeks of the human baby with their suctorial pads of fat are very different from what they are in the later child or adult, so does the character of the lips differ in the baby from what they will later be in the child or adult. The newborn baby's lips are characterized by a median papilla (which is sometimes mistaken for an abnormal condition). This papilla, on each lip, enables the baby to secure a better hold upon the nipple.

In the trend to prolong postnatal life, which is characteristic of all primates, the period which shows the least change between the apes and man is the fetal stage, or period of gestation. The duration of man's infantile, juvenile, and adult phases has more than doubled, but the intrauterine phase has remained the same. Man's development within the uterus has accelerated in some respects, but in most features—such as the formation of the bones, the size of the brain, and the myelination of peripheral nerves—it is clearly retarded when compared with that of other primates. Man produces absolutely and relatively the largest infant at birth of all primates, but the ossification of the bones of the hand lags far behind that of macaques and somewhat behind that of chimpanzees. At birth the human infant's brain is 25 per cent of its adult size, whereas the macaque's and the gibbon's brains at birth have already achieved 70 per cent of their adult size.

After birth, in man, the brain grows rapidly, the maximum growth period being the first three years of life. By the age of three the human brain is 75 per cent of its adult size. After that the brain "spurt" subsides, and further growth occurs at a rate equivalent to that of the rest of the body. In nonhuman primates similar "spurts" in body weight growth do occur, but they start earlier in the postnatal period and do not last so long. The retardation and prolongation of the brain-growth period in humans is a reflection of the complexity of the neuronal organization and connections in the adult.

It would seem that regressive evolution is achieved at a far more rapid pace than progressive evolution. One such example is the development of the human brain. While the earlier stages took tens of millions of years to evolve, its present form, with the enormously increased surface attained by way of the many folds and convolutions of the neocortex, took only a few hundred thousand years. It seems to be a law of nature that once a single successful specialization becomes well established, it tends to develop faster and faster, and sometimes of its own accord even beyond the limits of usefulness. Thus we see in man signs of evolutionary regression of the body in favor of absolutely extraordinary growth of the brain.

The absolute size of the human brain at birth, when it weighs an average of 350 grams, can be correlated with the fact that the human gestation period has not become extended in the same way as have all the other periods of his life. If the intrauterine period were to be prolonged by, say, three months, it would mean that the brain would weigh approximately 526 grams when born. But if that were to be the case the size of the infant's head would be too large for the birth canal. The gestation period is terminated in primates, including man, when the size of the head is compatible with a safe delivery.

It would seem that natural selection for increased pelvic dimensions in man would have been a way in which nature could have met this dilemma, but the pelvic dimensions are circumscribed by the demands of walking upright on two legs. So two evolutionary trends, the increased size of the brain and the adaptations of the pelvis for bipedalism, are at odds. As is

Regressive Evolution

the case with most adaptations, the solution has been a compromise.

We are able to judge the relative (as opposed to the absolute) growth of the brain in various primate species by establishing a ratio between the size of the palate and the volume of the brain. This has proved to be a more satisfactory index than brain volume. In doing this we find a progression from

> the gorilla where, for each sq. cm. of palate surface there are 5.8 cu. cm. of brain volume
> the adult male chimpanzee where, for each sq. cm. of palate surface there are 8.5 cu. cm. of brain volume
> the suckling male chimpanzee where, for each sq. cm. of palate surface there are 20 cu. cm. of brain volume
> the hominid (pre-man) where, for each sq. cm. of palate surface there are 30–38 cu. cm. of brain volume

to the eighth-month fetus of the chimpanzee, *as well as in modern grown man,* where this ratio is 60 cubic centimeters of brain volume for each square centimeter of palate surface.

Here we have the amazing fact that modern adult man's brain capacity relative to his palate surface area is identical with that of the chimpanzee fetus.

There is another point: While it does not necessarily have to happen that fetalization occurs wherever there is usually only one baby born at a time, yet it is only when such is the case that it is an advantage. Where several young are born at a time, in a litter, any retardations would be a drawback, and mutations promoting fetalization would not become established, for there is intense competition among the litter group within the womb for nourishment and oxygen, so that in that case rapid development is an advantage. Thus the fact that man normally produces one offspring at a time is a factor contributing to the possibility of his evolution by means of retardations.

There is only one feature that appears to go against this trend toward anatomical fetalization: the earlier onset of menstruation. One would expect, if childhood were being prolonged, that menstruation would commence at a later and later age. But, as we explained in the chapter on the sexual manifestations of infantilization, specific cultural practices have promoted the reverse. This is supported by the observation made by Margaret Mead that in contemporary primitive societies the onset of puberty remains stable at a later age.

Further evidence of man's close kinship to the apes was reported in December 1969 by A. C. Wilson and V. M. Sarich. On the basis of the fossil evidence, the evolutionary lines that have produced man, apes, monkeys, horses, and donkeys began to diverge from a common ancestor about seventy-five million years ago. At the time the divergence began all must have had about the same type of hemoglobin (the blood constituent that carries oxygen). The differences that are apparent today are considered an accurate reflection of the extent of evolutionary change.

Man and chimpanzee have hemoglobin structures in which the complete sequence of subunits is the same. There are about 300 of these subunits, called amino acids, in the hemoglobin molecule. This new report stated that there are no differences in sequence between normal human and chimpanzee hemoglobins; there are only two differences in sequence between man and gorilla, but twelve between monkey and man, and forty-three between horse and man.

The new analysis shows that man, apes, and monkeys are about equally distant from the horse and donkey. It also shows that man and the apes are no farther apart in this respect than horse and donkey—two species known to be able to produce living, although sterile, offspring when they interbreed.

Another consequence of this new evidence may be to place the time that the progenitors of mankind split off from those of the African great apes much later than had been thought —perhaps to only five million years ago. Most anthropologists have estimated that the time of divergence was as far back as thirty to thirty-five million years ago, which was about the time when man's ancestors became distinct from those of the old-world monkeys. In this case the evidence of the blood would support the view of the speedier evolution by neoteny than would have been possible by random mutation and selection.

An interesting sidelight to this is that the baboon, a terrestrial monkey, cannot hang from its arms as can man. This would tend to support the theory that man's ancestors descended from the trees later than did the baboon's, and also the idea of the rapid development of our species.

At this point it needs to be stated that while regressive evolution is responsible for the basic trends which have formed man into the creature he is, nevertheless the universal processes of natural selection determined by adaptation to prevailing circumstances go on all the time. This equally inexorable trend is considerably slower in its effects, and, in the case of man, less influential. But we do see its modifying action in some features. The most notable is probably the length of the legs in relation to the trunk. This apparently runs counter to the process of infantilization (paedomorphism) and is a change toward a more adult state (gerontomorphism). Besides this there are dual forces at work in the case of man's arms. His arm length has been reduced from that of his tree-living ancestors by a paedomorphic process, but in his individual development from child to man the ratio of his arm length to his body increases. This additional development tacked on at the end has been called anaboly by Sewertzow.

The evidence is powerful and convincing; many investigators have confirmed it. In many respects man is anatomically arrested at a fetal stage. We are forced to conclude that the series of anatomical arrests (fetalization) is a progressive and ongoing process which began with man's emergence as a separate species, and which not only continues right up to the present time, but will probably continue into the near and distant future.

We believe that paedomorphism arises whenever abnormal circumstances threaten the extinction of a species. This could be disease, unusual climatic changes, or the like. By this process a group of animals achieves a regeneration by shutting off its mature stage from the end of its development. In general the adult animal lives in a more complex environment than do its young. Therefore it would seem that the utilitarian value of paedomorphosis lies in permitting animals to recede from their customary mature habits to the ones of youthful life when survival is threatened, incidentally opening up new possibilities.

We further believe that this anatomical fetalization is intimately bound up with the prolongation of childhood in our species, and that all the manifestations we have described in this book, cultural and behavioral as well as anatomical, are in fact simply corollaries and additional expressions of it.

THE MECHANISM: HORMONES

Here again we have a language problem, in that apparently negative features become the means of promoting positive results.

One of the more outstanding, and at the same time surprising, characteristics of human development is that at each stage arrest, retardation, inhibition, interruption, delay, and timing are the principal tools which fashion the final forms. It is as though the hormones were possessed of intelligence and dictated to the organs just when is the most advantageous time (for the entire organism) for the organ to go into action.

Each one of these apparently negative features contributes to the uniqueness of man's body and behavior.

Everything which happens in the embryo and infant is geared not only to survival but also to preparation for the multitude of changes it must undergo to attain its mature form. For this purpose the most important regulator is the neuro-endocrine system which controls growth (increase in mass and height) and development (cell differentiation leading to specialized organs). However, when we use the words *regulator* and *controls* we have a mental image of orderliness, even spacing, and timing, but probably nothing in nature proceeds in such a way, and hormones are no exception.

The annual increase in the height typical of man is an example. It is produced by the interaction of hormones, of which some promote and some retard growth. From birth to the end of the first year the infant gains nine inches in height. This gain diminishes every year until in the year just prior to puberty, when the height gain amounts to less than two inches. At this stage the neuro-endocrine secretions reach a peak and there is a spurt in height of three to four inches. Then a gradual decline of the annual height increase follows until the epiphyses (the clefts in the long bones that allow for growth) close when full adult height has been reached.

Growth is an attribute of childhood. In this respect we find interesting data which tend to support the theory of infantilization. There has been an historically observable delay in the closure of the epiphyseal clefts allowing for a longer period of growth and the consequent increase in height of succeeding generations. Most of the suits of armor of medieval knights preserved in our museums would barely accommodate a husky twelve-year-old of today. It is an interesting sidelight that the beaver, the sea lions, and the cetaceans, also physically regressed animals, never stop growing. Although mature beavers are usually about three feet long and average thirty to seventy-five pounds in weight, in any case an unusually wide range, one record specimen weighed one hundred ten pounds. The epiphyses of the whales and sea lions *never fuse* with the shafts of their bones.

Like these animals, man also continues to grow even after he has matured sexually. His growth continues into the fourth decade of his life, so that from this point of view a man of forty is, at least physically, actually still adolescent. Most charts depicting growth simply stop at the age of seventeen or eighteen and do not go further, so that one has the notion that growth stops at this point, but this has been shown to be a misapprehension.

Garn and Wagner have published tables showing that stature increases until the age of thirty; muscle and skeletal mass increases through the fourth decade; and skeletal volume increases throughout life.

Tanner has established tables comparing the heights of children in the United States and Europe, and these show that children at the age of eleven in 1965 averaged nearly four inches taller than eleven-year-olds in 1905. Many physicians are made aware of this these days by anxious parents who think that their children are growing "too fast." Investigators cite a variety of reasons, such as nutrition, heredity, environment, socio-economic conditions, and psychological factors. Although it is true that these are probably contributing factors, we should not overlook the point that in some earlier periods, for example in ancient Greece, the upper classes at least had equally ample food of equal quality, if not better, because it was uncontaminated and not overprocessed—and the ancient Greeks were shorter than we. It is an axiom that once a successful evolutionary trend has become established, it will tend to continue. Environmental factors may accelerate or retard but will not stop it. The late Franz Boas, the famed Columbia University anthropologist who pioneered in measurement of human growth before the turn of the century, was the first to show the effect of the American physical and cultural environment on growth. He demonstrated a marked increase in stature of children of American immigrants over their parents' stature.

Paul K. Ito, amplifying Boas's studies, showed that environment and social influences can override genetic influences. He found that Japanese girls born and reared in California reached menarche an average of twenty months earlier than Japanese girls born in California but reared in Japan or those born and reared in Japan. He also noted that stature was influenced. Japanese women reared in the United States, whether born here or in Japan, reached a significantly greater mean stature than those reared in Japan.

Not only increase in dimensions, but also the timing of processes, occur at variable rates. Some youngsters, for no apparent reason, mature much later than the average, but nevertheless they become normal adults. Medically this condition is referred to as "delayed adolescence." Here too we have an historically observable and amply documented change. The average age at which the onset of menstruation occurs is earlier at a rate of one year in every thirty, as discussed in Chapter Eight.

In this context we have to include the slow pace of man's growth compared with other animals. A calf doubles its birth weight of about eighty pounds in forty-seven days. A horse doubles its birth weight, which is also about eighty pounds, in sixty days. Man doubles his birth weight (average seven pounds) in one hundred eighty days.

In nonhuman primates the temporary teeth are present at birth and continue their growth without interruption. Man, at birth, has no teeth. Following a rest period (another example of the retarding action of his hormones) of up to six months, he begins to grow his temporary teeth, which are not usually complete until the second year. There is then another rest period until the age of about six, when the permanent molars begin to break through.

The human ovary, which at birth measures seventeen by five millimeters, measures twenty by seven millimeters by the age of two. It reaches its adult size of twenty-seven by twelve millimeters at the age of five.

As we see, various parts of the human body come to full growth at widely different ages—height at twenty-one, teeth at about fourteen, ovaries at five, and other parts have equally varied ages at completion—yet, incredible as it may seem, like the work of a gifted composer who brings many themes together into a symphony, man's body achieves harmonious function eventually at adulthood.

All these facts point to the presence of highly efficient retarding agents, capable among other things of slowing the tempo of growth of the long bones. No other mammal has such protracted development, nor does any other mammal have a long life after the decline of sexuality.

Retarding agents are also at work with the ovary, which reaches its adult size at the age of five, but which is inhibited from functioning until the female reaches the age of sexual maturity at about thirteen.

Pregnancy, too, involves the retarding action of hormones. The placenta grows excrescences (called trophoblasts) which penetrate deeply into the maternal tissues. In its early stage this invasive growth is indistinguishable from cancer, yet at some specific point an inhibitory signal stops further invasion and the placenta then behaves in the same way as any other normal organ and respects its borders. Page and Tominaga discovered that the trophoblasts have an inherent quality of migrating toward sources of oxygen. They demonstrated this in a culture medium.

In the course of evolution, the early mammals had to cope with the problem that they could not prolong pregnancy much beyond the duration of one estrus cycle. Marsupials (kangaroos, wombats, etc.) abort an undeveloped fetus about twenty to thirty millimeters in length. The mother animal clears a trail from the birth canal to her pouch by smoothing down the hair with her saliva-moistened tongue. The fetus remains in the pouch for seven to eight months. As mammals climb higher on the evolutionary ladder, the placenta remains functioning for the full length of pregnancy. This can take place only through the agency of another retarding factor—the hormone progesterone, which is the key in preventing early expulsion of the embryo. Women who have had the experience of miscarriages will be familiar with this hormone, as it is frequently prescribed by their physicians to aid them in retaining their babies within the womb to full term.

Kovacs presented evidence that human pregnancy should last twenty-one months. At about one year plus the nine months of intrauterine life, the human infant reaches the same maturity as other mammals have reached by the time of their birth. This applies to all phases of development, such as the regulation of body temperature, coordination of muscles, ability to digest food, conversion of cartilage into bone, enzyme development, and so on. This makes the human infant at least one year premature at birth, and therefore maternal care of an unusually high order must be given to allow for the survival of this fragile offspring. On the other hand, it is not possible for structural reasons for the pregnancy to continue far beyond the allotted nine months, because the growing head of the fetus even at this stage barely accommodates itself in the narrow passage of the birth canal. One adaptive change has occurred, though. Whereas the anthropoid apes show no distinction in shape and size between the male and the female pelvis, in humans the female pelvis shows a greater dimension than the male.

E. W. Page has stated that some women habitually give birth postmaturely and deliver twelve-pound newborns. If one were to preserve this genetic line by means of Caesarean sections repeated over several generations, one would ultimately breed a variant species of man with a longer gestation period. During the pregnancy of the human female there has to be an harmonious interdependence among uterus, placenta, and endocrine glands, so that birth will take place at the last possible moment before the fetal head becomes too large to pass through the bony structure of the birth canal. Grosser, in 1933, realized that the evolutionary design of the placenta may have reached a dead end. He wrote:

No doubt the human type of placentation is to be considered as a product of evolution and even as the terminal production of a phylogenetic line, not to be continued or even to be surpassed. But such extremes have always been ... dangerous to their bearers. ... In geologic times, many species have become extinct, and always they were the highest and mightiest existing. Always some organ or organ system developed in an excessive way. Rather than adaptation, one must admit orthogenesis—the inherent tendency of organisms to persevere along a line of development that the species has entered upon. ... In man, orthogenesis has led to the development of two very highly specialized organs, the brain and the placenta. One or the other will ultimately lead to the extinction of man.

The ability of the body to thrive in unfavorable environmental conditions, resist infections, neutralize external and internal poisons, and repair injuries and regenerate harmed tissues to normal functioning is mediated by an interplay between the various supporting and inhibiting activities of the endocrine glands. Whenever normal endocrine function is disturbed, as it sometimes is by, for instance, infection or cancer, the suppressing element often fails to operate. *When this happens, the retarding factors being removed, the human organism proceeds through the same further stages as its anthropoid ancestors did and we see the emergence of features similar to theirs.*

A tumor of the pituitary gland in an adult leads to the appearance of facial features somewhat resembling those of the apes. Since the growth of the long bones has already stopped, these are not affected, but the effect of the increased production of growth hormone from the pituitary tumor has its effect on the skull, which has open sutures until the fourth decade of life, and also on the soft tissues. One sees the emergence of features for which humans have the inherent potential, but which in present normal circumstances are suppressed. These are heavy eyebrow ridges, a pronounced underslung jaw, thickened nose and lips, and spadelike hands. This condition is referred to medically as acromegaly.

If the victim of the pituitary tumor is a young person whose epiphyseal clefts are still open, he will continue growing and become a seven- to eight-foot giant. In such cases of pituitary gigantism it has been observed that the sexual organs are usually subnormal. This is not surprising, since normally developed sexual glands would act as inhibitors and counteract the effects of the tumor.

Disturbances of other endocrine glands, either interfering with their capacity to retard biological processes or causing the discharge of excessive quantities of hormones, may result in any of the following abnormalities:

1. Excessive hairiness. In this case the propensity of the hormones to promote fetalization by retarding development at the fetal, hairless stage, and prevent growth of a pelt, is reduced, enabling the potential of the species toward a pelt to develop.

2. Small head. This is due to a lack of the hormone which prevents too early closing of the cranial sutures. The condition is called microcephaly.

3. Precociously developed sex organs. The normal delay for sexual maturation does not take place. In the well-known experiment, when tadpoles are fed thyroid hormones which remove the inhibition of the sexual maturation of the larval forms, the result is the appearance of miniature frogs.

A similar phenomenon is the diapause in insects. This refers to the state of suspended animation which permits insects to survive extremes of low temperature during the winter. One aspect of the property which puzzled observers is the fact that it emerges not when cold weather appears, but when warm summer days and favorable environmental conditions are still prevailing.

Beck devised a series of ingenious experiments in which he altered the length of their day while maintaining a constant temperature for certain insects. By varying their exposure to light it became quite evident that these insects ready themselves for the state of diapause not because of a drop in temperature but primarily in response to the shortening of daylight hours. The duration of daylight, more commonly referred to as photoperiods, could not in itself initiate such changes were it not for the presence of a hypothesized biological timeclock.

In 1933 Makita Kogure of Kyushu University demonstrated that silkworms kept in darkness or on a limited number of artificial daylight hours grew into moths the eggs of which developed into silkworms without interruption of the growth cycle and with no intervening diapause. But when the larvae were kept under prolonged photoperiods the adult moths produced eggs that went into diapause exactly as in nature.

Experiments carried out at Nagoya City University, Japan, revealed that a hormone produced by a nerve ganglion in the female silkworm larva is responsible for the interaction with variable light exposure. Without the presence of this hormone proper preparation for survival during the winter would be impossible.

Wigglesworth of Cambridge University and Williams of Harvard discovered a hormone, subsequently labeled ecdysone, secreted by glands in the insects' thoracic tissue, which influences growth. Insects in the diapause do not produce ecdysone, but if they are injected with it they resume normal growth almost immediately.

This hormone, produced by larvae, delays maturation. When the hormone is stopped after such a delayed maturation, the larva becomes a giant insect. It is interesting that the early underfeeding of rats also delays maturation, and that if they are fed suitably later, they live twice as long as those fed well all the time.

From these experiments it will be seen that in insects too there is a retarding hormone, which was discovered through its sensitivity to light. At an appropriate moment in the course of the year this inhibition is arrested and growth then takes place.

We commonly attribute to hormones the ability to promote a specific action which brings about a positive change in the body. As we have seen, however, there are hormonal substances which have the ability of either *retarding* the time at which another hormone begins to exert its influence, or *releasing* other hormones which have been held back, so to speak, in storage.

The failure to release one hormone while others continue to be released is probably the most important mechanism in the process of fetalization. In this way it is possible for new species to emerge after comparatively few generations.

For this reason it is important to highlight some of the attributes of the hormones.

The earliest forms of life had their own primitive chemical regulatory agency that facilitated their growth and metabolism. Hormones, produced by our endocrine glands, are direct descendants of these. Hormones possess an unusual potency. Adrenalin affects organs in a concentration as low as one part in five hundred million; one ounce of thyroid extract satisfies the needs of a human being for a lifetime. They promote complex changes in cellular composition through their presence in the tissues. There is a parallel in the inanimate world, in which an inert substance such as platinum brings about a mixing of molecules which otherwise would not combine. A drop of blood put into a beaker filled with hydrogen peroxide causes an immediate eruption into a fizzing liquid (by inducing each molecule to give up one atom of oxygen). In a similar way hormones initiate myriads of transformations within an organism that lead to the conversion of food into energy and building blocks for the body. The hormones of even the most advanced animals have retained their original configuration. Their primitive nature makes them nonspecific to any single species. Insulin produced by a cow is perfectly effective in man.

Since hormones are discharged directly into the bloodstream, they are effective without the intervention of the nervous system. This is important in the development of any fetus, for the nervous elements do not develop until the end of gestation. In man myelination (the growth of the sheath of the nerve through which its nutrition is supplied) is not completed until the end of the sixth month of life. Hormones float freely throughout the bloodstream of the entire body and ultimately reach their target organs by means of a special affinity. While all parts of the body are regulated by hormones, their most significant influence is in the areas of growth, reproduction, behavior, and energy requirements. The nervous system and the endocrine glands work in tandem to exercise a modulating effect on the functions of the body's organs. The nervous system is responsible for rapid reactions and the endocrine glands for slow and sustained effects. The two systems overlap considerably in their spheres of influence, and modify each other.

There is also the little-known fact that the nervous system itself also secretes hormonal substances. Two types are known: (1) Transmitter substances, which are brief-acting over a short range (acetylcholine and noradrenaline) and (2) Neurosecretory hormones, which act over greater distances and have a prolonged effect. These activate the anterior-pituitary gland in turn to produce hormones that then connect with the target organs. This is the end of a chain of signals which often starts in the brain. There is one exception, the antidiuretic hormone which acts directly on the kidneys, bypassing the anterior-pituitary, to retard loss of water.

When civilized man is in a situation of stress, he rarely reacts by fleeing or fighting. Instead he controls (inhibits) the instinctual muscle responses. In the earlier primates, instinctual responses, which comprise muscular, visceral, and hormonal actions, are well coordinated. In civilized man they are disrupted. Social demands made upon him permit only a narrow range of responses, making it necessary to suppress many instinctual muscular reflexes. Many social stimuli are interpreted by his body in terms that are no longer applicable to modern environment. Anticipated disapproval by a superior may, in a particular individual, provoke responses which duplicate those of an early primate confronted with a threat to its life. Methods of upbringing profoundly modify the neuro-endocrine mechanism. While one family urges its children to avoid any physical violence, another encourages its children to stand their ground and fight an opponent. It is easy to see that the children from these two homes will mobilize different neuro-hormonal patterns when facing a bully.

Man reacts not only to actual danger, but also to symbolic representations of threats to his existence, and he reacts to both in a similar way.

Measurable changes in endocrine function (for example, the presence of catecholamines in the urine) accompany emotional states, so that one actually has a concrete gauge of what is thought of as a nonphysical reaction, such as a feeling or sensation or emotion.

Emotional stress modifies neuro-endocrine discharges. For instance, children raised in troubled homes show a stunted growth pattern as compared with children from the same socio-cultural background and receiving the same nutrition but raised with love and affection. As soon as the troubled children are transferred to a more favorable environment they resume their normal growth pattern.

If an animal's behavioral responses are persistently and significantly different from those of its fellows, these different responses will alter the hormonal pattern of its growth and reproduction from the pattern usual for the species. This can happen when a branched-off group is confronted with new environmental conditions. It will ultimately also modify the appearance and reactions of these animals, and thus prepare the ground for the development of a new species.

A portion of the midbrain called the hypothalamic region is probably the most important mediator between the nervous system and the endocrine organs. A great deal of research on this area is in progress. Investigators have found that some nerve cells secrete hormonal substances which act as a series of "releasing agents." These hormones move to the posterior part of the pituitary gland, where they are stored. At appropriate times they induce the anterior part of the pituitary to produce several other hormones (these are corticotrophin, acting on the adrenals; luteinizing and follicle stimulating hormones acting alternatingly on the ovaries; thyrotropin stimulating the thyroid; a growth hormone; and melanocyte hormones, producing pigmentation).

We have gone into such details of some of the functions of hormones because they play a major part as the mechanism by which the processes described in this book, and which constitute its thesis, are carried out. Either failure to produce the hormones' releasing factors or a change in their timing mechanism may contribute to a very large extent to the development of man as a species by retarding some areas of his growth and retaining some fetal features of his primate ancestors.

The midbrain (hypothalamic) region is, like the rest of the brain, richly supplied with blood, and therefore it too is very vulnerable to blood-borne virus infections affecting the nervous system. We shall show in the next part of this chapter that virus epidemics afflicting our early forerunners may well have been the chief determining factor in bringing about conditions inducing hormonal changes that resulted in the formation of a new branch—Homo sapiens—by a process of regressive evolution.

Diseases affecting the other endocrine organs are of less importance from an evolutionary point of view, but nevertheless have some influence.

A deficiency of thyroid causes a slowing of growth and development; the conversion of cartilage into bone in the formation of the skeleton is delayed; sex organs remain small and fail to reach functional capacity; teeth are late in appearing. In Addison's disease, which is an affliction of the adrenal glands, there is a re-emergence of normally suppressed pigmentation, darkening the skin of the mucous membranes.

An increase in the size in the outer layers (hypertrophy of the cortex) of the adrenal gland leads to precocious sexual development. In females with this condition there is also an accentuation of masculine features, such as increased muscular development, deepening of the voice, luxuriant growth of body hair, and increased size of external genitalia. When this condition befalls prepubertal boys, their secondary sexual characteristics become accentuated while the testes remain immature. Because of their unusual physique they are sometimes referred to as "Infant Hercules."

The adrenal glands and the precursors of the sex glands begin their growth very close together in the human embryo, and they continue as a functional unit into later life. The adrenals play an important role in the earliest stages of growth; in fact, in the third month of fetal life they are the most conspicuous organs in the body cavity. At birth their size is about one-third that of the kidney, but in the adult they form a small cap on the top of the kidney.

An increase in the size of the testes of a prepubertal boy leads to sexual precocity and to the premature appearance of the permanent teeth. On the other hand castration before puberty leads to a eunuchism characterized by excessive growth.

Removal of the pineal gland accelerates sexual development while depressing growth.

Removal of the thymus gland causes a stunting of growth. When an extract of thymus gland is fed to tadpoles, we see a delay in metamorphosis leading to overgrowth in the larval stage.

It will be readily seen that the retarding action of hormones, either by delaying the release of growth hormones or by neutralizing them for a certain amount of time, is one of the major contributions to an evolutionary branching off of species. Any interruption of development from the embryo to the fully grown animal opens the door to the emergence of a new branch. Variations in the timing of these interruptions can also offer sufficient differences of features to produce a large number of subspecies. Among many subspecies there is a chance that the most viable forms will survive in the end. *This mechanism allows for bypassing the necessity to assume an astronomical number of mutations and eons of time to arrive at a new species.*

THE CAUSE: THE VIRUS: DEUS EX MACHINA

It appears that all the forms of life we know today have arisen gradually from simpler ones. The evidence for this, on the basis of fossil remains and biological findings, is overwhelming. Yet to make such a statement tells us nothing about the causes which bring this process about. Neither fossils nor living forms can tell us anything of the mysterious forces which induce the transitions from one stage to another. Nor do we have evidence of what was and is the motivating factor that impels these modifications into ever more complex, rather than into simpler, structures.

The hummingbird, with its whirring wings and the lightness of its body, seems to have found the ideal framework for hovering over the nectar of flowers. A modern engineer, commissioned to design a helicopter, can find no better solutions. The shape and proportions of the whale's body afford it a perfect vehicle for rapid movement at great depths in its aquatic environment, and the builder of a submarine has no choice but to follow similar principles of marine design. There is an apparent symmetry between all creatures and their immediate surroundings. Every minute detail of their bodies seems to be especially constructed so as to fit like a key into the lock of their environment.

Darwin believed that nature determined the form and function of the species. Just as two sharp-edged rocks placed in a tumbler and shaken long enough will become smooth through their interaction, so will environment influence the animal and, to a lesser extent, the animal its environment (man, of course, being the exception in that nowadays he influences his environment more than he is influenced by it). Darwin explained the progressive development of species in terms of natural events, or processes, that go on all the time. He first published his theory on the origin of species in 1859. He had been familiar with the work of animal breeders, whose goals were set by the preferences of their clients, and he observed that these breeders were able to modify any species to any desired forms by selective mating. Pigeon fanciers were numerous in England at the time, and their hobby produced more than one hundred fifty varieties of the bird. Some of them were so different from the others that they could have been mistaken for separate species; yet they had all stemmed from a common ancestor, the wild rock pigeon. Darwin came to the conclusion that for changes to take place there had to be *variability* in the traits of the progeny of the breeding pair, the *ability to inherit* these variations, and a conscious end in the mind of the breeder to guide his *selections*.

In this setting Darwin was able to observe how a species could subdivide into varieties capable of forming new lines. In contrast to the artificially imposed selection, Darwin sought an elucidation of the theme underlying nature's selections. He was aware that all life forms produce more progeny than necessary to maintain their species. For example, it has been estimated that less than one acorn in every hundred that fall from the parent tree lives to grow into another oak. More than 99 per cent of all acorns provide a staple in the diet of weevils and squirrels, nests for the eggs of white moths and eventually food for their larvae, shelter for wasps and centipedes, the debris eventually enriching the humus of the soil and so only indirectly contributing to the growth of the trees. Darwin considered this superabundance of life a tool of nature to ensure the survival of a few. Only by struggling for survival could these few stay ahead to become the parents of a new generation. By this means only the fittest perpetuated their kind, and the fittest were necessarily those which happened to possess the most favorable adaptation. On the whole, Darwin believed, the weaker tended to be killed off or to die out before they reached their breeding period. Many experiments in recent years, both in the cultivation of plants and the breeding of domestic animals, have tended to confirm the strength of this assumption. However, although natural selection can be seen as a factor in some instances, we do not know to what extent this method applies in the whole of evolution. Even Darwin did not believe that his theory covered all the forces at work.

An earlier naturalist, Lamarck, believed that animals themselves exercised volitional control over the direction of their evolution. The determining factor was the usefulness of an adaptation. He thought that if a species found the modification of any organ to be an advantage, it would be modified. Bernard Shaw, who held strong views on most matters, supported the Lamarck view in this controversy. (As a professional Irishman, of course, he would naturally have felt obliged to oppose the Englishman Darwin, especially when the protagonist of the other side of the argument was not English!) Shaw expressed Lamarck's idea graphically when he wrote: "If you like eating the tender tops of trees enough to make you concentrate all your energies on the stretching of your neck, you will get a long neck, like a giraffe."

As against Darwin's concept of the survival of the fittest, Lamarck had earlier proposed that the use or disuse of organs was the reason for their growth or atrophy, and in consequence was the guiding factor in the direction of evolution. He thought that such changes acquired during the course of an individual life could be transmitted to progeny. This was the heart of his theory of evolution by the inheritance of acquired characteristics.

Shaw notwithstanding, most scientists today dispute the possibility of this contention, although a case may sometimes be made in single instances as, for example, when a cave-dwelling animal gradually loses the use of its eyes. Darwin's theory of natural selection, on the other hand, still seems to offer a more satisfactory explanation in the light of present knowledge, but we are not sure how far-reaching a force it is. Does it perhaps only accentuate or diminish another process which is going on in any case, as the waves above a strong undertow give the illusion of being the ocean's sole movement? To this day there is no satisfactory explanation of the nature of evolution's undertow.

This brings us to the bedrock of our thesis. There is one agent in nature that could conceivably be part of both the surface wave and the subsurface undertow of evolution: the virus.

We speak of mutations as the factor which promotes evolution. But mutations cannot arise without an agent to provoke them. One could visualize that from time to time solar flares

Regressive Evolution

might have generated particularly powerful radiation which could possibly have contributed to changes in the genes. There might also be other cosmic or terrestrial influences of which we are not yet aware. Is it not much more likely, however, that invasion of the body cells by the ubiquitous virus, a factor that has been present as long as life itself, has been the most important triggering agent? Viruses obviously may limit the population through disease but, more importantly, they affect the gene pool. Among those animals that survive a viral epidemic it is inevitable that some will be left with a permanent alteration of their chromosomes, which would then be transmitted to following generations.

We believe that if there is an intelligent principle guiding evolution then the microorganisms which cause gene mutation are its servants.

To explain the nature of the virus we have to go back all the way to the time organic chemicals first formed into chains which became the precursors of life. In this twilight zone between animate and inanimate matter some particles, because of the chemical properties of their constituents, combined with others to form particles which were then capable of self-duplication. These particles still exist in two forms, as genes and as viruses. The distinction between them is far from clear. At present there are three theories as to what viruses are. One suggests that they have evolved from very simple cells by adopting extreme parasitism. Another is that the viruses are indeed parasites, but that they have evolved only from the large-molecule stage. The third theory, the only one that has any experimental support, is that they may be parts of the cell's genetic elements which have escaped. Some scientists refer to viruses as free-floating genes. They contend that the viruses arose originally from cell chromosomes with the predestined aim of changing cells, by genetic recombination, in the manner most desirable for evolution. The gene is described as "a hereditary determinant which, in its alternative forms, is responsible for differences in a particular trait." Of course, flexibility and generality are necessary in writing of this field of investigation, in the face of rapid advances which are being made. But one thing is certain, that viruses can provoke mutations in genes just as they are able to incorporate other chemical combinations into their own structure and thus mutate themselves.

In essence both genes and viruses bear in their chemical structure an extreme condensation of information. The hereditary material carried in the genes of germinal cells leads to the formation of a new animal or plant in the pattern of its species. For the free-floating virus this possibility is aborted, since the condensed information has no place to go unless it invades a living cell. When it does this, it recruits the chemical material it needs to multiply itself from the host cell. Sometimes the virus may coexist within the host cell, causing little or no damage, but at others it may lead to the death of the cell. It is in this coexistence between virus and cell that the wellspring of mutation may be found.

What exactly do we know about viruses?

The Russian biologist D. Ivanovsky searched for the cause of the mosaic disease which afflicts tobacco leaves. In the course of his research, in 1892, he crushed the leaves of an infected plant and passed them through a filter fine enough to retain bacteria. The filtrate which resulted was capable of infecting other tobacco plants, indicating that whatever the infecting agent might be, it was of smaller size than bacteria. Subsequently other diseases, such as the hoof-and-mouth disease of cattle, were discovered also to be caused by a "filterable" agent. It was not until 1935 that W. M. Stanley, in the

United States, isolated and purified the tobacco mosaic virus. It appeared to be a living entity consisting of particles; yet these could also be crystallized as if they were inorganic matter. Later biologists discovered that a virus is a large complex molecule containing a protein and a nucleic acid. (When we use the term *large* it may assist the imagination to remember that a bacterium can have a virus infection.) It is probably a concourse of atoms halfway between an inanimate molecule and the most primitive living organism. It stands, so to speak, on the frontiers of life.

Although the virus can be crystallized like a chemical, it does possess many biological properties. Outside the host cell its appearance for all practical purposes is like that of any nonliving protein molecule. Once it has found its way into a cell, though, it becomes a living entity. Unlike other living organisms, it does not grow or divide; it simply multiplies into identical particles at the expense of its host, leading to what we call a virus disease.

Viruses are dispersed and spread by direct contact, through food and water, or by carriers such as ticks, flies, and mosquitoes. Some viruses, such as those that are carried by insects to plants, multiply both in the cells of the carrier and in those of the infected plant. They make no distinction between plant and animal life and are able to use the material of the cells of either equally well, pointing to the essential oneness of all life.

The virus begins its invasion by attaching itself to the wall of the host cell. It injects its strands of nucleic acid through the wall while its protein coat remains outside. This nucleic acid (DNA) attracts to itself its chemical counterpart from within the cell, causing a rapid multiplication of newly formed viruses. Sometimes the virus remains dormant, but if it does multiply the host cell eventually splits open and releases the newly synthesized viruses which are now ready to invade other cells. The reproduction of the virus is under the sole direction of the nucleic acid—the protein plays no part in heredity. The invading virus uses the available nucleotides and proteins of the host to build new viruses, so that the host cell becomes depleted and eventually dies.

The composition of the tobacco mosaic virus was the first to be deduced from X-rays and electron microscope studies. Some two thousand identical protein molecules form a symmetrical coil in the shape of a cylinder, in the center of which is embedded a single strand of RNA composed of six thousand molecules.

Whether one considers viruses animate or inanimate matter depends upon how one defines life. Viruses do not respond to stimuli and do not convert food into energy as is the case with all entities we customarily consider "living"; on the other hand, they have genetic properties and can mutate. We probably have to think of them as intermediary forms halfway between inert matter and life.

Viruses are ubiquitous and can infect all existing living things, probably with no exception. They are not always damaging: the encephalitic virus which is deadly to humans is harmless to fowl, and many disease-producing viruses multiply harmlessly in their insect carriers. Of special interest to us in connection with our theory are the viruses which affect the nervous system. Certain of these, such as herpes simplex, measles, and rabies, prefer to invade the limbic system of the brain. The consequence of either acute or subacute inflammation of the brain tissue of this region is a severe behavioral disturbance, manifested chiefly by loss of energy and apathy. Besides this, the unique metabolic requirements of the limbic system—a greater need for oxygen and sugar—render it especially susceptible to those diseases which affect the brain.

The limbic system governs the critical relationship between behavior and memory; it is necessary for the use of stored information in respect to planned, or any goal-directed, activity. The resulting malfunction would have a profound effect upon arboreal primates, as we have previously indicated.

Periodic outbreaks of viral infections of the brain in various parts of the world caused by the common viral illnesses of childhood now produce the greatest number of psychiatric illnesses. Most patients with viral encephalitides, particularly those that are insect-borne, display mental symptoms early in, during, or after the acute phase of the illness. Vague personality disturbance with irritability, weakness, and even mild confusion may herald the onset of viral disease, preceding fever, headache, and other symptoms by a few days.

An epidemic of St. Louis encephalitis in Florida in 1962 afflicted many people. Emotional complaints typical of neurasthenia were reported as being the most common sequels of the epidemic regardless of the age of the victim or the severity of the case. Many of these patients remained disabled for months after the illness had subsided.

Continued reports from Japan indicate that encephalitis japonica in childhood produces intellectual impairment as well as serious behavioral disturbances.

Those viruses which primarily affect the skin and cause herpes simplex and herpes zoster can also produce encephalitis or meningitis. In mild cases, particularly during the stage just before the actual onset of the illness, the patient's diffuse complaints of nervousness, coupled with the impact of his irritability on his family and friends, have been known to lead to a mistaken diagnosis of neurosis. Many patients with herpes zoster show signs of general nervousness, lack of stamina, insomnia, and a whining crabbiness for one or two months after the skin lesions have healed.

A graphic description of ravages caused by the influenza virus on a primitive community was given by the Australian External Territories Minister in his report on an outbreak in New Guinea. When the disease struck the highly susceptible population of the inland regions of New Guinea, the Australian authorities found themselves battling the gravest medical emergency in the area's history. The death toll was close to two thousand as counted in hospitals, which might reflect as many as six to seven thousand actual deaths, either from the influenza itself or from the consequent pneumonia. It is believed that the epidemic affected more than 1.75 million of the territory's 2.25 million people. The public health director for New Guinea and Papua estimated that cases occurred in nine-tenths of the whole area. An epidemiologist at the Sydney University school of tropical medicine pointed out that a recent Hongkong flu epidemic in Australia produced only mild illness in some 15 per cent of Sydney's population. But because the people of the inland regions of New Guinea have such low resistance, the epidemic there was expected to have a severe effect on 95 per cent of the population in some areas. "These people will find it very difficult just to carry on with their day-to-day lives," he commented. The population affected was one of mountain tribesmen, described as latter-day Stone-Agers. Whole villages were affected and were unable either to help themselves or to seek outside assistance. Many died within twenty-four hours; the mortality rate during the outbreak was ten times the territory's normal death rate. Although this epidemic occurred among a very primitive people, they did have the Australian authorities to help them in some way to fight it. They received help from doctors, shipments of vaccine, and hospital care whenever possible. One may imagine the effect of the disease on such a population in times when there was no outside help during an outbreak.

Other viruses, such as those which cause encephalitis, poliomyelitis, or rabies, also cause brain damage, and as a consequence the animals afflicted with them frequently show disturbed behavior, affecting their adaptive capacity.

An example, as we mentioned in the chapter on the evolution of intelligence, could well have been the arboreal monkeys. They were perfectly well adapted to live in the trees. They had plenty of food and their skills and physiques were ideally suited to all kinds of movement in the branches. There was no reason for them to descend from the trees. Why should any of them have taken so drastic a course as to leave the familiarity, convenience, and comfort of their normal habitat to start out on doubtful and adventurous lives in unknown and untried territory?

We can only find an answer if we try to imagine what would happen if an epidemic of poliomyelitis or encephalitis struck a colony of arboreal primates. Unquestionably many of them would die. The few survivors would either lose their motor skills or be partially paralyzed as a result of the brain damage. For these there would be no other way but to leave the trees and attempt to adjust themselves to new modes of life. It may be a distressing thought, but these sickly primates were surely forerunners of man.

How do we envisage the many changes that took place as these brain-damaged apes were forced to descend from their tree homes? There is the matter of communication. It is extremely important for the young primate to be able to call its mother when in distress. With minor modifications these sounds can express the need for food, for proximity to the mother's body at nightfall, or they can be used to call the mother's attention to something that has aroused the baby's curiosity. Once they were living on the ground, the primates who could no longer use their native dexterity fostered in the branches

—visualize a victim of poliomyelitis—had to face the dangers of their new environment with a helplessness similar to that they had experienced as infants. One can well imagine that in such circumstances they would tend to regress to the habits of their infancy (as do victims of advanced cases of schizophrenia, which may be observed in any mental hospital today) and use similar sounds to communicate their needs and warnings. This method must have become a matter of life and death because of the double handicap—that of having been weakened by disease at the same time as living in an environment to which they were insufficiently adapted. Since such communication became necessary to their survival, these baby sounds had to be structurally reinforced until the vocal chords in succeeding generations became sufficiently modified to express a greater variety of signals. This in turn would have stimulated the expansion of certain regions of the brain, which would then have become the centers of speech. Such a sequence is not necessarily the sole origin of speech, since in very many species there is a mating language, a defense-of-territory signal, and there are hunting cries, and so on—but it was probably one of the more important contributing elements.

In this particular respect it is of interest that another regressed species, the dolphins and whales, have also developed a very sophisticated system of communication comparable to language, and those people who have kept otters as pets assert that the otters have a language which it is possible for humans to learn to understand. Scientific observers have also reported that badgers are able to make themselves plainly understood to men by their sounds, so that it would seem that the development of speech, along with a predilection to playfulness, are as much attributes of regressed species as the disproportionate growth of brain capacity and intelligence.

As the sickly primates attempted to survive in an unaccustomed and unfriendly locale they, as do any animals in situations of severe stress, regressed to a more primitive manner of adjustment. In other words they reverted to the behavior of their infancy. Those of them who could would have overcompensated by using the budding neocortex, and the exploratory curiosity natural to infants would improve their chances for making their way in the new surroundings. This new type of behavior, quite deviant from that practiced by their ancestors, became the guiding principle for subsequent evolutionary changes. The tendency was not only toward regression, but also to convert the regressive features into new mechanisms which would be beneficial to the newly emerging species. And, as we have noted, once a successful trend in evolution establishes itself, it continues its course. Thus regression, once it became established, took its inexorable course from the adult primate to the young infant and, in modern times, to the last stage of fetal development.

That playfulness is a marked feature of regressive patterns of behavior would also have had its consequences for the race. One of a primate litter might pick up a stick to push a crawling worm; another might drop a banana peel so that it falls on the head of a litter-mate on a lower branch. In the ground-dwelling primate the stick will become the instrument that will reach into termite hills to pull out insects for food or to help dig up roots, and eventually a long bone of a grazing animal replaces the stick, until a sharp flint is found and takes the place of the bone; similarly the playful aiming of the banana peel may lead to the throwing of stones to bring down fruit now out of reach, to kill animals for food, or to chase predatory beasts away. Upon awakening in his lair he would find the implements he had discarded the night before and remember their use. At one of these moments the thought would dawn on him that he would like to keep the stick to use again.

In this way he would make the transition from a creature living only in the present to one with the will and capacity to make provision for the future.

The combination of the increasing number of verbal signals, tools, and the playful manipulation of objects acts as a stimulant to the neocortex, subjecting it to continuous modification. Once the trend toward infancy and beyond that to the fetal stage was firmly established, any future viral diseases promoting mutations and consequent overcompensatory changes could proceed only in the direction already successfully determined.

As the ground-dwellers began to form new habits they would have appeared strange and different to the more mature tree-dwellers who had had no cause to regress. It would have been as if an adult animal were to observe a cub's games. He would be able to participate, but his mind would be on the more serious pursuits appropriate to his age and ways of life. This diversity would have had its most profound influence in the separation of the groups at their mating times. As the subspecies began to act more and more differently from the original line, they would cease to be sexually attracted to each other. As this isolation continued from generation to generation the new traits would become anchored in the gene pool. Before long we should find two apparently separate species, occupying the same territory, yet having very few features in common.

Every information-processing factor from the sensory organ to the neural centers becomes subject to modification by the innate utilitarian value of the nervous system in terms of survival. One cannot emphasize strongly enough the extent to which behavior becomes the guiding principle in separating new species from their ancestors. Mayr explained in his *Animal Species and Evolution:* "If we were to place the various isolating mechanisms of animals according to their importance, we should have to place behavioral isolation far ahead of all the others. A shift into a new niche or adaptive zone is, almost without exception, initiated by a change in behavior. Where a new habit develops, structural reinforcements follow sooner or later."

If we imagine a scientist from another world observing these two groups of the arboreal primate colony many years after such a viral epidemic, he would see significant differences in the behavior of the grounded members as contrasted with their tree-dwelling peers. The adult ground-dwellers would have more features in common with the *litters* of the tree-dwellers than with their contemporary adults. As this infantile behavior began to yield useful adaptations, our scientist would come to the conclusion that regression to an earlier stage in an animal's life could contribute to survival. Furthermore, if he were to extrapolate the gain in skills achieved by this method, he would then be able to predict the emergence of intelligent life.

But let us assume that this scientist was ignorant of the viral epidemic that had taken place many years prior to his visit. He would notice a gap, expressed only in behavior, between these two groups. If he had the same type of training as a modern anthropologist he would look for the missing link: namely, some individuals which were both arboreal and ground-dwelling. Not finding any, he would conclude that they must have died out, probably because they were evolutionary failures. On the other hand, if our scientist had witnessed the epidemic and its consequences, the transition from life in the trees to life on the ground would appear to him an uninterrupted sequence.

Many generations later the gap widens, and eventually the protohominid would appear on the scene. If the scientist were a permanent and long-living observer of animate existence on earth shortly prior to the appearance of intelligent life, he would note that there were long periods of time in which the ground-dwelling forerunner of man lived in equilibrium with its environment. Its habits remained unchanged throughout the duration of this span, creating the impression for the scientist that this must be the end of the line so far as this species was concerned. Then another virus epidemic would ravage the colony. Again, the surviving few are paralyzed and only able to sustain life for a little longer than those who succumbed to the disease on account of their inability to forage for food. But also again a very few, although handicapped, manage to hold on to a precarious life. Under the stress of not being able to meet the exigencies of existence with their disease-imposed handicaps they too, as their ancestors had, regressed to patterns characteristic of their youth and infancy. However, now that their adult patterns are on a level with the childhood habits of the nonregressed arboreal members of the species, their new regression will carry them toward a stage equivalent with the fetal development of that branch of their biological family, and of their own distant forebears. Once more, then, only the very few had had the ability to utilize the capacity of the neocortex to expand childhood characteristics into adult patterns suitable for survival. Our scientist would note another gap, and then another, until he reached historic times. Here he would see the frequent disappearance of populations in a veritable flood of epidemics lasting from earliest antiquity through the Middle Ages and right on into modern times when once more a new subspecies—modern technological man—made its appearance. He, too, is the outcome of regressive behavior. His playful, childlike pursuits have become the predominant feature of his life. And in modern man in the latter half of the twentieth century, we are witnessing another change. Owing to improved medical care and better nutrition many children have survived, and will live to breed, who would have perished as a result of viral diseases in previous generations. In our own lifetimes we see large numbers of children surviving childhood illnesses who would never have been able to live out their normal life spans had they been born in the days of our own childhood. They begin to form the nucleus of yet a new subspecies, regressing still another notch toward fetalization. Perhaps the appearance of deviant societies like those of the beatniks, the hippies, the flower children, and many others of these types all over the earth would prove to that patient scientist from another world that the process of regression continues unabated. He might also notice that regression does not proceed uniformly. Some of the human subspecies have lost their melanin pigment entirely while others are only in the process of doing so. But he would observe that all of them appear to move in the same direction. Only the pace differs. Those subspecies who are in ecologic equilibrium with their surroundings temporarily flatten this descending curve toward fetalization.

In warmer climates virus epidemics are inclined to spread along the major river valleys where ample water supplies favor the proliferation of insect carriers. The most fertile soil is found in such geographic locations, so these valleys became centers for early man when he took to agriculture. Here again, and right on into modern times, the cycle of weeding out by disease and overcompensation by survivors would repeatedly lead to new variations, and it could very well be that the inexplicable speed of the disappearance of Neanderthal man was due to a widespread epidemic rather than to hopelessness in the face of the arrival of better endowed Cro-Magnon man on the scene, as has been suggested.

Viruses are, of course, by no means the only disease agents important in the evolutionary process. Bacterial and plasmodial diseases contribute their share. In this latter category is malaria, which Sir William Osler called "the greatest single destroyer of mankind." The malarial plasmodium also causes brain damage.

Stanley Garn, in his *Culture and the Direction of Human Evolution,* wrote: "The biochemical evidence clearly points to culture (i.e., way of life) as the directional force in recent evolutionary change." And

while malaria is the immediate agent of natural selection . . . it is man and his way of life that made malaria an important disease. . . . Not scattered nomadic tribesmen, hunters, etc., but the inhabitants of settled villages have traded mosquito-free poverty for an enriched if more malarial existence. Population size is crucial in disease selection. Small, isolated or nomadic populations are effectively isolated both from each other and from infectious diseases. With the advent of agriculture, especially cereal-crop agriculture, larger populations constitute a disease reservoir.

Continually on the move, African Bushmen do not overtax the ability of the dung-burying beetle to do an adequate sewage-disposal job. But stable agricultural populations have a permanent sanitary problem to the point where intestinal parasites become an important cause of death. Nomadic peoples outwalk both parasites and vermin, but villages set in forest clearings with mud houses and granaries all attract mice, rats, cockroaches and other domesticable insect vectors of disease. . . . So it is that the great technological advances that made civilization possible brought with them diseases in turn, some carried by man, some by flies and mosquitoes, some by rodents and some by snails. Each of these communicable diseases, malaria, typhus, typhoid, paratyphoid and many others, became actual or potential directors of human evolution.

The proportions of this factor were pointed up by Paul F. Russell, Chairman of the World Health Organization's Committee on Malaria, who estimated that the total number of contemporary cases of human malaria, as recently as 1952, was about 350 million, or roughly 6.3 per cent of the world's population.

Medical authorities also believe that in view of the large numbers of Westerners who have been shuttling back and forth to the Far East at the present time, whether in the course of vacations or business activities, or in connection with the wars in Korea or Vietnam, the psychic manifestations of malaria, including the cerebral type, will be seen more frequently in the West and that they will present diagnostic problems. It has been pointed out that a deficient oxygen supply to the brain produces personality disturbances as well as many neurologic signs and symptoms. Several patients of one doctor reporting on his cases had experienced frank psychotic episodes during the recovery phase from malaria.

The question occurs that among so many disease-caused mutations, could there not have been some that were beneficial in their effect? This is not very likely, since most organisms are so very well adapted to their environment that any change could only be for the worse. The progress of evolution could only be achieved by the overcompensatory development of other parts of the anatomy to make up for the loss of use of those damaged or handicapped by disease and mutation. In man we see this overcompensation in the rapid growth of his brain. This was his instrument in the struggle back to the perfect adaptation of his forebears.

The process of overcompensation is always present in nature. Animals that live in the dark and therefore no longer need the use of the eye compensate—or, more exactly, overcompensate—for the missing function. Bats emit pulses of high-pitched sounds and are able to determine the size and nature of objects accurately by means of this hyperacute acoustic system. The image of a flying insect is perceived by hearing quite as accurately as we should perceive it by seeing. Compensation alone would not be enough, since the acoustic elements in the possession of most animals would be of little help if they were suddenly deprived of their sight. Only a consistent refinement of the sensory perception, taking over from the one atrophied, could ultimately lead to a satisfactory substitute.

The underlying need for overcompensation has to be pressing—of the order of a life-or-death necessity. The processing of information, beginning with the ear and ending in the neural centers, receives top priority only in this way. An animal in the period of such a transition is literally straining to the very limits of its ability to perceive and distinguish sounds. The mental effort provokes an outpouring of hormones which intensify the alerting mechanism. Thus a mutual reinforcement takes place, which creates an extremely favorable climate for rapid learning and permanent retention of newly gained information.

An effective way to halt the spread of such viral diseases as smallpox, poliomyelitis, encephalitis, measles, yellow fever, and rabies is by immunization. In this process a vaccine is administered consisting of other viruses killed with formaldehyde—the Salk vaccine is an example—or, the more frequent method, the injection of attenuated viruses. These latter are not, as is commonly believed, a weaker form. Far from it. By passing through another host a mutation occurs in the virus, which nevertheless retains its ability to provoke the production of antibodies in man without causing disease. The vaccine which is used to render man immune from smallpox, however, will still cause the disease in cows.

Just as the virus itself undergoes mutation after being re-

Regressive Evolution

produced in the cells of a different host, so it may have a similar effect upon the genes of the man or animal into which it is injected as a vaccine. We may justly wonder whether the widespread use of vaccines may not also have contributed, or, for that matter, whether it is not still contributing, to a further acceleration of the prevailing evolutionary trend toward fetalization.

Another interesting example of the mutation of viruses as they pass through different host cells is offered by the virus causing a mild disease (myxomatosis) in Brazilian rabbits, which converted to an extremely virulent form for the Australian rabbit. This virus was successful in reducing the enormous rabbit population of Australia by 90 per cent. Meanwhile some of the diseased rabbits survived and overcompensated for the deficiency which made them so vulnerable to myxomatosis. We may yet see the emergence of a new variant of the rabbit family in Australia.

Virus diseases tend to appear in cycles, some as short as one year, others extending to three or more years. Highly infectious viruses will decimate a population, thus eliminating the hosts upon whom they can thrive, and in this way they may themselves sometimes disappear. On the other hand, viruses with a low degree of infectivity remain fairly constant, since they rarely cause death on such a widespread scale.

Although the relationship between cancer and viruses is not too clear, there is no doubt that many animal cancers are caused by viruses. There is a curious manifestation seen in the viruses which infect bacteria. They remain inactive until they come into contact with carcinogens (cancer-provoking chemicals) and then they begin to multiply, producing not cancer but other disease in the bacteria.

This is another piece of the jigsaw puzzle. It is now generally accepted that cancer cells originate from normal cells whose gene structure has been altered. And it is the gradual change in the genes which is responsible for the appearance of new species. Can we thus speculate that we are dealing here with a wide range of effects stemming from the interaction between the virus and the host cell? Can we speculate even further and assume that in the primordial oceans the free-floating carbon compounds assembled into long and coiled structures, some of which became self-reproductive while others remained in their original state; that the latter—the viruses—constantly interacted with their counterparts, the genes, in the former? Perhaps in this manner an endless spiral began in which at each turn a virus changed a gene structure in a living organism, eventually resulting in new species. There is no question of the widespread distribution of viruses or of their affinity to genes. It is difficult for our minds, trained as they are to see in nature an all-pervading trend toward perfection and at the present pinnacle of this trend man, the child of God, to accept the thought that perhaps life as we know it now is the result of an ongoing process of disease—even that life is a disease of matter. It may be that this is not the answer to the puzzle of what is the guiding undertow in selection for evolution, but this theory can certainly explain a larger array of manifestations in simpler terms than can previous theories.

To come back to the Darwinian theory, discussed briefly at the beginning of this chapter: One of the strongest arguments against the idea of evolution by natural selection is the fantastically large number of random mutations that would be necessary to produce from land-living forebears an animal capable of, say, aquatic life—an adaptation made at one stage in their history by the predecessors of the whale. Literally thousands of genes would have to be altered, in some harmonious relationship and in comparatively short order, by pure chance, to produce the qualities necessary for even the preliminary stages of transition to life in the sea. Even a lesser adaptation would require a combination of such a large number of favorable mutations occurring simultaneously, or within a short time, as to make the odds against its occurrence astronomical.

Here we have the forebears of the whales, land animals—and then we have the whale. What happened in between? In similar instances where we have found two disparate forms of life, one deriving from the other, and have so far not found fossils of connecting links, the scientists in this field (paleontologists) have simply concluded that eventually they will be able to locate some. Is there not a possibility, however, that these so-called "missing links" were so short-lived (in terms of numbers of generations, not of their individual lives) that there were not enough of them to leave fossil traces?

In the present state of our knowledge there is only one possibility that could account for such a sudden transition. The few survivors of a species afflicted by severe virus epidemics, who have regressed as a result of physical and genetic damage, will tend in the long run to assume the forms of the fetal stages of their ancestors, in this case of the primitive eutherians. In this way one can more easily understand the relatively rapid emergence of an aquatic descendant. There is a regressive continuity all the way to the ancestral fetus comfortably immersed in its amniotic fluid. In other words, the whale is a primitive eutherian arrested at a fetal stage; like man, who has passed through similar stages of regression, it has also grown to greater size and become the possessor of a very sophisticated brain in its journey along the way. This development could take place in a comparatively short time from a geologic point of view, and would eliminate the necessity of having to account for an apparently vast number of mutations.

After all, a comparison of the fetus of any animal with its adult form presents a vivid demonstration of the rapid differentiation produced by normal growth in a single life span.

The life of an animal begins with an infinitesimal globule, the fertilized egg, and before it reaches its adult stage it goes through numerous transformations. It takes fifty-six generations of cells to produce a grown man out of a fertilized egg. Each stage brings such radical changes that development could be described as a succession of different creatures. If a modification takes place only in a young stage, it may promote little or no change in the adult stage. De Beer refers to this as clandestine evolution. If, however, retardation should take place at that stage where the change has occurred, a very abrupt modification will take place and initiate a subspecies in a completely new direction. This accounts for the fossil gaps and missing links previously referred to.

That any adult form differs greatly from its fetal form is so obviously true of all species that it is hardly necessary to give an example, but a telling one is the lamprey. Lamprey infants so little resemble their adult form that for many years they were thought to be a different species. Adult lampreys were called cyclocoetes and the newly hatched larvae ammocoetes. During extensive metamorphosis into adulthood the heads of the young are partially destroyed—skull, muscles, nerves, pharynx—as is their intestinal tract, then remodeled. They live as larvae for three to four years, buried in the sand, as sedentary as clams, filtering sea water through a maze of cilia, eyeless (though with active pineal "eyes" which are sensitive to light), enroute to their final shapes. Another example is the axolotl, which is the tadpole stage of a newt. In this stage it sometimes becomes sexually mature before changing into a newt so that some features of its structure, such as the bones of the skull, never become properly developed. In the vegeta-

Regressive Evolution

ble world, one has only to look at the acorn and the oak. If any species were mutated so as to arrest its development in one growing stage, its appearances might be so radically different as to be at first unrecognizable, and after a series of such mutations over several generations would certainly be so.

It might be intriguing to attempt such an act of creation in a laboratory experiment by feeding some caterpillars with suitable hormones—those which retard development and those which induce sexual maturation. Imagine a butterfly, arrested at the caterpillar stage of its growth, that has managed a one-sided continuation to maturity only of its sexual development. We should then have what would in a comparatively short time become a new species.

A fact that would tend to confirm this interpretation is that the phase of most rapid growth takes place within the uterine cavity, so that any animal regressing to this stage should experience similar inordinate growth. This was certainly the case with the cetaceans. It could also have been a contributing factor to the monstrous size of some of the dinosaurs. In the absence of any evidence we may speculate that they became arrested at the embryonic stage of their species shortly before emergence from the egg. At this point the possible limits of their regression may have been exhausted, and thus they came to the end of the line.

It is not without interest in this regard that the emu, the ostrich, and the cassowary all show many features of regression (loss of capacity to fly being the most obvious) and also grow to the largest size of the family of birds. The penguin, although not so very large as these, is also a regressed species. Like the ostrich's, its plumage remains throughout life in the condition of the down plumage of the chicks of flying birds.

We offer the view that the Darwinian theory of the survival of the fittest is true, but that it accounts only for the evolution that has taken place in small steps over eons of time. To account for those major changes in species that appear suddenly, and without any evidence of stages linking the new species to earlier forms, we believe it is necessary to look to the viruses, which promote evolutionary change in two ways. First, they decimate animal populations by disease and force the survivors to overcompensate for their handicaps by the development of new adaptations, largely achieved with the necessary speed by the arrest of certain features at earlier stages of growth, a process that has been called fetalization. Second, in their similarity to genes, and in their parasitic methods of reproduction, the viruses mutate the genes of their hosts directly, causing alterations in hereditary characteristics.

In this manner the viruses, with a certain degree of assistance from other diseases (notably malaria), have been the most important factor in guiding the direction of our anatomical evolution, and indirectly might be said to be responsible for the rapid growth of our brain structure, our intelligence as a species, our civilizations, cultures, and all those attributes of man which are sometimes considered to separate him from other beasts.

THE RESULT: NEW SPECIES

The evolution of man is a descent in more ways than one. At first it is a descent from the trees, then a descent from more mature to less mature forms. Perhaps the ancient Greeks, with their marvelous insights, had some kind of awareness of this process, for they claimed an origin for their lineage in cloud-dwelling gods whose behavior in many ways was clearly adolescent and saw themselves as their children. The Jewish and Christian religions, too, conceive of men as the children of God and attribute their origin to a childlike, innocent pair, Adam and Eve. In this case the descendants reverted back to what is a later stage in human development, the display of aggressive adolescent behavior in Cain's murder of Abel, but the dream for the future is to recover the perfect peace of youngest childhood, when the lion may lie down with the lamb and we may all re-enter Eden. It is quite extraordinary how the earliest myths of peoples seem to embody facts supported much later by scientific research, as though men were possessed of some unconscious but built-in racial memory.

All of his forerunners as well as modern man himself seem to have appeared on the scene rather suddenly. Our paleontologists are constantly seeking fossil records of intermediary forms, but many of the gaps are still quite wide. Some fortunate finds of such devoted researchers as the Leakeys have narrowed some gaps, but man's complete lineage is not yet confirmed by fossil finds.

It takes rather a special set of circumstances to preserve a living form as a fossil. There must be river beds, mud flats, lake shores, desert regions, floods, avalanches, snowstorms, volcanic eruptions, or similar conditions that might suddenly overtake and bury an animal. A dead animal is normally disposed of very efficiently by being eaten, by decaying, or by decomposing.

Also contributing to a lack of fossil remains of some stages is the fact that many of the deviant branches produced by any line are short-lived; they are unsuccessful and die out. In fact more than one hundred twenty genera of extinct primates have been identified to date. Of known primate groups which are considered of generic significance, nearly two-thirds do not survive today. Since the numbers of individuals composing the surviving intermediary forms were therefore probably not very great, the chances of their having encountered circumstances that would lead to preserving them as fossils are rather remote.

Most students of evolution take for granted that intermediary forms must have endured for lengthy stretches of time to allow the odds for the favorable mutations to have materialized. However, if evolution were achieved by retardation at earlier stages of development, then a far shorter time would be required to achieve new species. This would further reduce the numbers of members constituting the linking species, and again reduce their chances of being preserved to our time as fossils. The very fact of the scarcity of fossil "links" would thus tend to confirm the occurrence of speedy transitional stages by regressive evolution. Only by retarding development at a fetal or infantile stage can there be relatively radical changes within comparatively few generations. After all, the infant animal, in behavior and body build, and the adult animal are as different as any two distantly related species.

Modern man obviously did not descend directly from the fetal stage of a distant tree-dwelling, nonhuman primate. A series of discontinuous stages, each one characterized by arrested development at a youthful phase of the immediate ancestors, eventually led to Homo sapiens. That modern man at the height of his maturity has so many features in common with the eight-month-old chimpanzee fetus is then the logical outcome of a continuing process, based on the principle of orthogenesis, the principle that whenever an evolutionary trend is successful it continues until it exhausts its potential. In all the physical traits we have described, man resembles the fetal ape more closely than he does the adult. Even the prolonged dependency and growth periods are simply prolongations of fetal dependency and growth periods.

It is reasonably clear that our organisms represent an inheritance acquired as a consequence of interaction between our basic hereditary combination of genes and the environment experienced during the course of development. It is during the process of *individual* development that mutations occur, but any mutation which causes a relative retardation in the development of some part of the descendant's body, so that the descendant fails to pass through several of the growth phases of the ancestor, will result in the descendant exhibiting a pattern of growth which in the adult stage represents a retardation of the ancestral fetal or juvenile pattern. Many such cases are known to zoologists and geneticists. Such neotenous mutations may spread rapidly in a small population, and it has been suggested that under such conditions the fetal or juvenile developmental stage of any of the types that preceded man could have become consolidated in the descendant groups very quickly.

Perhaps it will be easier to visualize this concept if we state it in the form of a schematic chart. We shall arbitrarily assume a tree-dwelling primate as the "Adam" of the line, whom we shall call T. He was followed by various stages and species of protohominids, all of which we shall compress under the initial P. Then came various hominids, of some of which we have knowledge through fossil finds, although others surely existed of which we have no trace; all of these we call H. Finally comes man in all his varieties, whom we call M.

We then divide the life spans of the individuals of these four groups into four stages for each. These would be:

    a for the fetus stage
    b for the infantile stage
    c for the juvenile stage
    d for the mature stage

Thus a mature tree-dweller would be T-d, an infant hominid H-b, and so on.

If we now assume that virus epidemics arose periodically

throughout evolution then, as we have suggested in the earlier parts of this chapter, they will not only have decimated the numbers of these groups, but will also have produced genetic changes affecting the release of hormones. This will have set up retardations or have resulted in nontypical and nonviable deviant forms. The nonviable and the unsuccessful nontypical forms will die out. We are left with the noninfected individuals (who will continue their own line unaltered), and those surviving but affected by processes of retardations.

The result of a viral epidemic can thus be illustrated as follows:

T-a (tree-dweller fetus): Will most likely die in the womb and be aborted, be deformed, as in German measles, or not survive after being born.

T-b (tree-dweller infant): Has only a limited chance of survival. Paralyzed or sick, falling from a tree, it would have little chance to live to breed and thus be unlikely to found a line.

T-c (tree-dweller juvenile): If it survives a not-too-severe infection, this group has the best chance of becoming the forerunner of a species. With the youthful vigor it possesses it is more likely to be able to overcompensate in its new environment for the defects acquired by the infection.

T-d (tree-dweller mature): Survivors of the infection in a few instances may produce mutants, forming some variations in the species.

Regressive Evolution

In this way the juvenile tree-dweller becomes the initiator of a line (because of the alterations of his genes by the infection) which leads in relatively few generations to the protohominids. Thus T-c leads to P.

At some time during their span of existence the protohominids will probably experience similar recurrent epidemics. The cycle repeats itself. We have P-c as the most likely survivor, with genetic alterations resulting in further retardations, and in turn it becomes the progenitor of the hominid species.

In the next cycle, H-c leads to the sudden appearance of modern man, roughly thirty-five thousand years ago. The whole development would be charted like this:

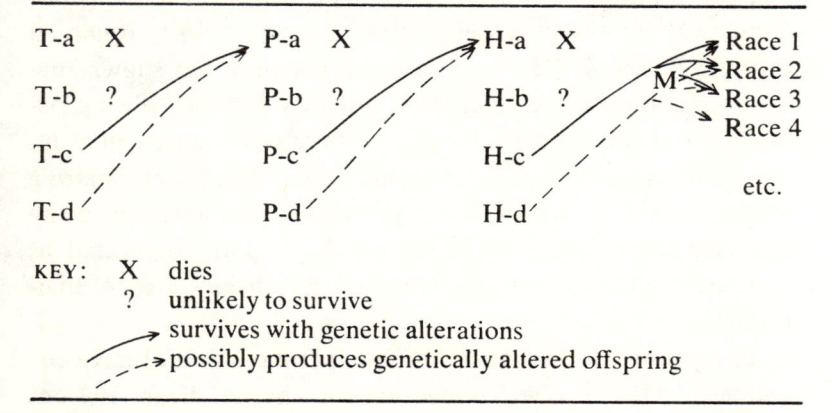

```
T-a  X           P-a  X           H-a  X           → Race 1
                                              M →  → Race 2
T-b  ?           P-b  ?           H-b  ?           → Race 3
                                                   → Race 4
T-c              P-c              H-c
                                                        etc.
T-d              P-d              H-d
```

KEY: X   dies
      ?   unlikely to survive
      →   survives with genetic alterations
      ⇢   possibly produces genetically altered offspring

Modern mature man (M) thus derives many of his physical features from the retardations achieved by the juvenile hominids (H), who are the distant offspring of juvenile protohominids (P), who had also undergone retardations, which brings us back to the tree-dweller (T).

It is understood, of course, that the terms *hominid* and *protohominid* cover many parallel or intermediary species.

It will also be noted that it is the juvenile at each phase that has the greatest chance for surviving an epidemic. It is precisely the juvenile form whose body is undergoing profound hormonal changes. Therefore the form of the descendant will depend very much on the exact age at which the infection struck the progenitor.

Let us follow the hypothetical juvenile tree-dweller in his life on the ground. His companions for all his activities will be not the conservative family group from which he would learn the traditional behavior of his species but fellow disabled juveniles. With the faculties they have retained they are obliged to improvise an existence without the role models of the elders of their line. Their instinctual ritual behavior must be modified by three different factors all reinforcing each other. These are their illness, their new environment, and the lack of example and restraining pressure of the elders of their group. This last factor was interestingly demonstrated at the Yerkes Regional Primate Research Center at Atlanta, where it was shown that the young animals were far more unruly when they lived separately from their elders than when they were reared in company with the elders of their group, who exerted a modulating effect on their behavior. (This probably has relevance to the disturbances initiated by today's unruly youth, separated as they are from their seniors, whether in college or gang environments.)

The young are by nature more experimental, and have the greatest ability to overcompensate for any handicap. Besides the natural tendency of their age to experiment, these young are forced by circumstances to improvise new habits of life.

A disturbance in a specific region of the brain, such as one which might be caused by an encephalitic illness, will not bring a stereotyped response. Although it is an aberrant stimulus from within, it becomes incorporated with the total experience of the animal. Another very revealing experiment carried out by Dr. Bryan Robinson at the Yerkes Regional Primate Research Center showed this very clearly. Electrodes were implanted in the appropriate parts of the brain of a rhesus monkey. The experimenter then sent radio waves to selected electrodes that activated a portion of the monkey's brain. These cause the animal to do some specific thing, such as fight, cower, or mount a female. In this particular demonstration, three monkeys squatted quietly in a cage, two males and one female. The two males wore the electronic head units. When Dr. Robinson sent out a wave to stimulate an aggressive response in the dominant male, it leaped at the other male, who cried out in fear and raced around the cage with the first one in hot pursuit. The female leaped to the top of the cage and hung there, out of danger. After about ten seconds the technician cut off the stimulus. The monkeys quieted down and sat together again as if nothing had happened.

This was not a stereotyped reflex. If it had been, the stimulated monkey would have attacked anything—the cage or the female—but it did not. It selected the subordinate male as a victim, showing that it had integrated the abnormal brain stimulation with its previous experience, and retained its inhibitory reflexes (it did not attack the female). It had adapted the emerging emotion (rage) to its prevailing environment.

Similarly, when virus infections damage specific portions of the brain, the resultant behavior of our juvenile tree-dwellers will be integrated with their past experience and adapted to their current environment. Genes do not determine behavioral traits, but do influence the responses of the developing organism to its environment. That is to say, there is no inheritance of fully developed characteristics or anomalies in behavior, only a transmission of predispositions, or specific *potential* responses to environment. The giraffe did not survive because he had a long neck, but because he used his neck to reach higher and higher branches, and random mutations which coincided with this need were favored. The same is also particularly true of brain-damaged human adolescents. Identical damage in individuals of different cultural backgrounds results in totally different responses. When our juvenile tree-dwellers breed, however, they can only transmit to their offspring the new responses to the environment which they themselves have worked out. This has to be a juvenile society, modifying inherited characteristic behavior traits—a Pliocene version of the *Lord of the Flies* situation.

We observe in modern times that the firstborn children of adolescent parents show a greater degree of emotional immaturity throughout their lives than the later-born. The predominantly juvenile societies of the earliest protohominid victims of infection would have set an example of different behavior patterns to their offspring, and thus to succeeding generations. This behavior would have been subject to two sets of modification: the first in response to the new environment, the second the result of their altered adaptational capacities. In these circumstances those mutations would be utilized which served their needs. Changes by natural selection, preferred use or disuse, and behavior would reinforce them, for at the same time that regressive evolution changes various parts of its anatomy into earlier forms the total organism is nevertheless concurrently subject to the over-all basic trends to survival by natural selection, adaptation to environment, and to some modification by disuse or preferred use. But since regressive evolution is the overriding trend, of all the changes which occur those would be adopted that tend to reinforce it (orthogenesis).

The cumulative effect of the long series of retardations accounts for the great number of similarities between modern man and the fetuses of present tree-dwelling primates.

How can we account for the great variety of types of modern man? We see Caucasoid, Negroid, Mongoloid, Australian, and other types, and these general classifications cover very broad categories within which are many variations.

We know, as explained in the earlier part of this chapter, that the normal retarding effects of the hormones are uneven in their timing mechanisms. One could conclude that an absence or diminished amount of pigment indicates the largest degree of regression. This would apply to the Caucasoid races. In the degree of hairiness, on the other hand, these races are less regressed. We see the reverse in the Negroid races, where the pigmentation would indicate a lack of retardation, but the relative hairlessness points to a greater. These and similar variations among the different races of Homo sapiens would derive from the various stages of development at which their hominid forebears suffered the virus infections which resulted in mutation of their genes, and also in the nature of the mutation. The responsible retarding hormones must have operated in many combinations to produce the racial differences we see.

De Beer stated: "It is now realized that the ancestor of modern man could not have been Neanderthal man because he appeared later in time than the earliest types of modern man. But if the human ancestor were similar to Pithecanthropus, or Australopithecus, modern man would have descended from them by the retention of features in the juvenile forms of their skulls, which is what is meant by neoteny."

All races of modern men do not exhibit neotenous mutations in the same degree. Ashley Montagu has written of this aspect of evolution in these terms:

Mongoloids, for example, are rather more fetalized than Caucasoids. Negroids exhibit some fetal traits that Caucasoids do not. The varieties of mankind that fall into these broad classifications of major groups were at one time very small populations, and it is evident that in these populations neotenous mutations occurred somewhat differently in each. In this way we could readily explain the appearance of such neanthropic-like types as Swanscombe and Fontéchevade before the advent of such an apparently morphologically [in form] more primitive type as Neanderthal. The fact that Neanderthal man got to look more "primitive" than he appeared to be in his earlier phases of evolution, suggests that our conceptions as to what is "primitive" and what "advanced" in human morphology are in need of careful study.

As long ago as 1923 Keith, commenting on the ideas of Bolk, remarked that "man's outstanding structural peculiarities have been produced during the embryonic and foetal stages of his developmental history." In 1925 he wrote: "This intra-uterine period is one which gives every opportunity for the working out of new inventions." In 1927 he wrote, even more positively: "It is during the intra-uterine phase that nearly all revolutionary changes have been introduced."

It is of particular interest here that the rate of evolutionary change in a group of pithecanthropines that was geographically isolated (Java Solo man) was rather slow when compared with that which appears to have occurred in other hominid groups in other parts of the world. It has been suggested that this may be an example of what Simpson has called bradytely—a lack of appreciable change over a long period of time. The fact that a geographically isolated group evolved at a slower rate than other groups would tend to support our contention that virus infections were probably the trigger for many mutations. An isolated group of creatures would have been less exposed to infectious epidemics and might therefore have suffered fewer retarding mutations, at least for so long as it remained isolated.

It is generally assumed that the ancestors of all men originated in the Early Pleistocene or Late Pliocene, so that many of the really important changes that led to his taking on the form he did must have happened in the Pliocene (which preceded the Pleistocene). It is also generally assumed that our species arose in Africa. As there were significant climatic changes in Africa in the Pliocene—principally the withdrawal of rainfall farther and farther north, converting vast areas of forest land into savanna—it has also been suggested that it was this factor which caused our ancestors to adapt to life on the ground. However, it seems to us that those capable of doing so would have migrated, so to speak, with the trees, and that while the climatic change may account for the beginning of a wider dispersal of the species, it does not account for the reasons that the ones who stayed behind did so. We think it is more likely that those individuals who remained in land that became savanna did so because they were incapacitated in some way and incapable of remaining with their companions in forests, no matter to which latitudes the forest receded. Having remained behind, they would have tended to become separated not only by reason of being on the ground but also because their erstwhile companions then lived wherever the trees were, and this fact would reinforce the consequences of any mutations.

Simpson discussed the varieties of evolutionary rates in his work *The Major Features of Evolution*. He notes that it is now fairly well understood that there has been the widest possible variation in the evolutionary rates of living forms, and points out that an increase in the rate occurs whenever a species occupies a new territory. In this connection it occurs to us that a traveler today, when he visits an unfamiliar country for the first time, frequently suffers infections from "bugs" which are not present in his own part of the world and to which his body has not built up immunity. Thus North Americans who vacation in Mexico, or north Europeans who visit Spain, frequently suffer from infections of the intestinal tract which do not inconvenience the local populations. On the other hand, Mexicans report that they suffer similar discomforts when they visit California. Judging from the wide distribution of fossil man upon the earth and the wanderings of peoples, the occupation of new territory seems to have been a not infrequent activity of many prehistoric human populations. It therefore seems to us that the lack of immunity of the migrating populations to the infectious agents of the new areas was another way in which disease-caused mutations hastened anatomical changes in them. Such populations were small, so genetic changes could have been rapidly established. Man, as a mammal of quite ordinary inherent variability, therefore owes his present great intergroup variation not only to the fact that he has adapted to a large number of different habitats (not only physiographic, but also socio-cultural), but also to the fact that he has been subjected to a greater number and variety of disease processes than more sedentary species.

Incidentally, perhaps we should look at the chimpanzee as a vivid illustration of an in-between stage exemplifying the regression of a tree-dwelling species. He is equally as at home in the trees as on the ground. He displays a high degree of intelligence (capacity for learning, discrimination, and memory), pronounced playfulness, and some sense of humor.

Another version of an in-between stage would be the baboons, who have developed highly structured societies and extremely sophisticated forms of group living.

The sudden appearance of radically new patterns of behavior—and this includes man, the chimpanzee, and the baboon—is not in keeping with gene theory, but fits well with the theory of regressive evolution. It is through the process of fetalization that the greater portion of the brain remains uncommitted in childhood so that a capacity for learning can extend over a longer span of life.

The capacity for learning of these three species rests on one

Regressive Evolution

basic principle: the suppression of inappropriate responses and delay in reactions. Thus the brain (nervous system), like the endocrine glands, achieves many ends by holding back, retarding, and inhibiting.

From what has been observed it appears that the behavior of a regressed species will be of a type more characteristic of the youthful stage of a preceding form than the equivalent anatomical configuration. It would appear that behavior, so to speak, runs ahead of anatomy, and in doing so indicates the direction of its modification. At the beginning of each stage the behavior of the full-grown animal is inappropriate for its degree of physical maturity, and more closely approximates the playfulness of the very young. But in the course of many successive generations the playfulness becomes incorporated into adaptive mechanisms, by which time the slower anatomical changes have caught up with the social changes and adaptations to environment. In such a way, in time, new species emerge.

What is more, we can conclude that this process is continuing. We may in fact be in the midst of a transition that may have started in our century and will become more pronounced in the next few centuries. Twentieth-century man is more youthful in appearance than his nineteenth- and eighteenth-century counterpart. A forty-year-old woman was "old" in appearance then, whereas today a forty-year-old woman thinks of herself, and appears to be, hardly changed from her postadolescent years. A fifty-year-old man or woman until recently was an old person, whereas today he is usually in the prime of life. Although this phenomenon relates more to the behavior of modern man, we are now seeing the very beginning of anatomical changes. Among other things man is continuing to grow in height until the age of about twenty-one, about four years longer than he grew fifty years ago.

The evidences of the acceleration of the process of infantilization that we can now see on all sides may very well be partially due to an aspect of our advancing medical knowledge that has to a certain extent been overlooked. When we cure, as we do today, most of childhood's virus diseases (such as poliomyelitis, encephalitis, measles, German measles, chicken pox, or mumps), we are preserving many children who, as short a time as one generation ago, might have died as a result of these illnesses. These children are likely to have undergone gene changes (mutations) as a result of their infections. Thus we are progressively increasing the number of individuals with altered genes who survive to breed another generation. Margaret Mead, addressing a meeting of child psychiatrists in New York, drew attention to the fact that in the histories of the disturbed children referred to them they would almost invariably find a record of such childhood diseases. She implied that delayed effects of the diseases had some bearing on the fact of these children's psychiatric disturbances.

In the context of regressive evolution an interesting question crosses our minds. Would it be possible for the human species to arise again?

From a purely theoretical point of view, patterns of development do recur again and again. At some future date a nonhuman primate that in the meantime has been advancing slowly in a progressive evolution by means of natural selection and adaptation to environment might again, following an epidemic, become the progenitor of a regressive species, with a similar potential to become a "Homo sapiens." On the other hand, the resulting parallel end product, although again intellectually superior to its precursors, would assume the features of the fetal forms of a species in the meantime grown different from the tree-dwelling progenitor of modern man, and might be as different, or as similar (whichever way one cares to look at it) as, say, Cro-Magnon and Neanderthal man.

THE HISTORY

L. Bolk, a professor of anatomy at the University of Amsterdam, held a lecture on April 15, 1926, at the twenty-fifth meeting of the German Anatomical Association in Freiburg, Germany, in which he proposed a novel theory of the origin of man. He was aware that his view deviated strongly from prevailing opinions. He had kept his conclusions to himself for a long time, until he was convinced that they were correct.

Bolk cited a statement in the closing chapter of Oscar Hertwig's *Das Werden der Organismen* as a starting point for his idea. The sentence was:

"Wie zur wissenschaftlichen Naturerklärung keine Universalursache ausreicht, so gibt es auch keine einzige allgemeine Formel, aus der sich das Werden der Organismen begreifen lässt." ("In the same way that no universal cause is valid to explain nature scientifically, so there is also no single general form from which one can trace the development of organisms.")

Bolk did not begin his investigation with a search for similarities or dissimilarities between man and the other primates. On the contrary, at that time he believed that man was a unique phenomenon with specific internal mechanisms that differed in some ways from those of the other primates. He stressed that anthropologists until that time, in attempting to establish similarities between nonhuman primates and man as an indication of the degree of closeness of their relationship, had paid little attention to the various parts of anatomy in terms of evolving in a progressive or regressive direction. It was on the occasion of the lecture referred to that he brought forward the facts that we outlined in the first part of this chapter. He stated that these facts had indicated to him that our ancestral nonhuman primate forebears possessed the physical characteristics of modern man for a short phase just prior to their birth. Therefore the process of becoming human consisted of an arrest at this fetal stage. The uniformity of this process of fetalization points to a basic cause which was not adaptation, nor was it a struggle for life or selection.

When a fetal state becomes permanent there must be present a factor which prevents the animal from continuing its development to maturity. This retardation is brought about by the action of the endocrine glands. He stated that the characteristics which were suppressed by the action of hormones in the genesis of man must be present in a latent state in modern man. Therefore we carry within ourselves the potentials of our ancestors.

When there is a malfunction of any of the endocrine glands, the retarding influence it exerts is removed, and features emerge which are characteristic of nonhuman primates (as we detailed in the second section of this chapter). Bolk also demonstrated that some nonhuman primates, too, show retardation on the basis of the third deciduous molar. He thought that the Nordic races showed the greatest degree of fetalization, and he pointed out that the Negroid baby resembles the white baby far more than the respective adults resemble each other.

This lecture was published in the form of a monograph entitled, *Das Problem der Menschwerdung* (The Problem of Becoming Man).

There had been some notions along these lines as far back as 1866, when von Baer described the development of mature germ cells in a larval body, referring to this as paedogenesis. In 1896 J. E. V. Boas went a step further when he discovered elements of youthful anatomical features of the ancestors becoming prominent in the adult stage of the descendant. In 1909 A. Sedgwick stated: "The evidence seems to show, not that a stage is added on at the end of a life-history, but only that some of the stages in the life-history are modified ... one would not expect often to find, even if new stages are added in the course of evolution, that they are added at the end of the series, when the organism has passed through its reproductive period.... Inasmuch as the organism is variable at every stage of its independent existence and is exposed to the action of natural selection there is no reason why it should escape modification at any stage." That is to say, a new characteristic in evolution is not necessarily tacked on to the end of the animal's previous complete development, but may arise in any of the stages of its growth.

Other anthropologists came to similar conclusions. In 1883 Kollman called it neoteny, Jaekel, protogenèse, and Giard, foetalization. O. H. Schinewolf used the term proterogenesis, and A. N. Ivanov described the phenomenon as bradygenesis, Garstang first used the term paedomorphosis in 1922. Devaux expressed the same views as Bolk. The concept of gerontomorphosis was presented by de Beer in 1940. Except for the last, all these terms have approximately the same meaning as paedomorphosis and paedogenesis, except that, as Ashley Montagu has pointed out, fetalization, strictly speaking, would refer exclusively to fetal stages, while paedomorphosis, etc., would apply to the young stages. Since the term neoteny implies both these stages, it is on the whole preferable, as it is the more comprehensive.

So far as we know, this is the first time all these concepts have been put together, a cause for the observed facts proposed, and the anatomical findings related to man's increasingly prolonged behavioral youthfulness. We see the whole as an ongoing process of regressive evolution, which we have termed progressive infantilization.

CHAPTER SEVENTEEN

The Future

If a theory has any kind of intrinsic veracity, it should enable one to make predictions; and so the theory we have been enlarging upon, if it is granted some validity, leads us to draw some conclusions about the further development of our species.

To draw a comparison between the various stages of man, one must take some fixed point. Let us compare man's ancestor, man himself, and his future protagonist at the point of reaching their reproductive years. We then find ourselves, as shown by the characteristic features of each of these representatives at the prime of their lives, viewing a descending gradient.

At the top we see in man's forerunner, the hominid:

1. Short childhood
2. Early physical maturation
3. Short life span,

in prehistoric and early historic man:

1. Transition from childhood to adult responsibilities gradually extended from the age of about seven to about thirteen (as shown by ancient puberty rites)
2. Age at which the long bone growth ceases progressively delayed from about thirteen to about sixteen
3. Average life span extended to the late thirties,

and in modern man:

1. Childhood prolonged until twenty to twenty-five years of age
2. End of the long bone growth beginning to be delayed until past the age of twenty (the graduating class of Yale University in 1960 stood two inches taller than the graduating class of 1905)
3. Average life span extended until about seventy-five.

Throughout this progression we notice a constant—that childhood corresponds to about one-third of the total life. Each succeeding stage resembles a more youthful period of the preceding stage, and in our time this process seems to be accelerating, for a man or a woman at the age of fifty today looks very much like a person of thirty of a few generations ago.

Since it has been observed that throughout nature a successful pattern of evolution continues until it exhausts its potential, we have to assume that the same will hold true for man.

The bridge from the past to the present brings us from the fetal ape who, through a series of retardations and prolongations of the succeeding stages of development, becomes a sexually mature creature while still anatomically and physiologically infantile. Behavior, however, takes the almost-impossible course of following two paths at the same time. On the one hand, but at an ever-slowing pace, it still follows the original instinctive responses of the species, while on the other, at an accelerating pace, it pursues the course of infantilization via intelligence and creativity. In these circumstances it is hardly to be wondered at that man's emotional problems at this point are many.

Here we are, then, on an island in the middle of a river, and another bridge to the future on the farther shore lies ahead of us. The shoreline is hazy and we can barely distinguish it, but some salient outlines are visible to us.

What is this creature on the island? At the outset of his journey, before he stepped onto the bridge he has just crossed, he was born able to stand and move under his own power. By the time he reached our island and is born as Man, he is born about one year prematurely by those standards. On the farther shore, man will probably be born even more prematurely. The gestation period will still be near enough to nine months, but because of the prolongation of the stages of development within the uterus, the infant will be born at an anatomically still earlier stage.

At this point we have to speculate. At present, in comparison with the anthropoid apes, we are a whole lifetime premature in many aspects. Suppose in the not too distant future our descendants are born six years more prematurely by today's anatomical standards. The first consequence will be a more than tripling of the nursing period, further extending the years of absolute helplessness. As a byproduct this will give an extended time for all growth, and as a result the individual will become still taller and bigger. But this very early period is the one during which especially the brain develops at a faster rate than the rest of the organs. This means that when the possibilities for the increase of surface by the convolution of the brain are exhausted, the pressure of the expanding brain, particularly its frontal portion, will increase the size of the skull. This

The Future

will be facilitated by a further delay in the closing of the sutures. Today they do not close until the age of about thirty-five to forty. Eventually they may remain open throughout life, allowing for the growth of the brain during the entire span of existence.

The counter trend to infantilization (gerontomorphism) apparent in today's man—the greater length of leg in proportion to the trunk—may not prove to be a successful trend in competition with the overriding paedomorphism, and may come to a halt. On the other hand, the stretching out of the growth period will increase the size and weight of the whole body. In today's man the legs grow fastest after birth. In the man of the future the lower limbs will grow at the same rate as the rest of the body, or perhaps a little more slowly. This will force the proportionately shorter limbs to become sturdier and stockier.

What, then, can this man of the future look like? From what we have seen in the journey across the first bridge to the island where we now stand, the continuing journey to the farther shore can only lead to one end by the time of his arrival there.

He will be a man larger than today's. His head will be considerably greater in proportion to his total body. His legs will appear shorter in proportion, but have grown sturdier to bear the weight, or else have become bowed. In continuation of the overriding paedomorphic trends, he will be hairless, devoid of molars, and his back may be slightly more stooped, continuing the fetal curvature.

What do we have here? An amazing likeness to today's newborn baby blown up to a man's proportions. Man of the future is therefore likely to be a physically grown, sexually mature, mentally overdeveloped, version of today's neonate. This is not such an outlandish prediction as it seems at first sight. We have an example which can be seen today of another regressed species, the sperm whale. It has grown to great size and possesses great intelligence; its head is one third the total size of its body, and its limbs are lost or vestigial. What is more, in a quite startling parallel to our own race history, zoologists have noted that the cetaceans (whales, porpoises, dolphins) appeared quite suddenly in early tertiary times, like bats fully adapted by profound modifications of their basic mammalian structure for their highly specialized mode of life, and that *no intermediate forms are apparent in the fossil record* between the cetaceans we know and the ancient placentals of the cretaceous period. "Indeed," wrote E. H. Colbert, in his *Evolution of the Vertebrates,* "cetaceans are even more isolated than bats. They stand quite alone. Therefore it seems evident that, having separated from ancestral eutherians (mammals) at an early date, they enjoyed at the outset a series of extraordinarily rapid evolutionary changes that made them by eocene times completely adapted for life in the ocean." Dare we suggest that the cetaceans, like man, may have achieved their rapid transformation by similar processes of infantilization?

At this point we are somewhat reluctant to carry our thesis to its logical conclusion for the man of the very far distant future—if indeed we may still refer to him at all as man. But, since we have embarked upon it, we shall continue our journey. It is possible, of course, that man will become a nonviable species, doomed to extinction. On the other hand, should he, like the cetaceans, manage to make a transition back to an aquatic life, the water may relieve his limbs of the burden of his disproportionately grown body and give him a new lease on evolution. Further fetalization would aid him in this eventuality, since at a very early stage of human development we still possess gills and, after all, the amniotic fluid has a chemical content similar to that of sea water. If we wish to be still more speculative we might even add that such a trend could prove to be a useful preadaptation, enabling men's distant descendants to survive when the next melting of the polar ice caps again causes the inundation of a large part of today's land masses, while continuing erosion tends toward a further encroachment of the oceans upon the continents.

Scientists from Woods Hole Oceanographic Institute have reported that two of their drilling profiles indicated that the North Atlantic is now spreading about a centimeter a year, and the South Atlantic at twice that rate. What could possibly happen in an evolutionary sense when the land masses re-emerge in the next cycle of geologic time, boggles even our most speculative imaginings!

In the meantime, our concern is with man as we know him and his nearer posterity. A trend we should not overlook is that it is almost inevitable that he will lose most of his self-preserving and self-procreating instincts. As we have indicated at various points of this work, the older paleocortex, which governs our instinctual behavior, is being superseded with increasing rapidity by the intellectualizing neocortex. More and more, instincts are being replaced by learned behavior. We have to teach our children not to play with fire, not to swallow pins, pennies, or poisons, to keep out of danger. Animal babies know these things instinctively. A newly hatched gosling runs for cover as soon as it is aware of the shadow of a buzzard. Darwin noted, in his *Descent of Man,* that the orang in the Eastern Islands and the chimpanzee in Africa avoid poisonous fruits, but that our domestic animals when taken to those lands at first eat but later avoid them. In other words, domesticity has blunted their instincts, forcing them to substitute the learned behavior of experience.

Along with all the other present instincts, sexual activities, too, will eventually have to be taught entirely. Our descendants may be so completely governed by the neocortex that if left to themselves, and not instructed, they might be unable to carry out the copulatory act. The increasing prevalence of sexual difficulties even today points to a partial loss of these instincts in our own time. The phenomenon of sexual instruction in today's schools may be another indication of a trend. It may not take too long before the subject is entered on the report card along with physical education!

As the process of infantilization follows along these lines, man's pursuits will change correspondingly. Emphasis on work will lessen and the pursuit of pleasure increase. Play, comprising more and more intellectual activities, will occupy man's time. Debating, pure research, philosophizing, theorizing, writing, art, and other creative outlets may provide his favorite diversions.

A progressive de-emphasizing of technological and material culture may ultimately lead to its complete abandonment by man. On the other hand, there is the possibility that, like the ants and the bees, he may develop a specialized worker caste. Such a possibility was envisioned and partly carried out by the ancient Athenians. Plutarch wrote, in his biography of Pericles:

Admiration does not always lead us to imitate what we admire, but, on the contrary, while we are charmed with the work, we often despise the workman. Thus we are pleased with perfumes and purple, while dyers and perfumers appear to us in the light of mean mechanics. . . . If man applies himself to servile or mechanical employments, his industry in those things is a proof of his inattention to nobler studies. No young man of high birth or liberal sentiments would, upon seeing the statue of Jupiter at Pisa, desire to be Phidias [the sculptor] . . . or wish to be Anacreon or Philetas, though delighted with their poems. For, though a work may be agreeable, esteem for the author is not the necessary consequence.

And Plato took a poor view of applied science. According to Plutarch, "Plato inveighed against them with great indignation, as corrupting and debasing the excellence of geometry, by making her descend from incorporeal and intellectual to corporeal and sensible things." Whoever applied mechanical instruments in geometry had to "make use of matter, which requires much manual labor and is the object of servile trade."

This demonstrates an ultimate rejection of the mature activity of work, and the glorification of the infantile pursuit of pleasure and play.

Aristotle carried this repugnance for the remotest semblance of work even further, just as any child does. In their approach to science the ancient Greeks viewed experimental testing as an occupation requiring manual labor, which was the occupation of slaves, not of free men. Aristotle defended the institution of slavery, comparing the master's rule over the slave with the rule of man's intellect over his body:

Nor can we doubt that it is natural and expedient for the body to be ruled by the soul and for the emotional part of the soul to be ruled by the intellect or the part in which reason resides, and that if the two are put on an equality the consequence is injurious to both.

There is too great a parallel here to overlook the possibility of such attitudes toward the development of science in the future. The emphasis is likely to be on pure science—the exercise of reason—not to mention speculation, rather than its application in technology.

Since the infantilization of our species will render it physically dependent upon technology, our descendants will have to find a way to man the machines they will need for survival. By that time the same process will have made them as nonaggressive as newborns, and they will have neither the inclination nor the capacity to wage war to acquire slaves, nor would they have the force to coerce any of their fellow men into a slave caste. Even were they to do so their fellow men, by reason of their similar nature, would be unable to fulfill such a function. But by applying the principles of paedomorphism to other species that are intelligent, but not by then so far regressed as themselves, they might eventually use a domesticated descendant of the anthropoid apes to man (or ape) their necessary machines. In our own time we have begun a phase of having robots take over those tasks we no longer care to perform. When the time comes that man does not care to work at producing robots, he may not be averse to training animal workers, just as today's child would object to doing a day's work but enjoys playing with and teaching tricks to his puppies and other domestic pets. By retardation he might produce another race of apes with sufficient intelligence (but not too much) to serve him as a worker caste.

The population explosion, which so worries all responsible people today, may find its own solution. With the reduction of the sexual and maternal instincts along with the others, and the paternal instinct additionally weakened by the loss of maturity and responsibility already observable in our own time, there will be a tremendous reduction in population. The problem then may very well be the maintenance of the species rather than controlling its proliferation.

Ultimately we may see future man living in small groups as his earliest ancestors did, having the features of the newborn of today. In spite of his enormous size he will have the same placidity and passivity, and so be almost totally nonaggressive. Strife, wars, and dissensions will cease, since he will no longer have the reflexes necessary to engage in such activities.

In the meantime some other species may have gained ascendancy, not because of greater intelligence but perhaps because of physical strength or greater adaptability.

Lecomte de Noüy wrote:

During the whole age of the reptiles, about one hundred million years, the mammals vegetated. They were small aplacental animals, a few inches long, resembling the marsupials of today. Some of them existed on insects, others were carnivorous, and still others, rodents. The enormous dinosaurs, weighing up to eighty tons, could crush dozens of them underfoot without even being aware of it. Who could have foreseen in those days, that the future belonged to these little beasts who, by their constant temperature, the proportionally greater development of their brain, and their mode of reproduction, represented an immense progress over the colossal reptiles with their rudimentary intelligence and their slavery to certain conditions of temperature and humidity? About fifty million years ago the gigantic saurians had disappeared and the mammals were beginning their reign which has been extended and consolidated up to our era.

The species that gains ascendancy in the future, then, would not necessarily be any of the apes. It might be a species as insignificant and little regarded today as were the mammals in the time of the dinosaurs.

CHAPTER EIGHTEEN

A Summing Up

Man's deepest awareness of himself and his feelings about his place in the universe are nowhere so completely revealed as in his religions.

In his most primitive phases man considered himself pursued and hunted by natural forces he could neither control nor understand, much as he pursued and hunted other species for his own purposes. His earliest religious rites consisted largely of efforts to propitiate those forces in an effort to gain from them what he needed rather than to be subjected to their, to him, inexplicable whims.

As man's understanding of his environment extended, concurrently with his infantilization, this perspective changed among most peoples to a personification of natural forces as gods, and later to the concept of God the Creator, Generator, and Father. In some Oriental religions, where this progression is not quite so clear, we find nevertheless such concepts as the philosophy of nirvana (an aim, through rebirth and successive purifying lives, ultimately to regain non-entity—a total unity with the cosmos—as a child not yet born is still a part of its parent).

Man has on the whole, through the past several millennia, felt like a child of God very simply because in his deepest being he has thought of himself as a child, and has needed so to think of himself in relationship with a force which he could believe would guide and protect him, and not destroy him.

In modern times, a profusion of new ideas has undermined these beliefs that have been the foundation of his existence through the ages and which he cherished above life itself.

The Copernican system of astronomy removed Earth from the center of the universe. Darwin's theory took man off the pedestal on which he had believed himself to stand as God's unique and favored creation, making him simply another species of the animal world. Freud showed that man is driven by psychological forces over which he has little, and sometimes no, control. Einstein conceived the formula which defined matter and energy as interchangeable. In the wake of such shattering concepts as these, perhaps we shall be forgiven for adding the thought that man is not on the highest rung of the evolutionary ladder and proceeding onward to ever-higher forms, but rather that he is a product of regressive evolution moving backward in terms of his physical endowments while overcompensating for his deficiencies with a hypertrophied neocortex.

Along with the toppling of long-held ideas about the nature of the universe, man's thoughts of himself and his own position in it have undergone a vast change. From his conception of himself as a child of God, he has come to feel that he is himself master of the universe. Like the infant, he has a sense of omnipotence over his immediate environment and the feeling that he can control all the forces it contains. This feeling is reinforced by the products of his technology so that to him the world has become an extended nursery, with everything in it his plaything.

True, in order to maintain his security within a social order, man-child has had to acquire coping mechanisms to enable him to co-exist with his fellows. But these coping mechanisms are brittle, and at the slightest stress they shatter.

Any society, no matter what the culture, as soon as it outgrows its extended clan structure, shows evidence of strain. Ceaseless rivalry simmers between factions within the culture and between cultures. The thin veneer of mature responsibility to the society peels away as soon as a personal need, real or imaginary, is felt. Our lives are disrupted by endless breakdowns in vital services through strikes. Effective planning for eventual needs of populations is seldom achieved because of the inability of the planners to submerge narrow interests for the common good. The eruption of disorder is world-wide, and not confined to any technological condition of the society, political orientation, or racial or national group.

There is absolutely no common ground to account for this universal lack of responsibility except the biological immaturity of man himself. While the mature animal of any species has instincts which impel it to preserve its group, the young of any species expect all their personal needs to be gratified immediately, without reference to the needs of the group. In fact, the young are not even aware of the group as a whole, but only of those individuals which form part of their immediate surroundings, and they only *relate* to their mothers and siblings. In man, the "passing the buck" or "leave it to George" philosophy is an extension of the child's expectation that anything that needs to be done will be done without his participation in the effort. The world-wide trend toward the socialization of all services is a further indication that man is placing government in the role of Mother (albeit not always a loving one). Special groups make nonnegotiable demands and are satisfied only when they are obtained in full, regardless of their possi-

A Summing Up

ble effect on, damage to, or disruption of the whole society. Such practices were entertainingly parodied in an English film, *I'm All Right Jack*. These traits are in no way different from the child's expectation of the fulfillment of its desires without question, or thought, of how this fulfillment is obtained. The child wants what it wants when it wants it, without consideration of the needs of others, and man-child does not outgrow this pattern.

One recognizes that the social infantilization of man has not proceeded at an even pace. There have been periods of comparative stability, and others when the trend has advanced headlong.

The branching off of new species from our anthropoid ancestors by paedomorphism may not have been confined to man. The majority of such branches must have died off, because the odds against their survival were too great. There is just a possibility that the ground-dwelling baboons may be such a surviving line. The baboons have lost their ability to use their arms for swinging in the trees, have adapted to life on the ground, and have developed an advanced social order replete with methods of communication and a high degree of social responsibility such as is seen in man only on rare occasions. Their infantilization is apparently proceeding at a slower pace than man's, and perhaps we may attribute to this the comparative stability of baboon society in contrast with man's. It is a rather fascinating exercise to speculate as to what baboon society of the future will be like as compared with man's, both having followed similar paths although at different speeds.

Science deals not only with hard facts but also with general ideas. To bring the two together into an harmonious union is the work of the theoretical scientist. The theoretical physicist, through his speculations, prepares the ground for applied physics. The theoretical biologist can suggest areas for new investigation and experimentation. Biology and medicine have lagged behind other disciplines in this. They have tended to follow pragmatic paths and establish theories as a result of experience, rather than using logically arrived-at ideas as guiding lights pointing the way to new paths.

It is the task of the theoretical scientist in any discipline to correlate apparently unrelated facts by means of abstract notions. It is as though he were from a treeless planet and, on ours, came across a pile of branches left by a woodcutter who had removed the trunk. He would see a connection between the separate branches on the ground, but it would require a great leap of knowledgeable imagination for him to be able mentally to construct the idea of the tree.

Reichenbach stated that it was characteristic of ancient and medieval philosophy to believe that there is a "seeing with our minds" analogous to seeing with our eyes. As we see shapes and colors with our eyes, so we see ideas and general laws with our minds. This was the basis of Plato's theory of ideas. Since physical things exist, they can be seen; since ideas exist, they can be seen through the eye of the mind. Mathematical vision was construed by Plato as equivalent to sense perception.

Aristotle, too, emphasized that "as the senses are always true as regards their proper sensible objects, so is the intellect as regards what a thing is." Today we should probably not be so sure of the evidence of our senses, but we should still be inclined to agree with Aristotle that it is possible to perceive the essence of a reality through the medium of the mind.

There is always the possibility, and one must be aware of the pitfall, that theoretical scientists may be unduly influenced in the formulation of their ideas by phenomena which seem to be overriding in their own time, but which in the long run turn out to have been passing phases.

We seem to see an exponential increase in the momentum of the process of infantilization in recent (and especially in our own) times. Aware of the pitfall we have just alluded to, we nevertheless believe there to be an adequate concrete explanation for this. The knowledge and ability of the medical profession to prevent and cure diseases on a scale never before known has created a vast reservoir of survivors carrying mutated genes to future generations. The consequences are not necessarily immediately apparent in one or two generations, but the accumulation of such factors will certainly have a long-range effect. We are now roughly in the third generation of improved medical care, and it is conceivable that the momentum we note is in some part the effect of it. Not only do the cured sick contribute to the changed genes of the following generations, but the healthy too, inoculated and vaccinated as we are, make these artificially induced gene alterations population-wide.

This development has reached such proportions that in the United States the National Foundation for Genetics and Neuromuscular Diseases has established a network of centers to counsel families and treat patients with genetic disorders. With the decline of infectious diseases as causes of death in children, genetic diseases have risen in importance. Today an estimated ratio of one in five childhood deaths is caused by a genetic disorder.

Everything in nature follows orderly patterns. At each stage of history observers become aware of some of them. At later stages, as the horizons of knowledge widen, it is seen that some of these patterns fit into larger schemes. New explanations are found. It frequently happens that earlier theories are not invalidated but enlarged, or seen as facets of a greater whole. In this work, for example, we have attempted to show that evolution takes more than one path.

A good example of our approach is afforded by the work of the Russian chemist Mendeleyev. For many years he collected all the information he could find on the properties of the elements. Scientists before him had attempted to group them. Octaves, triads, and helical curves were some of the many groupings that had been tried in efforts to accommodate the known facts, but they were all without satisfactory result. Mendeleyev initially was not seeking to systematize the knowledge, but only to record it. He carefully noted the information he gained on cards, and filed them away. As he leafed through them again and again in the course of adding to them, he began to perceive that they fell into an order. A colleague of his presented his findings at a meeting of the Russian Chemical Society in 1869, since he himself was sick at the time and unable to do so. This colleague unrolled Mendeleyev's chart, on which he had arranged in columns the sixty-three then known elements. Each column contained a periodic sequence of lighter to heavier elements which shared particular properties. There were a number of blank spaces. The opening sentence of Mendeleyev's report on the periodicity of elements was "The properties of the fundamental substances are dependent in a periodic way on the magnitude of the atomic weights of the elements." Later discoveries filled in the blank spaces and extended his chart with descriptions of elements, unknown in his time, whose properties were predicted on the basis of his work. To arrive at this fundamental insight, Mendeleyev had drawn on the research of many scientists from all over the world.

We, too, have used this method. We have collected and drawn on the experience, research, and writings of workers in many fields, from many countries and spread over many centuries.

It was apparent to all of them that there was an order in evolution, but that man did not fit into the sequence in a satisfactory manner. Darwin himself noted missing links in the chain leading to man. Like Mendeleyev, we were collectors of data, in an attempt to find a correlation between man's prolonged childhood and the widespread prevalence of behavioral and social immaturity on the one hand and possible anatomical and physiological concomitants on the other.

In going through the information as it accumulated in our files, two dominant themes forced themselves on our attention. The first of these themes was that all has its place in the natural order. Not only the fit and the stable, but also the sick and deviant, play participating roles in evolution. Remarkably, not only do the sick and the deviant participate, but they have a very special place in nature. It is they who provide the testing grounds for nature's trials. It is not from the normal, the well-adjusted, or the healthy average specimen of any species that new forms arise, but from the mutant, the aberrant, and the sick.

One could draw an analogy with the experiences in life of any individual. On the whole it is not the humdrum rounds of one's normal day-to-day existence that contribute the most to our emotional or mental stature, or even to our joy. They tend to fade out of our memories. They are boring. What remains in our minds are the isolated, unusual, nontypical events we experience, even though these may as often be disturbing or painful as rewarding or joyous. It is through these "deviant" joys or trials that we modify previously held opinions, gain new insights, plumb previously untapped depths or scale heights of emotions, or call out of ourselves hitherto unrecognized capacities. The humdrum parts of our lives are certainly easier on us, and more comfortable, but our greatest heights are achieved in the "special" circumstances.

In the same way, nature seems to rise to new heights of inventiveness when the disabled are obliged to overcompensate; a new order emerges when an established order is disturbed and falls into chaos. The new forms and methods may or may not turn out to be improvements on the old, but they are tested, tried, and have their day. A stable order rarely improves and usually degenerates. Its chief virtue is the easy comfort of its very stability, but its defect is in stagnation, lack of effort, boredom.

Perhaps we should draw some comfort from this realization, for surely out of the chaos, revolutions, and upheavals of all kinds that we witness in the world around us today, new orders and new norms will emerge.

The second theme that stood out was the all-pervasive importance in the genesis of man of delays, inhibitions, retardations, interruptions, and other brakes in the course of the orderly processes of growth. This theme is readily verifiable in its anatomical and physiological aspects, some of which we have detailed. We can to some extent observe and measure delays in growth and retardations and inhibitions of development caused by hormonal agents. In behavior such factors are less readily observable, but if we regard human actions with the "eyes of the mind" we may discern similar processes at work. The ability to delay a response allows a person time to think, to control emotions, and to consider alternatives, all of which abilities are unique to human beings. These abilities are not instinctive. They are a result of learning time gained by delaying maturity and are a concomitant of infantilization.

As the patterns of these two themes emerged they provided a framework within which many otherwise inexplicable facts fell into place and suggested explanations for diverse phenomena.

One inescapable conclusion was that man is not the pinnacle of evolution. Man, as a product of regressive evolution, owing his intelligence to a series of circumstances in which disease played an important part, is not a conventional concept, nor is his dethronement easy to accept. Knowledgeable editors who read the proposed outline of our book at first reacted with the sentiment that the idea of man taking shape by regression was depressing. But every aspect of our theory results from the scientifically demonstrated findings of many scholars in many times and places, all duly filed in our metal and mental cabinets.

Our source material has been accepted as valid by specialists who have spent lifetimes working in each of the fields we have touched upon. The results of their work are not debatable unless or until new facts are brought to light that might modify or extend them. Only our conclusions are at issue here. We feel that if the reader applies the theory we have presented to the human scene, he will find explanations for many occurrences and actions that until now have been the subject of contradictory views or have been considered entirely inexplicable.

While we are on the subject of interpretations, we realize that the word *infantilization* may conjure up a disparaging image, as a parent admonishing a youngster not to be childish implies undesirable comportment. We should like to reiterate that we are using the word as a description of a process that has two edges. While man's social immaturity and difficulties may be laid to it on the one hand, on the other man's highest achievements are also the attributes of the childlike capacity to learn, the delight in discovery, and the creative curiosity that have become essential parts of man's make-up. What is more, the necessity of protecting human young throughout their prolonged period of helplessness has led to the emergence of a striving toward morality and ideals that is an indirect benefit of the same process.

We may be accused of attempting to explain too much—in fact, of reductionism. There is no doubt that many of the points we have touched upon admit various explanations. Given the same set of facts, any number of people will give an equal number of different explanations for them, based on their bias, predilections, knowledge, and personal experience. Their conclusions will be what seems to be the most obvious to each of them. However, the obvious explanations of biological facts, particularly in the realm of human activities, quite often turn out to be not the true ones, or ones that are only partially true.

For example, it can be maintained that the over-all increase in man's size should be attributed at least as much to better nutrition as to genetic causes. There is no doubt that there may be either contributing or detracting factors, or both at the same time, operating in specific areas. In the matter of nutrition, for example, we may enjoy greater abundance, but we also ingest much overprocessed and a great deal of chemically contaminated food. In the matter of clothing, we certainly have a desire to keep warm or protected when we cover ourselves, but these factors do not negate the probability that clothing has an earlier and more deeply rooted significance in rank and role delineation.

What we have here attempted is to convey to the reader a view of the thread we have found running through so much of what man does, the way he behaves, the things he likes, and last but not least, found structurally embedded in his anatomical configuration.

In this thread of infantilization we feel that we have found a key that opens a lock to a greater understanding of our inordinately powerful, creative, gifted—and unruly—species.

Bibliography

Abdell, Walter. *The Collective Dream in Art.* New York: Schocken Books, 1957.

Ackerman, Nathan. "The Diagnosis of Neurotic Marital Interaction," *Social Casework,* XXXV, No. 4:141, 1954.

Adler, A. *Social Interest.* London: Faber & Faber, 1938.

Alexander, F. *Fundamentals of Psychoanalysis.* London: Allen & Unwin, 1949.

Alland, Alexander, Jr. *Evolution and Human Behavior.* New York: American Museum of Natural History, 1967.

Allee, W. C. *The Social Life of Animals.* London: Wm. Heinemann, 1939.

Angelo y Gonzales, A. W. "Is Myelinogeny an Absolute Index of Behavioral Capability?," *J. of Comparative Neurology,* 48:459, 1929.

Ardrey, Robert. "Control of Population," in *Life,* Feb. 20, 1970.

Ariés, Philippe. *Centuries of Childhood.* New York: Alfred A. Knopf, 1962.

Aristotle. *The Works of Aristotle* (ed. W. D. Ross), Book 1, 5. London: Oxford.

Arvay, A. "Cortico-hypothalamic Control of Gonadotrophic Function," *Major Problems in Neuroendocrinology* (ed. E. Bajusz). Basel: Karger, 1964.

Ashley Montagu, M. F. *The Direction of Human Development.* London: Watts, 1957.

———. *Introduction to Physical Anthropology.* Springfield, Ill.: C. C. Thomas, 1960.

Bajusz, Eörs (ed.). *An Introduction to Clinical Neuroendocrinology.* Baltimore: Williams & Wilkins, 1967.

Barry, H. and I. L. Child. "A Cross Cultural Survey of Some Sex Differences in Socialization," *J. of Abnormal & Social Psych.,* 1957.

Beck, S. D. "Insects and the Length of Day," *Scientific American,* February 1960.

Bender, L. and H. Yarnell. "An Observation Nursery," *Amer. J. of Psychiatry,* 97:1158–74, 1941.

Bennhold-Thomsen, C. "Über die Acceleration der Entwicklung der Heutigen Jugend," *Klin. Wsche.* 17:865, 1938.

Bergler, E. *The Basic Neurosis.* New York: Grune & Stratton, 1949.

Bleibtreu, John N. *The Parable of the Beast.* London: Gollancz, 1968.

Blos, P. *The Adolescent Personality.* New York: Appleton-Century, 1941.

Boas, Franz, *et al. General Anthropology.* New York: D. C. Heath, 1938.

Bolk, Ludwig. *Das Problem der Menschwerdung.* Jena: G. Fischer, 1926.

Born, Max. "My Life and Views," quoted in *Time,* Jan. 19, 1970.

Brady, J. P. "Epilepsy and Disturbed Behavior," *J. Nerv. & Ment. Dis.,* 138:468, 1964.

Brown, Maxwell. In *Violence in America: Historical and Comparative Perspectives.* (A report to the National Commission on the Causes and Prevention of Violence, by 27 specialists), New York: Praeger, 1969.

Buettner-Janusch, John (ed.). *Evolutionary and Genetic Biology of Primates,* Vols. I and II. New York: Academic Press, 1963.

Bullock, E. and L. Segneira. "The Relations of the Adrenals to the Sex Organs," *Tr. Path. Soc.,* 66:189, London, 1905.

Burkitt, Miles C. *Prehistory.* London: Cambridge, 1921.

Butler, Robert A. "Curiosity in Monkeys," *Twentieth Century Bestiary,* by the Editors of *Scientific American.* New York: Simon & Schuster, 1955.

Bychowski, G. and J. L. Despert. *Specialized Techniques in Psychotherapy.* New York: Basic Books, 1952.

Canaday, John. *Mainstream of Modern Art.* London: Thames & Hudson, 1959.

Capell, Martin D. "Games and the Mastery of Helplessness," *Motivations in Play, Games & Sport* (ed. R. Slovenko and J. A. Knight). Springfield, Ill.: C. C. Thomas, 1967.

Carpenter, Philip. *Microbiology.* London: W. B. Saunders, 1967.

Churchill, Winston S. *A History of the English Speaking People.* London: Cassell, 1956–8.

Clarke, E. Gladys. "Cookery," *Encyclopaedia Britannica* (1929).

Colbert, Edwin H. *Evolution of the Vertebrates.* New York: Museum of Natural History.

Coogan, Joseph P. "Simian Society," *S K & F Psychiatric Reporter,* May–June, 1968.

———. "The Remote Control of Animal Behavior," *S K&F Psychiatric Reporter,* July–Aug., 1968.

Csikszentmihalyi, Mihaly. "The Rigors of Play," *The Nation,* Feb. 17, 1969.

Cuenot, L. "L'homme néoténique," *Bull. l' Acad. Roy. Belg.,* 31:1945.

Curtis, Helena. *The Viruses.* Garden City, N.Y.: Natural History Press, 1965.

Dahrendorf, Ralf. "Society and Democracy in Germany," quoted in *Time,* Oct. 10, 1969.

Dart, R. A. "The Makapansgat Protohuman Australopithecus Prometheus," *Amer. J. Phys. Anthrop.,* 6:259–284, 1948.

Darwin, Charles. *Descent of Man* (Thinkers Library No. 12). London: Watts, n.d.

de Beer, Sir Gavin. *Embryos and Ancestors* (3rd ed.). Oxford: Clarendon Press, 1962.

de Latil, Pierre. *La Pensée Artificielle.* Paris: Gallimard, 1952

Demos, John. *A Little Commonwealth.* New York: Oxford, 1970.

Devaux, E. *Trois Problèmes: L'espèce, l'instinct, l'homme.* Paris, 1933.

Dewing, Arthur. "Principles of Art," *Encyclopaedia Britannica* (1929).

Dobzhansky, T. *The Biology of Ultimate Concern.* London: Rapp & Whiting, 1969.

―――. *Mankind Evolving.* New Haven: Yale Univ. Press, 1962.

Dollard, J., et al. *Frustration and Aggression.* New Haven: Yale Univ. Press, 1939.

Downs, J. F. and H. K. Bleibtreu. *Human Variation.* London: Collier-Macmillan 1969.

D'Souza, Victor D. Paper read to 8th International Congress of Gerontology at Washington, D.C., as reported in "Over 65," *Medical World News,* Sept. 26, 1969.

Duckworth, W. L. H. *Morphology and Anthropology.* Cambridge: Cambridge Univ. Press, 1904.

Dupin, Jacques. *Introduction to Works of Miró.* London: Thames & Hudson, 1962.

Durant, Will. *The Story of Philosophy.* London: Benn, 1962.

Eaton, J. W. and R. J. Weil. *Culture and Mental Disorders.* Glencoe, Ill.: Free Press, 1955.

Eibl-Eibesfelt, Irenäus. "Über die Jugendwicklung des Verhaltens eines Dachses unter Besonderer Berücksichtigung des Spielen," *Zeitschrift für Tierpsychologie,* Vol. 7. Apr. 7, 1949.

Eisenstein, Victor (ed.). *Neurotic Interaction in Marriage.* London: Tavistock, 1956.

Erikson, Erik M. *Gandhi's Truth: On the Origins of Militant Nonviolence.* London: Faber & Faber, 1970.

Evans, Joan. "Jewellery," *Encyclopaedia Britannica* (1929).

Farb, Peter. *Man's Rise to Civilization.* London: Secker & Warburg, 1969.

Fenichel, O. *The Psychoanalytic Theory of Neurosis.* London: Kegan Paul, Trench & Trübner, 1946.

Field, Henry. *The Track of Man*. London: Peter Davies, 1955.

Frank, Philipp. *Philosophy of Science*. Englewood Cliffs, N.J.: Prentice-Hall, 1957.

Franks, J., et al. "The Role of Anxiety in Psychophysiological Reactions," *A.M.A. Archives Neurol. & Psych.* 81:227, February 1959.

Fraser, Dean. *Viruses and Molecular Biology*. New York: Macmillan, 1967.

Frazer, J. G. *The Golden Bough: A Study in Magic and Religion*. London: Macmillan, 1945.

Friedenberg, Edgar. *Coming of Age in America*. New York: Random House, 1963.

Freud, Anna. "The Concept of Developmental Lines," *Psych. Stud. Child*, 18:245–261, 1963.

———. *The Ego and the Mechanisms of Defence*. London: Hogarth Press, 1937.

Freud, Sigmund. *Beyond the Pleasure Principle*. London: Hogarth Press, 1920.

———. *The Complete Psychological Works of Sigmund Freud*. London: Hogarth Press, 1953.

Fromm, E. *Escape from Freedom*. New York: Farrar & Rinehart, 1941.

Galton, F. *Hereditary Genius*. London, 1892.

Gardner, Helen. *Art Through the Ages*. London: Bell, 1959.

Garn, Stanley M. and Betty Wagner. "The Adolescent Growth of Skeletal Mass in its Implications to Mineral Requirements," *Adolescent Nutrition & Growth* (ed. Felix P. Heald).

Garn, Stanley (ed.). *Culture and the Direction of Human Evolution*. Detroit: Wayne State University Press, 1964.

Garstang, W. "The Theory of Recapitulation: A Critical Restatement of the Biogenetic Law," *J. of the Linnean Soc. of London, Zoology*, 35:81.

Gasser, S. M. "The Classification of Nerve Fibers," *Ohio J. of Science*, 41:145, 1941.

Gates, R. R. *Human Genetics*. New York: Macmillan, 1946.

Gastaut, H. *The Epilepsies*. Springfield, Ill.: C. C. Thomas, 1954.

Glaser, G. H. "Limbic Encephalitis," *J. Nerv. Ment. Dis.,* 149:59, July 1969.

Grey Owl. *Pilgrims of the Wild.* London: Lovat Dickson, 1934.

Grinker, R. R. and co-workers. "Mentally Healthy Young Males (Homoclites)," *Arch. Gen. Psych.,* 6:405, June 1962.

Grosser, O. "Human and Comparative Placentation including the Early Stages of Human Development," *The Lancet,* 1:1054, 1933.

Gudernatsch, J. F. "Feeding Experiments on Tadpoles," *Amer. J. Anatomy,* 15:431, 1914.

Guerrant, John L., *et al. Personality in Epilepsy.* Springfield, Ill.: C. C. Thomas, 1962.

Hadden, Jeffrey K. "The Private Generation," *Psychology Today,* October, 1969.

Haldane, J. B. S. *The Causes of Evolution.* London: Longmans, 1932.

Hallowell, A. Irving. "Hominid Evolution, Cultural Adaptation and Mental Dysfunctioning" in *Transcultural Psychology* (CIBA Symposium). Boston: Little, Brown, 1965.

Harris, G. W. "The Central Nervous System and the Endocrine Glands," *Triangle,* Basel, 6:241, 1964.

Heald, Felix P. (ed.). *Adolescent Nutrition and Growth.* New York: Appleton-Century-Crofts, 1969.

Hediger, H. *Wild Animals in Captivity.* London: Butterworth Scient. Publ., 1950.

Henderson, R. W. *Ball, Bat and Bishop: The Origin of Ball Games.* New York: Rockport Press, 1947.

Herbert, S. *The First Principles of Evolution.* London: Adam & Chas. Black, 1913.

Hertwig, Oscar. *Das Werden der Organismen.* Jena: G. Fischer, 1922.

Hildreth, Gertrude H. *Educating Gifted Children.* New York: Harper, 1952.

Hinde, Robert A. *Animal Behavior.* New York: McGraw-Hill, 1966.

Bibliography

Hoffmann, Paul. "A With-It Center for Warsaw Young People," *The New York Times,* Oct. 11, 1969.

Horney, K. *The Neurotic Personality of Our Time.* London: Kegan Paul, 1937.

———. *Neurosis and Human Growth.* London: Routledge & Kegan Paul, 1950.

Howells, William (ed.). *Ideas on Human Evolution.* Cambridge, Mass.: Harvard Univ. Press, 1962.

———. *Mankind in the Making.* Garden City, N.Y.: Doubleday, 1959.

Hsiung, G-D., *et al.* "Susceptibility of Primates to Viruses in Relation to Taxonomic Classification," *Evolutionary & Genetic Biology of Primates.*

Huizinga, Johan. *Homo Ludens: A Study of the Play Element in Culture.* London: Routledge & Kegan Paul, 1950.

Huxley, J. S. *Evolution: The Modern Synthesis.* London: Allen & Unwin, 1942.

Huxley, T. H. *Life and Letters.* London, 1900.

James, William. *Vareties of Religious Experience.* London: Collins, 1960.

Janowitz, Morris. In *Alternatives to Violence.* New York: Time-Life Books, 1968.

Jonas, A. D. *Irritation and Counterirritation.* New York: Vantage Press, 1962.

———. *Ictal and Subictal Neurosis.* Springfield, Ill.: C. C. Thomas, 1965.

——— and D. F. Klein. *Alpha Eridani,* unpubl. mss.

Joyce, Thomas Athol. "Dress," *Encyclopaedia Britannica* (1929).

Keith, A. *A New Theory of Human Evolution.* London: Watts, 1949.

Klee, Paul. *Paul Klee on Modern Art.* London: Faber & Faber, n.d.

Kluckhohn, Clyde and Henry A. Murray. *Personality in Nature, Society and Culture.* London: Jonathan Cape, 1949.

Koestler, Arthur. In *Alternatives to Violence*. New York: Time-Life Books, 1968.

Konody, Paul G. "Art and Nature," *Encyclopaedia Britannica* (1929).

Korn, Noel and Fred Thomson (ed.). *Human Evolution*. New York: Holt, Rinehart & Winston, 1967.

Kovacs, F. "Biological Interpretation of the Nine Months Duration of Human Pregnancy," *Acta. Biol. Magyar,* Tudom. Acad. 10:331, 1960.

Kropotkin, Piotr A. *Mutual Aid, A Factor in Evolution*. London: Wm. Heinemann, 1902.

Kuhlenbeck, Hartwig. *The Central Nervous System of Vertebrates*. London: Academic Press, 1967.

Kysar, J. E., *et al.* "Range of Psychological Functioning in 'Normal' Late Adolescence," *Arch. Gen. Psych.,* 21:515, November 1969.

Leighton, A. H. *Transcultural Psychiatry* (ed. Ciba Foundation). Boston: Little, Brown, 1965.

L'Etang, Hugh. *The Pathology of Leadership*. London: William Heinemann Medical Books, 1969.

Liddell, D. W., *et al.* "Latent Epilepsy as a Factor in Tension States," *J. Nerv. & Ment. Dis.,* 121:215, 1955.

Lilly, John C. *The Mind of the Dolphin* (*A Non-Human Intelligence*). Garden City, N.Y.: Doubleday, 1967.

Lorenz, Karl. In *The Evolution of the Organism*, 2d ed. (ed. G. Heberer) Stuttgart, 1954, p. 131.

Lorenz, Konrad. *King Solomon's Ring*. London: Methuen, 1952.
———. *On Aggression*. London: Methuen 1966.

Lott, Dale F. *Threat and Submission Signals in Mature Male American Bison*. Philadelphia: Davis, 1969.

Lowe, P.R., "Studies and Observations Bearing on the Phylogeny of the Ostrich and Its Allies," *Proceedings of the Zoological Society of London,* 185, 1928.

———. "On the Primitive Characters of the Penguins," *Proceedings of the Zoological Society of London,* 483, 1933.

Lyford, Joseph P. "Who's Brainwashing Whom?" *The Center Maga-*

zine, Santa Barbara, Cal.

Macaulay, Lord T. *Lays of Ancient Rome.* London: Dent.

MacCurdy, George Grant. *Human Origins.* London: Appleton, 1924.

MacLean, Paul D. In *Alternatives to Violence.* New York: Time-Life Books, 1968.

Maier, N. R. F. and T. C. Schneirla. *Principles of Animal Psychology.* New York: Dover, 1964.

Mandelbaum, H. "Diencephalic Epilepsy and the Diencephalic Syndrome," *Ann. Intl. Med.,* 34:911, 1951.

Mann, Thomas. Preface to *The Short Novels of Dostoevsky.* New York: Dial Press, 1945.

Marsh, O. C. "Recent Discoveries of Extinct Animals," *Am. Naturalist,* 10:436–440, 1876.

Matz, Friedrich. *The Art of Crete and Early Greece.* New York: Greystone Press, 1962.

Maxwell, Gavin. *Ring of Bright Water.* London: Longmans 1960.

———. *The Rocks Remain.* London: Longmans, 1963.

Mayr, Ernst. *Animal Species and Evolution.* Cambridge, Mass.: Harvard Univ. Press, 1963.

McDonald, J. M. *Psychiatry and the Criminal.* Springfield, Ill.: C. C. Thomas, 1958.

MD Magazine. "Castor Canadensis" (editorial), February 1968.

Mead, Margaret. Third Annual Lecture of the Society for Adolescent Psychology at New York Academy of Medicine, Oct. 30, 1969.

Medical World News. "Influenza Ravages New Guinea" (editorial), Nov. 21, 1969.

———. "People Pollution" (editorial), Dec. 19, 1969.

Menninger, Karl. *Love Against Hate.* New York: Harcourt, Brace, & World, 1952.

Miller, D. R. and G. Swanson. "Defense Against Conflict and Social Background," *Symposium Am. Psychol. Assoc.,* September 1953.

Mittelman, B. "The Concurrent Analysis of Married Couples," *Psychoanalytic Quarterly,* 17:182–197, 1948.

Modern Medicine. "Collective Violence" (editorial), Nov. 17, 1969.

Moorehead, Alan. *Darwin and the Beagle.* London: Hamish Hamilton, 1969.

Mulholland, John H. "On Resistance to New Concepts," *Roche Medical Image & Commentary.*

Munroe, Ruth L. *Schools of Psychoanalytic Thought.* London: Hutchinson, 1957.

Murphy, G. *Personality: A Biosocial Approach to Origins and Structure.* New York: Harper & Bros., 1947.

Murphy, Lois. Unpublished lectures given at Veterans Administration Hospital Forum, Topeka, Kan., Mar. 25, 1959.

Napier J. R. and P. H. *A Handbook of Living Primates.* London: Academic Press, 1967.

Neal, Ernest. *The Badger.* London: Collins, 1962.

Nesbit, J. F. *Insanity of Genius.* London, 1891.

Noüy, Pierre Lecomte de. *Human Destiny.* New York: New American Library, 1947.

Offer, D. "Normal Adolescents," *Arch. Gen. Psych.,* 17:285, September 1967.

Omachi, Chiyo. Address before the 8th International Congress of Gerontology in Washington, D.C. as reported in "Over 65," *Med. World News,* Sept. 26, 1969.

Oparin, A. I. *Genesis and Evolutionary Development of Life.* New York: Academic Press, 1968.

Opler, M. K. and J. L. Singer. "Ethnic Differences in Behavior and Psychology," *Intl. J. Soc. Psych.,* 2:11, 1956.

Page, Ernest W. "Some Evolutionary Concepts of Human Reproduction," *Obst./Gyn.,* Vol. 30, No. 3, September 1967.

———. and G. Tominaga. "Accommodation of the Human Placenta to Hypoxia," *Amer. J. Obst. Gyn.,* 94:679, 1966.

Peiper, Albrecht. *Cerebral Function in Infancy and Childhood.* London: Pitman, 1964.

Penfield, W. and T. Rasmussen. *The Cerebral Cortex of Man.* New York: Macmillan, 1950.

Piaget, Jean. *The Construction of Reality in the Child* (tr. Margaret Cook). London: Routledge & Kegan Paul, 1955.

Plutarch. *The Lives of the Noble Grecians and Romans.* New York: Heritage Press, 1941.

Porter, Robert T. "Sports and Adolescence," *Motivation in Play, Games and Sports* (ed. Slovenko and Knight). Springfield, Ill.: C. C. Thomas, 1967.

Portman, Adolf. *Animals as Social Beings.* New York: Viking, 1961.

Powicke, Frederick. "The Middle Ages," *Encyclopaedia Britannica* (1929).

Pycraft, W. P. "Nest," *Encyclopaedia Britannica* (1929).

Reich, W. *Characteranalysis.* London: Peter Nevill, 1950.

Reichenbach, H. *The Rise of Scientific Philosophy.* Berkeley: Univ. of Cal. Press, 1951.

Reif, Rita. "For Adults, the Toys Captivate," *The New York Times,* Sept. 30, 1969.

Reynolds, Sir Joshua. *Fifteen Discourses on Art* (Everyman Library No. 118). London: J. M. Dent, 1928.

Roche Report. "Frontiers of Clinical Psychiatry" (editorial), Vol. 6, No. 17, Oct. 15, 1969.

Roe, Ann and G. G. Simpson (eds.). *Behavior and Evolution.* New Haven: Yale Univ. Press, 1958.

Roessler, R. and N. S. Greenfield. *Physiological Correlates of Psychological Disorders.* Madison: Univ. of Wisconsin Press, 1962.

Róheim, Géza. *The Origin and Function of Culture.* New York: Nerv. and Ment. Dis. Monographs, 1943.

Rue, Leonard Lee, III. *The World of the Beaver.* Philadelphia: Lippincott, 1964.

Sager, R. and F. Ryan, *Cell Heredity.* New York: Wiley, 1961.

Schally, A. V., et al. "Neuro-hormonal Functions of the Hypothalamus," *Amer. J. Med. Sci.,* 248:79, 1964.

Scheffer, Victor B. *The Year of the Whale.* New York: Charles Scribner's Sons, 1969.

Schultz, A. H. "Studies on the Growth of Gorilla," *Mem. Carnegie Mus.,* 11:1–87, 1927.

———. "Chimpanzee Fetuses," *Amer. J. Phys. Anthrop.,* 18:61–79, 1933.

Schwab, John J. "Psychiatric Illnesses Produced by Infections," *Hospital Medicine,* October 1969.

Sedgwick, A. "The Influence of Darwin on the Study of Animal Embryology," *Darwin and Modern Science* (ed. A. C. Seward). Cambridge, 1909.

Sewertzow, A. N. *Morphologische Gesetzmässigkeiten der Evolution.* Jena, 1931.

Shakespeare, W. *Hamlet,* Act I, sc. iii. and Act I, sc. iv.

Shuster, Alvin. "Envoy's Biting Views of U.S. Aides in 1939," *The New York Times,* Jan. 1, 1970.

Simeons, A. T. W. *Man's Presumptuous Brain.* London: Longmans, 1960.

Simmel, G. "Über das Menarche Alter in Finnland," *Acta. Ped. Suppl.,* 84, 1952.

Simpson, George Gaylord. *The Meaning of Evolution.* London: Oxford, 1950.

Skolnick, Jerome H. *The Politics of Protest* (a report to the National Commission by 21 consultants and 34 researchers under direction of J. H. Skolnick), New York: Simon and Schuster, 1969.

Slovenko, Ralph and James A. Knight. *Motivation in Play, Games, and Sports.* Springfield, Ill.: C. C. Thomas, 1967.

Smith, Reginald Alexander. "Archaeology," *Encyclopaedia Britannica* (1929).

Spence, L. *Myth and Ritual in Dance, Game and Rhyme.* London: Watts, 1947.

Spranger, Eduard. *Types of Men: The Psychology and Ethics of Personality.* Halle: Max Niemeyer Verlag, 1928.

Stanek, V. J. *Pictorial Encyclopedia of the Animal Kingdom.* London:

Paul Hamlyn, 1963.

Stanford University. Report of School of Medicine Committee, *Science,* Apr. 25, 1969.

Sullivan, H. S. *Conceptions of Modern Psychiatry* (William Alanson White edition). New York: Norton, 1947.

Tanner, James M. "Earlier Maturation in Man," *Sci. Amer.* 218:21, 1968.

Taylor, G. R. *The Biological Time Bomb.* London: Thames & Hudson, 1968.

Thompson, C. *Psychoanalysis: Evolution and Development.* London: Allen & Unwin, 1952

Tilly, Charles. In *Violence in America.* Historical and Comparative Perspectives (a report to the National Commission on the causes and prevention of violence). New York: Praeger, 1969.

Towner, R. H. *The Philosophy of Civilization.* New York: G. P. Putnam's Sons, 1923.

Vishnevky, A. F. and K. P. Golyscheva. *"Zür Frage der Prädisposition,"* Zeitschrift für die Gesammte Exp. Med., Vol. 88, pp. 105–112, 1933.

Von Allesch, G. J. Preussische Akad. Wiss. Sitzb. der Phil.-hist. abt., *Naturwiss,* p. 774, 1921.

Walker, Ernest P. *Mammals of the World,* Vol. II. Baltimore: Johns Hopkins Press, 1964.

Watts, Alan. In *Alternatives to Violence.* New York: Time-Life Books, 1968.

Weiss, Paul A. *Dynamics of Development: Experiments and Inferences.* New York: Academic Press, 1968.

Wheeler, Harvey. In *Alternatives to Violence.* New York: Time-Life Books, 1968.

Wilkinson, Spenser. "War," *Encyclopaedia Britannica* (1929).

Wilson, Allan C., and Vincent M. Sarich. Report on Analysis of Blood Constituents and on DNA," *The New York Times,* Dec. 11, 1969 (by H. M. Schmeck).

Wilson, S. A. K. *Neurology.* London: Arnold, 1940.

Winick, Charles. "The Desexualized Society," *The Humanist*, Nov./Dec. 1969.

Wisbeski, Dorothy. *Okee: The Story of an Otter in the House*. London: Methuen, 1965.

Wissler, Clark. *Man and Culture*. London: Harrap, 1923.

Yerkes, R. M. *Chimpanzees: A Laboratory Colony*. New Haven: Yale Univ. Press, 1943.

Zuckerkandl, E. and I. Pauling. *Problems of Evolutionary and Technical Biochemistry*. Moscow: Nauka, 1964, p. 54.

Zussman, Shirley. *A Study of Certain Factors Influencing Husbands' Participation in Their Wives' Labor*. Unpubl. doctoral dissertation, Columbia Univ. Teachers College, 1969.